Cambridge IGCSE®
English

STUDENT'S BOOK

Also for Cambridge IGCSE® (9–1)

Series Editor: Julia Burchell
Keith Brindle, Julia Burchell,
Steve Eddy, Mike Gould and Ian Kirby

William Collins' dream of knowledge for all began with the publication of his first book in 1819.

A self-educated mill worker, he not only enriched millions of lives, but also founded a flourishing publishing house. Today, staying true to this spirit, Collins books are packed with inspiration, innovation and practical expertise. They place you at the centre of a world of possibility and give you exactly what you need to explore it.

Collins. Freedom to teach.

Published by Collins
An imprint of HarperCollins*Publishers*
The News Building
1 London Bridge Street
London
SE1 9GF

Browse the complete Collins catalogue at
www.collins.co.uk

British Library Cataloguing-in-Publication Data

A catalogue record for this publication is available from the British Library.

Series Editor: Julia Burchell
Authors: Keith Brindle, Julia Burchell, Steve Eddy, Mike Gould,
Ian Kirby
Project manager: Sonya Newland
Development editor: Sonya Newland
Commissioning editor: Catherine Martin
In-house editors: Hannah Dove, Helena Becci, Natasha Paul
Copyeditor: Catherine Dakin
Proofreader: Kim Vernon
Cover designer: Gordon MacGilp
Cover illustrator: Maria Herbert-Liew
Typesetter: Jouve India Private Limited
Production controller: Tina Paul
Printed and bound in Italy by Grafica Veneta

We would like to thank the following teachers for reviewing chapters of the book as it was developed:

Tabinda Shoaib, ELC International School, Selangor, Malaysia; Catherine Franklin, The British School of Rio de Janeiro, Brazil; Amanda Rundle, Girls' College, Bulawayo, South Africa; Amelia Kellerman, Village Montessori School, Centurion, South Africa; Richard Randelhoff, St Charles College, Pietermaritzburg, South Africa; Kate Martin, Acorn Academy, Cornwall, UK; Naomi Hursthouse, Steyning Grammar School, UK.

All exam-style questions and sample answers in this title were written by the authors. In examinations, the way marks are awarded may be different.

Contents

Introduction

The Collins *Cambridge IGCSE® English Student's Book (Third Edition)* offers a skills-building approach to the Cambridge IGCSE and IGCSE (9–1) First Language English syllabuses (0500 and 0990). Our book shows you how to make progress by modelling and giving you plenty of opportunities to practise the skills that underpin your course.

The Cambridge IGCSE prepares you for everyday and workplace communication in the English-speaking world, with a focus on being able to adapt what you say and write for a wide range of audiences and purposes. It is also a solid foundation from which to launch into further study of English Language or Literature.

Our book therefore encourages you to read a wide range of engaging literary and non-literary texts, to explore the way that language works within them to create meaning and influence readers, and to develop your own ability to write and speak in a range of different forms.

How the book is structured

Section 1: Building key skills

Section 1 introduces you to the fundamental skills that you will use throughout your course. Understanding these underlying skills will enable you to tackle a range of different tasks in Sections 2 to 5.

Many of the Cambridge IGCSE tasks require you to deploy a range of different skills together. For instance, the ability to summarise is impossible to achieve unless you have three basic skills: the ability to skim, scan and select. These fundamental reading skills are all introduced in Section 1, Chapter 1 and then the task of writing a summary is covered in Section 4, Chapter 6. Similarly, the key task of analysing writer's effects, which is taught in Section 2, Chapter 5, is prepared for through the study of selecting information, understanding explicit and implicit meanings and being able to recognise emotive and sensory language in Section 1, Chapter 1.

Your writing skills are also developed in the same way.

Accuracy is fundamental to any English course and we have included a specific chapter in the first section of this book, to help you improve your technical skills.

The ability to write in a range of forms and for a range of purposes and audiences is a vital part of success when attempting the extended response, directed writing, composition tasks and coursework tasks. Section 1, Chapters 3 and 4 therefore provide thorough coverage of these key writing conventions.

Section 2: Applying key skills

Each chapter of **Section 2** helps you to draw together and apply the skills introduced in Section 1 to respond effectively to tasks such as comprehension, summary writing, analysing language, directed writing and making an extended response to reading.

Section 3: Applying key skills in coursework

In **Section 3**, students opting for coursework will find out how the key reading, writing and technical skills developed in Section 1 can be used to best effect in their coursework assignments.

Section 4: Speaking and listening

Section 4 provides a dedicated chapter on Speaking and Listening to build your skills and confidence with clear guidance, activities and exemplification of the presentation and discussion tasks.

Section 5: Exam practice

Finally, **Section 5** offers extended exam practice to help you hone your examination technique under timed conditions.

Checking your progress

It is important to know how you are progressing, and we have therefore included activities throughout the book, which could be used as assessment opportunities. In Sections 2, 3, 4 and 5 these tasks are supported by sample responses at different levels to help you understand how you can improve your work. The sample tasks, responses and commentaries have been written by our authors, not by Cambridge Assessment International Education.

Throughout the book, there are regular 'Check your progress' features to help you assess the progress you are making.

We hope our skills-building approach helps you to unlock the fundamentals of your Cambridge IGCSE First Language English course and to become a confident, skillful communicator within and beyond the classroom.

Julia Burchell
Series Editor

Key reading skills

In this chapter, you will develop a range of fundamental reading skills that you can use throughout your Cambridge IGCSE course.

You will learn how to

- skim and scan to locate information
- select information
- understand explicit meanings
- synthesise information
- infer implicit meanings about character and setting
- identify emotive and sensory language
- recognise, analyse and evaluate facts, opinions and bias
- detect the form, purpose, style and audience of texts.

On their own, some of the skills may seem simple, but remember that they are building blocks to completing larger and more complex tasks later on. For example:

- tasks that ask you to find a word or phrase require you to skim, scan and select information
- tasks that ask you to explain or put something into your own words draw on your ability to understand explicit or implicit meanings
- tasks that ask you to retell or reuse a text in a more succinct way require you to synthesise.

Links to other chapters:

Chapter 5: Comprehension

Chapter 6: Summary writing

Chapter 7: Analysing language

Chapter 8: Extended response to reading and directed writing

Chapter 9: Composition

Locating information: skimming

There are two ways to find information in a text. The first is to *skim* and the second is to *scan*.

Explore the skills

You use skimming and scanning skills in everyday life as well as study. For example, you may skim and scan to find information from a train timetable or from websites.

Skimming means reading the whole text quickly, to get an overall picture of what it is about. Even a very quick skim-read can tell you a great deal about a text.

 1 Skim the following extract from the opening chapter of *The No. 1 Ladies Detective Agency* by Alexander McCall Smith, then answer the questions below.

> Mma Ramotswe had a detective agency in Africa, at the foot of Kgale Hill. These were its assets: a tiny white van, two desks, two chairs, a telephone, and an old typewriter. Then there was a teapot, in which Mma Ramotswe – the only lady private detective in Botswana – brewed redbush tea. And three mugs – one for herself, one for her secretary, and one for the client. What else does a detective agency really need? Detective agencies rely on human **intuition** and intelligence, both of which Mma Ramotswe had in abundance. No inventory would ever include those, of course.
>
> But there was also the view, which again could appear on no inventory. How could any such list describe what one saw when one looked out from Mma Ramotswe's door? To the front, an acacia tree, the thorn tree which dots the wide edges of the Kalahari; the great white thorns, a warning; the olive-grey leaves, by contrast, so delicate. In its branches, in the late afternoon, or in the cool of the early morning, one might see a Go-Away Bird, or hear it, rather. And beyond the acacia, over the dusty road, the roofs of the town under a cover of trees and scrub bush; on the horizon, in a blue shimmer of heat, like improbable, overgrown termite mounds.
>
> From *The No. 1 Ladies Detective Agency* by Alexander McCall Smith

a) What type of text is this?

b) Where is it set?

c) Does the passage feature a character?

d) Is this passage full of action?

e) What is the purpose of this text?

f) Is a strong attitude or message being presented by the text?

g) Is this passage very descriptive?

g) Is this passage very descriptive?

h) Do you get a sense of what might happen next/later?

Build the skills

Build the skills

You may need to skim a text in order to become familiar with it so that you can answer questions about it.

2 Would you now know where in the passage to look if you had to respond to the following, more specific, tasks?

a) Describe the kind of vegetation near Mma Ramotswe's office.

b) Does Mma Ramotswe employ any staff?

c) What sort of woman is Mma Ramotswe?

Develop the skills

Sometimes a text may be too long or complex to skim in one go. In this case, it helps to give each paragraph a heading.

3 Reread the extract. What headings would you give to its two paragraphs? Do the headings make it easier or harder to answer the questions in Task 2?

4 In the passage, both paragraphs could be annotated to show that they contain two sets of information. What would you write and where?

Apply the skills

5 Answer the three questions in Task 2 in full sentences, as if approaching part of a comprehension question.

Checklist for success

✔ Quickly skim-read the text to understand what it is about.

✔ Use annotations and headings to identify the content of each paragraph.

✔ Use these annotations to locate the information you need to answer the questions.

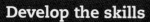

Locating information: scanning

Scanning is the reading skill that you use after you have skimmed the text. Scanning means looking for particular details or information. You dip in and out, reading certain words or phrases closely to check whether they are useful or not.

Top tip

In everyday life, scanning is like fishing around in your sock drawer looking for the other half of a matching pair!

Explore the skills

In real life, you scan when you are looking for something particular – for example, the cost of an item or the closing date for an application. To do this, you first decide what you are looking for, then find something that fits that requirement.

Key term

dialogue: a conversation between two or more people in a piece of writing

1 Copy and complete the table below by matching each numbered box with a lettered box.

Text	Information you need	What you would scan for
cinema home page	1 show times	A the words *donate*, *giving*; or types of information: how you can help, an address, telephone number, text number
take-away menu	2 their email address	B for example, their name, adjectives near their name, pieces of **dialogue** that they are in
advert for a Zumba class	3 the name of the instructor	C the words *boots*, *shoes*, *footwear*
a charity leaflet	4 how to donate	D the @ symbol
a novel	5 quotes about a character	E the phrase *pleased to inform you* or the word *regret*
a receipt	6 the price of a pair of boots to get a refund	F a word beginning with a capital or the words *instructor*, *teacher*, *led by*
a letter	7 did I get the job?	G numbers in time format

Build the skills

When you are studying, you may need to select points for a summary, analyse the effects a writer has created or select information to use in a piece of directed writing. You may not have time to read the whole text again. To find the information, you need to *scan*.

The clue is always in the key words of the question. Look at the following question.

> Select four unpleasant aspects of the narrator's house.

Here, *unpleasant* and *the narrator's house* are the key words. First, you need to 'unpick' the word *unpleasant*.

> unpleasant = not nice, would be uncomfortable to live with, would make daily life hard

Then make a mental checklist of what you are looking for:

- I am looking for details about a building.
- I am going to be scanning mainly for comments about it that do not sound nice.
- I should look out for descriptive details (**adjectives/adverbs**) with negative meanings.

As you scan, your brain will ask itself whether the words you are reading fit the checklist.

Here is the extract that goes with the question.

I live in a corner of [the city [...] in a cramped hundred-square-foot shack which has (a) no natural light or (b) no ventilation, with a corrugated metal sheet serving as a roof over my head. It vibrates violently whenever a train passes overhead. There is no running water and no sanitation. This is all I can afford. But I am not alone [...]. There are a million people like me, packed in a two-hundred-hectare triangle of swampy urban wasteland, where we live like animals and die like insects. Destitute migrants from all over the country jostle with each other for their own handful of sky in [the world's] biggest slum. There are daily squabbles – over inches of space, over a bucket of water – which at times turn deadly.

From *Q & A* by Vikas Swarup

Top tip

Remember that scanning is the reading version of matching socks, so you need to look carefully at the one in your hand before you can find its pair.

Key terms

adjectives: words that describe nouns ('the *red* car', 'the *closed* shop')

adverbs: describe a verb (usually an action)

2 Copy and complete the table below, which helps you to sift the words and phrases from the first few sentences of the *Q & A* extract on page 11 to decide what is and is not relevant.

Words read	Is this about a house?	Are the words used unpleasant?	Other thoughts
I live in a corner of [the city]	no, about an area		corner sounds like a trap – not nice
in a	yes, 'in' suggests we are going to get a description of a house next		
cramped		yes, means too small for comfort	
hundred-square-foot	yes, about its size		I am used to a bigger room so I would not like this
shack	another word for a house	this word means not well made or temporary, so yes	
which has (a) no natural light			
or (b) ventilation			
with a corrugated metal sheet serving as a roof over my head			
It vibrates violently			
whenever a train passes overhead			
There is no running water			
and no sanitation			

Develop the skills

Scanning the rest of the sentence around the key words will usually help you find the correct information. This is called using the context. It is particularly important in a selective summary, when you have to summarise information on a particular aspect of a text. Use the whole sentence to clarify factual information, such as the person or place being described.

3 How could you use the whole sentence below to work out the specific meaning of the word *migrants*?

> Destitute migrants from all over the country jostle with each other for their own handful of sky in [the world's] biggest slum.

Apply the skills

Sometimes you will need to skim a whole sentence or paragraph in order to identify the gist, or a general feeling. You will then go back to scan for the words that are key to creating this effect. This is particularly useful when approaching questions that look at how writers achieve effects.

4 Use the strategies that you have learned to scan for relevant information to answer the following question about the extract on page 11.

> How does the writer suggest that life is not easy for the narrator?

Checklist for success

✔ Use the key words in the question to help you decide what is relevant and what is not.

✔ Find relevant, short words, phrases or details that answer the question.

✔ Make sure that you understand the precise meaning of each word, phrase or detail by looking at the context of the whole sentence around it.

Selecting information

Once you have the gist of a text (skimmed) and have located the information you need (scanned), you need to *select* what information to use.

Explore the skills

Select only the *most relevant* information.

1 Read the following question and extract. Then identify the unnecessary material in the two sample answers below.

> Name two aspects of Portugal that Jack Petchey wanted others to experience.

> In 1970 45-year-old Jack Petchey stood on a hilltop overlooking one of the most beautiful bays on Portugal's Algarve and envisaged a time when people would come and marvel at the same view, walk on those white-gold sands and swim in that perfect sea – and they would do it all from the comfort of a luxury holiday resort complex.
>
> From *P-Leisure Magazine*

> Petchey wanted people to have his experience of the white-gold sands and to swim in the perfect sea. He wanted them to 'marvel at the view'.

> Petchey liked the hill above a lovely bay and the amazing view that he was enjoying so he wanted to share it.

Build the skills

Look at the two sample answers to this question.

> What made Jack Petchey decide to build Club Praia da Oura?

> Jack Petchey decided to build the club because he enjoyed that part of the Algarve coast and he wanted other people to be able to enjoy it too.

Top tip

Being concise and using your own words are important in summary and directed writing tasks. Simply copying out sentences from the passage will make your response weaker.

> Jack Petchey decided to build the club because one day he was out for a walk and the view reminded him how lovely it was on the beach and in the sea and he wanted other people to be able to do it too so they needed somewhere to stay.

Top tip

Never include descriptive detail, examples, anecdotes or quotations in a short answer or a response to a summary question.

2 Using the statements below, find examples of what makes one answer more effective than the other.

- It removes specific examples.
- It removes descriptive detail.
- It ignores irrelevant additional details.
- It combines different examples into larger points.

Develop the skills

Writers often develop their ideas by adding **anecdotes**.

Key term

anecdotes: short stories to exemplify or back up a writer's or speaker's points

I really don't like cats; they scare me. If I see one coming I run. Well okay, I step hesitantly backwards and wait for them to pass, never losing eye contact with their slinky panther-like frames. They're mysterious, aloof creatures. Give me a soppy canine anytime. One look at its face and you know it all: 'keep away, I'm not in the mood' or 'yes, yes, yes, let's play now!' It all started when I was a small child and I was left in the garden on my own. Next door's cat came walking up to me. It looked harmless enough; in fact it looked cuddly and kind, so I put my arms out and pulled it towards me. Yowl! It made a terrible noise, and swiped me across the cheek with its paw. I began to wail even louder than it had! So there you have it: the reason I hate our furry friends, in a nutshell.

3 What is the main point here? Where does the anecdote start and finish?

Sometimes you will need to use your own words to answer a question concisely.

4 Rewrite the following sentence in your own words. In particular, think about using alternative verbs and adjectives (**synonyms**).

> It looked harmless enough; in fact, it looked cuddly and kind.

Key term

synonyms: words that are identical, or very close in meaning, to other words

Apply the skills

5 Answer the following question on the passage above. Summarise concisely in your own words, grouping ideas together in longer sentences.

> How does the writer feel about cats and why?

Synthesis

Synthesis is a skill you will need when responding to a directed writing task. Synthesis involves locating information from different sources and combining it in your own text.

Explore the skills

Synthesis is the skill of bringing information together from a range of sources and making sure that it is clearly organised for purpose.

In everyday life, you often need to consider a wide range of written information on a topic. For example:

- if you were planning to purchase a new mobile phone, you would probably check the details of several phones in store or on the internet
- if you were planning a holiday, you might gather information about a country from holiday brochures, the internet and guidebooks.

However, synthesis is not simply about collecting information from different locations. It is also about sorting relevant information into a clear and concise order.

You may need to gather information from several places and use it in one piece of writing. Directed writing and extended responses to reading tasks ask you to draw your answers from all parts of one, or sometimes two, texts. Summary questions ask you to look at one text at a time, but you still need to use information from across the whole text.

> **Top tip**
>
> Synthesis is a little bit like cooking a meal. It would be very inefficient to start cooking while the ingredients are still jumbled up in your shopping bags. Good cooks unpack their ingredients and organise them according to when they are needed and which items will be combined with each other.

1. Look at the ingredients below. Some are used to make tortillas (simple pancakes made of flour and water) and others to make the fillings of chilli, salad, sour cream, cheese and salsa. Sort the ingredients into two lists: one for the tortillas and one for the fillings.

red onion, finely sliced	cheddar cheese, grated	two hot green or red chillies
fresh tomatoes	fresh coriander, chopped · sour cream	cucumber
one cup of water	lettuce · juice of one lime	plain flour
tinned tomatoes	minced lamb	

Build the skills

If the question is a simple one, you may only be looking for one type of information from the text or texts. For example:

> Summarise the problems caused by extreme weather conditions as shown in the passage.

It is tempting in these circumstances to simply start reading and to write out your answer as you go along. However, this can waste time and your answer will be weaker if similar points are repeated in several places in the text.

This is even more of a problem if you need to use two or more texts in an extended response to a reading task. For example:

> Imagine that you are a journalist putting together a script for a radio broadcast about the kinds of aid that are needed after a natural disaster. You have read the extract below and you have also made the following notes (on page 18) taken from an interview with an aid worker from an international charity.
>
> In your broadcast, you should explain:
>
> • what kinds of problems arise from natural disasters
> • what can be done in advance to make recovery easier
> • what needs to be done after the disaster has occurred.

Extreme winds, such as those found in hurricanes, tornadoes and some thunderstorms, can overturn caravans, tear off roofs and topple trees, causing extreme distress to many people and financial hardship to whole communities. Some of the strongest tornadoes can demolish houses completely, leaving people homeless, and vulnerable to disease and criminal harm. People may be knocked down or struck by debris and many places may lose electricity. Flooding and storm surges can destroy buildings and roads, contaminate water supplies, halt other essential services and drown people. Large hail stones can damage cars and roofs, and destroy crops, but rarely kill people. Heat waves can lead to drought, which causes crop loss as well as health issues and death from dehydration.

Interview notes

Need supplies, fresh water, medicines, tents

Disease spreads fast when pipes are broken

People should not rely on the state, they can get private insurance

Rapid response teams need to be formed to remove debris and search for/treat survivors

Rough terrain vehicles needed Extra police presence helps to reduce looting

After you have digested the question, first scan the text to locate information. Then go back over the text and categorise the information into the different types requested in the question. You could use colour-coding to group similar pieces of information together, so that when you write your answer, you only make each point once.

2　Reread the passage on page 17 and list all the different statements about problems caused by extreme weather conditions.

Develop the skills

It is important to group ideas together as you are reading, to save time.

3　Look back at the list of problems caused by extreme weather conditions you generated for Task 2. Group the information into between five and nine different categories. Each time you come across a new piece of information, decide whether it should go under an existing heading or whether you need to create a new one.

You can go through the same process with two or more texts. Simply add to the categories you have created, or add details to existing ones.

Apply the skills

When making notes for a directed writing task, you should use the bullet points given in the question to help you decide on the category headings.

 4 Consider the whole extended response to the reading task on pages 17 to 18. Make a complete set of notes for the task, using the interview notes as well as the passage that appears with the question.

Checklist for success

✔ Use the question to help you decide on your categories for making notes or annotations.

✔ Decide on the best method of recording information from a text so that it is most useful for summary questions or directed writing tasks.

Top tip

Making notes can also help to keep your answers balanced. In directed writing tasks, it is a common mistake to focus too much on one text and forget to use points from the other. By making notes, you will ensure that both texts are fully covered.

Explicit meaning

You will be asked to find words with explicit meanings, or provide explanations for them, in several different assessment type tasks. Sometimes the information that you are scanning for is very obvious, or explicit. For example, you might be looking for a precise piece of information, such as a name or number in a non-fiction piece, or the narrator may reveal something about a character, place or feeling in a direct way in a piece of fiction.

Top tip

Understanding explicit meaning is also important in extended response to reading and directed writing tasks. For these, you will have to gather and select information from the texts provided and adapt it for a different purpose. (See Chapter 8.)

Explore the skills

Summary tasks and low-scoring 'closed' comprehension or short-answer exam questions often test your ability to identify explicit information. You also need to be able to find and adapt explicit information in response to reading and directed writing tasks. To do this, use the following four steps of basic scanning skills (explained on pages 10–13):

1 Look carefully at the question.
2 Decide exactly what you are looking for.
3 Jump to the rough location of that information.
4 Cross-examine what is there to see if it matches your checklist.

1 Read the extract from *The Salt Road* by Jane Johnson on page 21. Then use the four steps above to identify a word or phrase from the text that suggests the same idea as the words underlined.

   a) Izzy's wigwam consists of cotton <u>hanging from</u> a bamboo pole.

   b) Izzy <u>would rather</u> be outside.

   c) Izzy found the house impossible to <u>breathe freely in</u>.

   d) Izzy's parents studied the evidence of <u>vanished cultures from long ago</u>.

   e) Izzy was not the kind of child to <u>go well with</u> her parents' lifestyle.

When I was a child, I had a wigwam in our back garden: a circle of thin yellow cotton draped over a bamboo pole and pegged to the lawn. Every time my parents argued, that was where I went. I would lie on my stomach with my fingers in my ears and stare so hard at the red animals printed on its bright decorative border that after a while they began to dance and run, until I wasn't in the garden any more but out on the plains, wearing a fringed deerskin tunic and feathers in my hair, just like the brave in the films I watched every Saturday morning in the cinema down the road.

Even at an early age I found it preferable to be outside in my little tent rather than inside the house. The tent was my space. It was as large as my imagination, which was infinite. But the house, for all its **grandeur** and **Georgian** spaciousness, felt small and suffocating. It was stuffed with things, as well as with my mother and father's bitterness. They were both **archaeologists**, my parents: lovers of the past, they had surrounded themselves with boxes of yellowed papers, ancient artefacts, dusty objects; the fragile husks of lost civilisations. I never knew why they decided to have me: even the quietest baby, the most house-trained toddler, the most studious child, would have disrupted the artificial, museum-like calm they had wrapped around themselves. In that house they lived separated from the rest of the world, in a bubble in which dust motes floated silently like the fake snow in a snow-globe. I was not the child to complement such a life, being a wild little creature, loud and messy and **unbiddable**.

[…] I had dolls, but more often than not I beheaded them or scalped them, or buried them in the garden and forgot where they were. I had no interest in making fashionable outfits for the **oddly attenuated** pink plastic **mannequins** with their insectile torsos and brassy hair that the other girls so worshipped and adorned.

From *The Salt Road* by Jane Johnson

Vocabulary

grandeur: grandness

Georgian: style of architecture from the period 1714–1811

archaeologists: scientists who study the past by looking at historical objects and sites

unbiddable: unresponsive to being told what to do

oddly attenuated: strangely long and thin

mannequins: models or dummies

Build the skills

Writers choose words very carefully for their precise meanings. As you read a passage, you need to think about the precise meaning of individual words and ask yourself why the author has chosen them. What other words (synonyms) might have been used instead?

2 Look back at the extract on page 21. Look up the words that have been highlighted, then copy and complete the table below.

Word	Precise meaning	Synonym	What the writer wanted to convey
infinite	having no limits or measurable extent	boundless	The girl is highly imaginative.
stuffed	very full		
yellowed			
dusty			

Develop the skills

You may be asked to explain the meanings of words and phrases. Try using a range of sentence stems to start this kind of explanation – for example:

The writer chooses the word…, which in everyday language means…

The word used by the writer, …, means…

The writer uses the phrase…, which is another way of saying…

3 Use each of the sentence starters above to write about three of the highlighted words in the extract.

Apply the skills

A range of questions will test your understanding of explicit meanings. (The following questions all relate to *The Salt Road* extract on page 21.) The most common are the simple 'closed' questions that appear in comprehension questions. For example:

> Give two reasons why the girl likes to go outside.
>
> How did the girl treat her toys?

Another comprehension question type requires you to explain the explicit meaning of the writer's words. For example:

> Explain how the girl liked to enjoy herself.
>
> Using your own words, explain what the writer means by 'In that house they lived separated from the rest of the world, in a bubble in which dust motes floated silently like the fake snow in a snow-globe.'

There will also be a summary question. For example:

> Using details that you have learned from the text, sum up what you know about the girl's childhood.

4 Answer the first four of the questions above in full sentences, using the extract from *The Salt Road* on page 21.

Implicit meaning: character

Sometimes the meaning that you are looking for is not immediately obvious from the explicit meaning of words alone. Words also carry with them suggestions and associations. You need to be able to identify and interpret this implicit information.

Explore the skills

When reading a text, you might be:

- looking for subtle aspects of a character
- trying to work out how a character feels about something or someone
- trying to define the relationship between two or more people
- exploring the writer's feelings or attitudes
- looking for a particular effect that the writer wants to create (for example, sympathy with a particular character).

This is called implicit meaning. Most of us are actually very good at finding implicit information in everyday situations. This is particularly true when we meet a new person. The process is called **inferring**.

Key term

inferring: reading between the lines and drawing conclusions from subtle clues

1 Look at the following question, then copy and complete the spider diagram below to record the clues that you use to reach your decisions.

> How do you know whether or not your teacher is in a good mood?

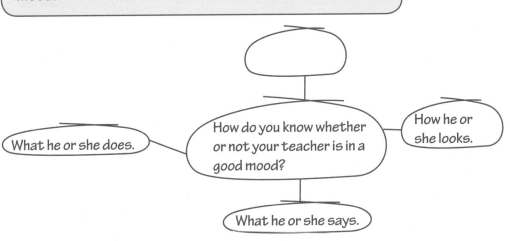

Build the skills

Writers give similar clues to guide their readers' responses to characters. You need to look for these clues and draw your own inferences from them. Consider this extract and then look at the table showing you how to draw inferences.

> 'It's no good!' Sasha groaned at her mother. 'I don't want Tracey at my birthday party and that's the end of this discussion!'

Phrase	Drawing out	Possible meaning
'Sasha groaned'	As if in pain – but she is not in physical pain, so she must be putting it on to make a point.	Sasha wants to make her mother feel that her attempt to persuade her is hurting her, to make her mother feel guilty and warn her to stop before she gets more upset.

2 Use the same approach to draw out what is implied about Sasha's attitude by 'that's the end of this discussion!'.

3 Read the continuation of the extract below, then answer this question.

> Explain how the highlighted phrases are used by the writer to tell us about the mother and the daughter.

> Her mother smiled, but her eyes were troubled as she scooped up the invitations from the table and began sliding them swiftly into the beautifully addressed envelopes. 'Well it doesn't seem kind to me to leave out just one girl in your class, sweetheart. I think you'll just have to accept that you can't have absolutely everything your own way…'. She looked up and tried to catch Sasha's eyes, which had already moved on to the photographs of elaborate cakes she had downloaded from the computer months ago.

Develop the skills

4 Read the extract from the opening chapter of *Great Expectations* by Charles Dickens on page 26.

As you read, note down what each character looks like, says and does, and how others react to him. Then think about the *effect* of what you are shown – what does it reveal about the two characters, Pip and the convict Magwitch?

Record your ideas in a separate table, like the one below, for each character.

Pip: What is said/done/how others react/words used to describe him	Effect: What it tells us about him	Effect: What it suggests about his relationships

'Hold your noise' cried a terrible voice, as a man started up from among the graves at the side of the church porch. 'Keep still, you little devil, or I'll cut your throat!'

A fearful man, all in coarse grey, with a great iron on his leg. A man with no hat, and with broken shoes, and with an old rag tied round his head. A man who had been soaked in water, and smothered in mud, and lamed by stones, and cut by flints, and stung by nettles, and torn by briars; who limped, and shivered, and glared and growled; and whose teeth chattered in his head as he seized me by the chin.

'O! Don't cut my throat, sir,' I pleaded in terror. 'Pray don't do it, sir.'

'Tell us your name,' said the man. 'Quickly.'

'Pip, sir.'

'Once more,' said the man, staring at me. 'Give it mouth!'

'Pip. Pip, sir.'

'Show us where you live,' said the man. 'Point out the place!'

I pointed to where our village lay, on the flat in-shore among the alder-trees and pollards, a mile or more from the church.

The man, after looking at me for a moment, turned me upside down, and emptied my pockets. There was nothing in them but a piece of bread. When the church came to itself – for he was so sudden and strong that he made it go head over heels before me, and I saw the steeple under my feet – when the church came to itself, I say, I was seated on a high tombstone, trembling, while he ate the bread ravenously.

'You young dog,' said the man, licking his lips, 'what fat cheeks you ha' got.'

I believe they were fat, though I was at that time undersized for my years, and not strong.

'Darn me if I couldn't eat em,' said the man, with a threatening shake of his head, 'and if I han't half a mind to 't.'

I earnestly expressed my hope that he wouldn't, and held tighter to the tombstone on which he had put me; partly, to keep myself upon it; partly, to keep myself from crying.

From *Great Expectations* by Charles Dickens

5 Use your notes to write a paragraph about each character.

Sometimes, meaning is implied by the literal meaning of an adjective or adverb. For example, in the sentence 'He flashed a warm smile in my direction', we associate warmth with friendliness or affection.

6 What is implied about the characters by the underlined phrases in the following sentences?

   a) Maria gave Tom <u>an icy glance</u>.

   b) He had a reputation for being <u>a smooth talker</u>.

   c) 'Can't you just <u>be straight</u> with me?'

   d) Counsellor Smith dealt with the objectors <u>somewhat heavy-handedly</u>.

   e) He greeted me <u>rather distantly</u>.

Apply the skills

In a task, sometimes the implicit information will be identified and you will be asked to find the words that create it. For example:

> Reread the description of Pip's first meeting with the convict Magwitch. Explain how the highlighted phrases are used by the writer to suggest that Pip is scared of Magwitch.

You may be asked to select words or phrases that have an effect on you, and to identify what this effect is. For example:

> Reread the descriptions of Magwitch in the extract. Select four powerful words or phrases from the extract and explain how each word or phrase is used effectively.

Top tip

You can explain the effect a writer creates by focusing only on the literal meaning – what the writer tells us directly. However, you will improve your skills if you also explain the implicit meaning – what you deduce from the subtle clues the writer gives.

7 Answer the two questions above in complete sentences.

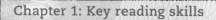

Implicit meaning: setting

Characters are not the only feature of writing in which you need to search for implicit meanings. You may also be able to infer meaning from the setting.

Explore the skills

You probably use your skills of inference in daily life, whenever you visit a new place.

1. Look at the following question, then copy and complete the spider diagram below to record the clues that you use to reach your decisions.

> When you first visit a new place what affects your attitude towards it?

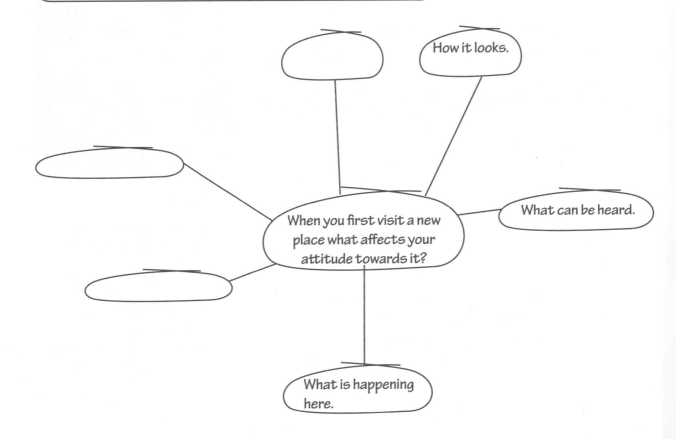

How it looks.

When you first visit a new place what affects your attitude towards it?

What can be heard.

What is happening here.

Build the skills

Writers give us similar clues to guide a reader's responses to places. They imply meanings through the details they give about settings to create a mood or atmosphere.

Read the paragraph below. Consider the effect of word choices, such as *buzzed*. This literally suggests a bee, which is thought of as continuously busy and energetic.

> The room buzzed with energy and everything appeared to be moving slightly as if to echo the **frenetic** hum of cheerful voices. Balloons gently swayed in the breeze, bunting swished above heads as couples danced or chatted with animation. Even the edges of the brightly patterned table cloths lifted as dresses swept by.

Vocabulary

frenetic: busy in an excited, uncontrolled way

2 Think of three words you could use to sum up the atmosphere in the room. Consider the following:

- How does the writer want you to feel about the event being described?
- Why might the writer have this intention?

Sometimes a writer will use **pathetic fallacy** in describing a place.

3 Add two more examples of this technique by making small changes to the passage.

4 Some settings already have particular connotations. For example, readers tend to see a cave as a mysterious or threatening place – what could be lurking within? However, in some contexts, it could suggest shelter.

a) Place the word 'jungle' at the centre of a spider diagram or mind map. Use this to explore words and ideas that you associate with the word 'jungle'.

b) What kinds of story might have jungle settings?

5 What is implied by the word 'jungle' in these sentences?

a) Mrs Jones's back garden was a jungle.

b) Living in an inner-city jungle, I grew up fast.

Key term

pathetic fallacy: when a writer reflects human emotions in natural features or objects: for example, *the balloons swayed happily* or *the leaden clouds hung heavy above the figure crouching on the moorland path*

Develop the skills

Read this extract from *Set in Stone* by Linda Newbery. A young man has arrived late at night and is searching for 'Fourwinds', a house deep in the countryside.

Darkness swallowed me; the branches arched high overhead; I saw only glimpses of the paler sky through their tracery. My feet crunched beech mast. I smelled the coolness of the mossy earth, and heard the trickle of water close by. As my eyes accustomed themselves to dimmer light, I saw that here, on the lower ground, a faint mist hung in the air, trapped perhaps beneath the trees. I must be careful not to stray from the path, which I could only dimly discern; but before many minutes had passed, wrought-iron gates reared ahead of me, set in a wall of flint. Though I had reached the edge of the wood, my way was barred. The gate must, however, be unlocked, as my arrival was expected.

I peered through the scrollwork of the gates. The track, pale and broad, wound between specimen trees and smooth lawns; I had some distance still to walk, it seemed. The mist clung to the ground, and the trees seemed rooted in a vaporous swamp. I tried the fastening; the left-hand gate swung open with a loud grating squeal that echoed into the night.

At the same moment another sound arose, competing for shrillness with the gate's protest: a sound to make my heart pound and my nerves stretch taut. It was a wailing shriek that filled my head and thrummed in my ears; close enough to make me shrink against the gate, which I pushed open to its fullest extent against the shadows of the wall. Whether the cry was animal or human, I could not tell. If human, it was a sound of terrible distress, of unbearable grief. I felt the hairs prickle on the back of my neck, my eyes trying to stare in all directions at once. Instinct told me to hunch low till the danger passed. Dropped into such strangeness, I had acquired, it seemed, the impulse of a wild creature to hide myself and survive whatever perils were near. The metal bit into my hands as I clung into the gate. Attempting to retain a clear head, I reminded myself that I was unfamiliar with the sounds of the countryside at night. It must be a fox, a badger, some creature yowling in hunger or pain.

From *Set in Stone* by Linda Newbery

The passage creates an atmosphere of foreboding without the writer saying directly that there is any threat. She does not say, 'I arrived at the house after a long journey and was really scared when I heard something screaming.' Instead, you work this out from the details she includes.

6 Copy and complete the following table on page 31 to help you analyse the different features the writer uses to create the mood in the extract. Add any further words or phrases that help to create this effect.

Top tip

In your own creative writing, remember to show rather than tell. This technique will help you imply subtle meanings of your own.

Word/phrase	Time of year	Time of day	Weather	Landscape	Object	Action	Sound
darkness							
branches							
mossy earth							
trickle of water							
faint mist							
wrought-iron gates							
a loud grating squeal							

7 The mood could be completely altered by changing the words and phrases. Add another column to your table with words and phrases that would make the approach to the house exciting and optimistic.

Top tip

Many writers use the factors in the top row of the table to create atmosphere. Try them out when you are writing your own descriptions.

Apply the skills

A range of questions will test your understanding of implicit meanings. Usually you will be asked to explain how words or phrases are used to suggest something. For example:

> Using your own words, explain how the highlighted phrases are used by the writer to suggest the narrator's experience and feelings.

> a sound to make my heart pound and my nerves stretch taut. It was a wailing shriek that filled my head and thrummed in my ears; close enough to make me shrink against the gate.

At a more sophisticated level, you may be asked to select words or phrases, and identify and explain their effects on you. For example:

> Reread paragraph 2 of the extract on page 30, beginning, 'I peered through the scrollwork of the gates.'
>
> Select four powerful words or phrases from this paragraph. Explain how each word or phrase selected is used effectively in the context.

8 Answer the two questions above in complete sentences.

Emotive language

One important type of implicit meaning that may occur in a text is emotive language – words or phrases that make the reader feel a particular emotion.

Explore the skills

Some words are very obviously emotive because of their explicit meaning. For example, the word *afraid* clearly tells us how someone feels and we immediately feel sympathy. However, sometimes the emotional effect is less obvious. For example, the word *graveyard* has negative **connotations** for most people. You might consider graveyards to be sad or even frightening places. The word might evoke your own memories or make you feel unhappy or uneasy.

1 What are the emotional effects of the following words? Is the effect created by the explicit meaning of the word or phrase, or by its connotations?

   a) sullen

   b) sunset

   c) red rose

   d) irritable

Build the skills

Different words have different connotations and levels of intensity. For example, there are many words that mean someone does not have very much body fat, but they all carry different connotations.

Key term

connotations: the emotional or sensory associations of a word or thing – for example, a flag can immediately make someone think 'my country'

Top tip

In cases where your personal interpretation is different from the usual one, it is safest to assume that the writer meant the word to be interpreted in the more normal way.

2 Consider the emotional effects of the following adjectives. Which have a positive effect and which have a negative one? Are any neutral?

a) thin

b) slim

c) slender

d) skeletal

e) scrawny

It is also important to consider *how* strong or weak the emotional intensity of a word is. For example, there are many words to describe feeling affection for something:

- keen on
- like
- adore
- love.

If you place these words on a scale of intensity, you will notice that some suggest a stronger feeling than others.

3 Where on the scale would you place the other two expressions in the list?

4 Draw your own 'intensity scale' for words related to *dislike*.

Develop the skills

It is also important to consider *why* a writer chooses to use a word with a particular emotional connotation or intensity, and what reaction they want from their reader.

5 What kind of emotional response do you think the author wants to create in each of the following sentences? How do the word choices achieve this?

a) The pack of ravening wolves bounded, snarling, razor fangs bared, closing in on the two terrified children.

b) As the rain began to lighten, and the sun shone bravely out from behind the clouds, a glorious rainbow spread in a huge arc across the sky.

c) The creatures slithered on their bellies, bulbous, pus-filled eyes pulsating at the ends of their long slimy stalks.

Read the following text from a short story.

The rounded bodies fell apart as he came into sight over the ridge, and displayed the pinkish object to be the partially devoured body of a human being, but whether of a man or woman he was unable to say. And the rounded bodies were new and ghastly-looking creatures, in shape somewhat resembling an octopus, with huge and very long and flexible tentacles, coiled copiously on the ground. The skin had a glistening texture, unpleasant to see, like shiny leather. The downward bend of the tentacle-surrounded mouth, the curious excrescence at the bend, the tentacles, and the large intelligent eyes, gave the creatures a grotesque suggestion of a face. They were the size of a fair-sized swine about the body, and the tentacles seemed to him to be many feet in length. There were, he thinks, seven or eight at least of the creatures. Twenty yards beyond them, amid the surf of the now returning tide, two others were emerging from the sea.

Their bodies lay flatly on the rocks, and their eyes regarded him with evil interest; but it does not appear that Mr Fison was afraid, or that he realised that he was in any danger. Possibly his confidence is to be ascribed to the limpness of their attitudes. But he was horrified, of course, and intensely excited and indignant, at such revolting creatures preying upon human flesh. He thought they had chanced upon a drowned body. He shouted to them, with the idea of driving them off, and finding they did not budge, cast about him, picked up a big rounded lump of rock, and flung it at one.

And then, slowly uncoiling their tentacles, they all began moving towards him – creeping at first deliberately, and making a soft purring sound to each other.

In a moment Mr Fison realised that he was in danger. He shouted again, threw both his boots, and started off, with a leap, forthwith. Twenty yards off he stopped and faced about, judging them slow, and behold! The tentacles of their leader were already pouring over the rocky ridge on which he had just been standing!

From 'The Sea Raiders' by H. G. Wells

6 Copy and complete a table like the one below.

- Identify the emotive words and phrases used in the text.
- Alongside each word, make a note explaining how the word would affect the reader.
- Consider why the writer wanted to create that effect.

Word/phrase	Effect on reader	Reason why writer wants to create that effect
partially devoured	We think of the shocking sight of the remains, and the savage power and appetite of the creatures.	He wants us to be disgusted and to fear for Mr Fison.
coiled copiously		

Apply the skills

7 Write up your notes as an answer to the following exam-style question.

> Select four powerful words or phrases from each of two paragraphs. Explain how each word or phrase is used effectively in the context.

You could use the following prompts to organise your answer:

- how the writer uses emotive language
- how the writer makes creatures seem alien
- how the writer uses physical details
- how the writer uses language to suggest threat.

Sensory language

Sensory language stimulates the reader's imagination so that they almost feel as if they are there. You can imagine exactly what you would be able to see, hear, touch, taste or smell at the scene.

Explore the skills

It can help to analyse sensory language in the form of a flow chart. You need to think not only about what a word means literally (its *denotation*) but also what associated ideas it brings to mind (its *connotations*).

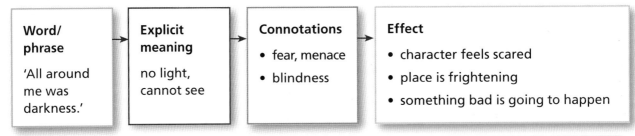

Word/phrase	Explicit meaning	Connotations	Effect
'All around me was darkness.'	no light, cannot see	• fear, menace • blindness	• character feels scared • place is frightening • something bad is going to happen

1 Make a flow chart for the following phrases:

   a) a wailing shriek

   b) I could smell the coolness of the mossy earth.

2 Read this description of a summer's day at the beach. Make a list of any words or phrases that stimulate the senses. You could use a table like the one started on page 37.

> Slush-grey and ice-white gulls scream and sticky toddlers wrestle over plastic spades, giggling carelessly. Their voices and the sweet smell of candyfloss wafts along the pebbled beach towards me. Striped deckchair canvases billow in the breeze and the commanding flags advertising ice-cream companies arch like stretching beauties as the warm wind catches them.
>
> The waves race towards us and their white crest curves up and over, scooping sand and stray flip-flops in its grasp. I lurch as the water sucks at my feet pulling me towards its grey-green depths, and grimace as the salt spray lingers on my stinging lips and tongue. There is no laughter in my mouth, just the harsh taste of loneliness.

Top tip

It is important to be able to spot words with a sensory appeal and explain their effects in writing. Sensory language is also a powerful technique to use in your own descriptive and narrative writing.

See	Hear	Touch	Taste	Smell
Slush-grey and ice-white gulls toddlers wrestle	scream	sticky	salt spray lingers	candyfloss wafts

Build the skills

3 Write a description of a person in the beach scene on page 36. Try to include at least three words or phrases to stimulate each of the senses. If possible, swap descriptions with a partner and see whether they can pick out your sensory details.

Develop the skills

Writers choose words very carefully to create precise pictures in the reader's mind.

Think about the difference between saying that the gulls were 'grey' and saying that they were 'slush-grey'. Which description helps you picture them most clearly?

Writers use adjectives, adverbs and even carefully selected nouns and verbs to create particular effects.

4 Look again at the description of the beach. Copy and complete the table below by picking out examples of each type of word and considering their impact on the reader.

Word/phrase	Noun	Adjective	Verb	Adverb	Effect
Slush-grey		√			Precise colour, makes us picture dirty snow. This does not sound positive and adds to the feeling of unease or unhappiness.

Apply the skills

5 Answer the question below.

Select four powerful words or phrases from the extract. Explain how each word or phrase selected is used effectively in the context.

Checklist for success

✔ Identify particular words and phrases relating to the senses.

✔ Consider the intended effects of this language and how it helps the writer to create a mood or convey the narrator's feelings.

Recognising fact, opinion and bias

To respond to texts in directed writing, you must be able to tell the difference between *fact* and *opinion*, and to understand **bias**. This will determine how you make use of the text in your own writing.

Explore the skills

Non-fiction usually includes facts and often includes opinions. A fact is a statement that could in theory be proven to be true – for example: *The Eiffel Tower is in Paris.* An opinion is a viewpoint that cannot be proven to be correct: *The Tower of London is well worth a visit.*

1 Decide whether the following statements are facts or opinions.

    a) Nothing matters more than family.

    b) Water covers 71 per cent of the Earth's surface.

    c) Women are on average shorter than men.

    d) Going abroad is a waste of money.

    e) Many people enjoy foreign holidays.

Build the skills

Read the following description of Dubai from a guide book. Look out for facts and opinions.

> For the visitor, there's far more to Dubai than designer boutiques and five-star hotels – although of course if all you're looking for is a luxurious dose of sun, sand and shopping, the city takes some beating. If you want to step beyond the tourist clichés, however, you'll find that Dubai has much more to offer than you might think, ranging from the fascinating old city centre, with its higgledy-piggledy labyrinth of bustling **souks** interspersed with fine old traditional Arabian houses, to the memorably quirky **postmodern** architectural skylines of the southern parts of the city. Dubai's human geography is no less memorable, featuring a cosmopolitan assortment of Emiratis, Arabs, Iranians, Indians, Filipinos and Europeans – a fascinating patchwork of peoples and languages that gives the city its uniquely varied cultural appeal.
>
> From *Rough Guides Dubai*

Key terms

bias: a strong favouring of one side of an argument or debate, often without representing the other side of it

Top tip

A statement presented as a fact could be incorrect, but that does not mean it is an opinion.

Vocabulary

souks: markets

postmodern: imaginative, rule-breaking

2 Create a table like the one below to show at least three more facts and three more opinions in the text about Dubai. Remember – opinions usually make a judgement.

Facts	Opinions
Dubai has 'designer boutiques and five-star hotels'.	Dubai is one of the world's best places for a beach and shopping holiday ('takes some beating').

3 Find words or phrases in your table that present a judgement, such as *takes some beating*. Use them in three sentences of your own to describe a place you know.

Develop the skills

Bias is describing something in a way that makes it seem better or worse than it actually is. Bias may be unconscious (as in bad reporting) or deliberate (as in a charity campaign or tourism promotion). Common forms are:

* presenting only those facts that support the writer's views
* using misleading statistics.

4 Look at these biased statements. Which misuses statistics, and how? Which is selective in its use of facts, and how?

a) Nettlefield United has never lost a home game.

b) The Antarctic is a great place to live, boasting 24-hour sunlight and wide-open spaces.

Now read this text from the Visit Dubai website.

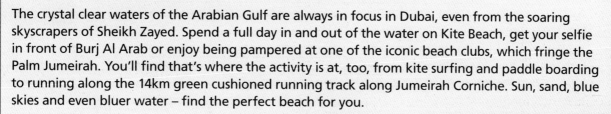

The crystal clear waters of the Arabian Gulf are always in focus in Dubai, even from the soaring skyscrapers of Sheikh Zayed. Spend a full day in and out of the water on Kite Beach, get your selfie in front of Burj Al Arab or enjoy being pampered at one of the iconic beach clubs, which fringe the Palm Jumeirah. You'll find that's where the activity is at, too, from kite surfing and paddle boarding to running along the 14km green cushioned running track along Jumeirah Corniche. Sun, sand, blue skies and even bluer water – find the perfect beach for you.

From www.visitdubai.com

5 In what ways does this text show bias? What information might have been included in a completely unbiased version?

Apply the skills

6 Write a description encouraging tourists to visit where you live. Include facts, opinions and bias.

Analysing and evaluating

In directed writing tasks, you may be asked to read one or more texts giving facts and opinions, then to write a letter, speech or report based on your assessment of them.

Explore the skills

To evaluate arguments, you first need to analyse them – to understand what they are and how they are constructed. For this, you need the reading skills you have developed so far in this chapter.

1 What do you understand by each of the following as a source of evidence for analysing and evaluating a text? How would you rank the importance and reliability of each one?

- The wording of the title
- **Topic sentences** introducing paragraphs
- Factual evidence
- Anecdotal evidence

Read the following extract from a newspaper article about the effect of social media on teenagers.

Key term

topic sentence: a sentence that introduces or sums up the overall idea or focus of a paragraph

Social media is harming the mental health of teenagers. The state has to act

The digital landscape has put increased pressure on teenagers today, and we feel it. There are so many social media channels: Facebook, Twitter, Instagram, Snapchat, Tumblr, you name it. I made a conscious decision to avoid Snapchat and Instagram because of the social pressure I saw them putting on my 14-year-old little sister. If my mum turned off the WiFi at 11pm, my sister would beg me to turn my phone into a hotspot. She always needed to load her Snapchat stories one more time, or to reply to a message that had come in two minutes ago because she didn't want her friend to feel ignored. If I refused, saying she could respond in the morning, I'd get the 'You're ruining my social life' speech. Even as a teenager as well, I sometimes find this craze a little baffling.

A new study has found that teenagers who engage with social media during the night could be damaging their sleep and increasing their risk of anxiety and depression. Teenagers spoke about the pressure they felt to make themselves available 24/7, and the resulting anxiety if they did not respond immediately to texts or posts. Teens are so emotionally invested in social media that a fifth of secondary school pupils will wake up at night and log on, just to make sure they don't miss out.

From 'Social media is harming the mental health of teenagers' by June Eric Udorie, *The Guardian*

title summarises

topic sentence introduces paragraph

factual evidence

anecdotal evidence

2 Using your own words, explain the main point Udorie makes in the first paragraph.

3 What evidence does she provide for this main point?

Build the skills

4 What important point does Udorie make in the second paragraph of the article?

5 What evidence does she give?

Develop the skills

To evaluate, you must judge, weighing up the points made. For example, you might judge that Udorie's argument is strengthened – or weakened – by what she reveals about herself.

Now read this extract from another article in the same newspaper.

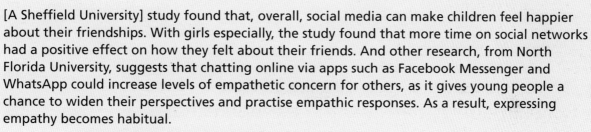

> [A Sheffield University] study found that, overall, social media can make children feel happier about their friendships. With girls especially, the study found that more time on social networks had a positive effect on how they felt about their friends. And other research, from North Florida University, suggests that chatting online via apps such as Facebook Messenger and WhatsApp could increase levels of empathetic concern for others, as it gives young people a chance to widen their perspectives and practise empathic responses. As a result, expressing empathy becomes habitual.
>
> From 'Social media gets a bad press, but it was a lifeline for me' by Grace Holliday, *The Guardian*

6 What main argument does Holliday put forward?

7 Comment on how convincing you find this argument, and why.

Apply the skills

8 Using material from both extracts, write the start of a speech to parents of teenagers, in which you weigh up the pros and cons of social media and start to reach your own conclusions.

Understanding the form and purpose of different texts

Form and purpose are important factors influencing a text. You should be aware of their effect on any text you read, and bear them in mind in your own writing.

Explore the skills

The *form* of a piece of writing is the context of where and how it appears. For example, it might be a review in a magazine, an informative web page, a letter or a diary entry. It will probably follow at least some of the conventions of its form. For example, a review will contain both information and evaluation.

1 How would you expect form to influence content in the following texts?

   a) an article in a free in-flight magazine

   b) a celebrity autobiography

   c) a newspaper review of a currently running play

The *purpose* of a text is what its author wants it to achieve. Some typical purposes are to inform, to advise, to persuade and to entertain.

2 Which of these purposes do you think would apply to the following types of text?

   a) a news report

   b) a holiday brochure

   c) an accident prevention leaflet

Build the skills

You should consider each element carefully when reading a text and in your own writing. When approaching extended response to reading and directed writing tasks, keep their form and purpose in mind at all times.

Read the following text on page 43 by the businessman and adventurer Sir Richard Branson. In 1987, he attempted to cross the Atlantic by hot-air balloon with his partner, Per Lindstrand. In this extract, after a disastrous attempt to land, Per has leapt into the sea to save himself but Branson remains in the balloon.

Top tip

Read Chapter 3 for more information about different forms of text.

Read Chapter 4 for more information about different purposes.

Alone in the balloon

Whatever I did in the next ten minutes would lead to my death or survival. I was on my own. We had broken the record but I was almost certainly going to die. Per, with no survival suit, was either dead or trying to swim on. I had to get somebody to find him. I had to survive. I cleared my mind and concentrated on the options in front of me. I hadn't slept for over 24 hours and my mind felt fuzzy. I decided to take the balloon up high enough so I could parachute off the capsule. I blasted the burners and then found my notebook and scrawled across the open page, 'Joan, Holly, Sam, I love you.' I waited until the altimeter showed 8000 feet and then climbed outside.

I was alone in the cloud. I crouched by the railings and looked down. I was still wheeling through the possibilities. If I jumped, I would be likely to have only two minutes to live. If I managed to open my parachute, I would still end up in the sea, where I would probably drown. I felt for the parachute release tag, and wondered whether it was the right one. Perhaps due to my dyslexia, I have a mental block about which is right and which is left, especially with parachutes. The last time I had free-fallen I pulled the wrong release tag and jettisoned my parachute. At the time, I had several skydivers around me, so they activated my reserve parachute. But now I was by myself at 8000 feet. I slapped myself hard across the face to concentrate.

From *Losing my Virginity* by Richard Branson

3 What is the form of this text? For example, is it an advert for ballooning? How do the following lines help you to decide?

   a) 'We had broken the record but I was almost certainly going to die.'

   b) 'I... scrawled across the open page, "Joan, Holly, Sam, I love you."'

   c) 'Perhaps due to my dyslexia, I have a mental block about which is right and which is left...'

4 Now think about the purpose of the text. What do you think the author wants to achieve with the following lines?

   a) 'Whatever I did in the next ten minutes would lead to my death or survival.'

   b) 'Per, with no survival suit, was either dead or trying to swim on.'

   c) 'If I jumped, I would be likely to have only two minutes to live.'

   d) 'I slapped myself hard across the face to concentrate.'

> **Top tip**
> ....
> A text will only have one form, but it may have more than one purpose – such as to criticise and entertain.

Develop the skills

Form and purpose are closely related. For example, an instruction booklet is short and easy to follow, because its purpose is to explain clearly. It will not tell funny stories or include poetic descriptions.

Read the following opening to a report in the *Metro Toronto* newspaper.

Confessions of a high-rise window cleaner

After cycling from Toronto to the West Coast and back, then sailing from Scarborough to Iceland, K.C. Maple was having trouble adjusting to the confined life within the tall towers of Toronto.

That was until he found a job that let him climb to the top and dangle off of them.

For the past two and a half years, the 24-year-old with long, blond hair pulled back in a ponytail has washed the windows of Toronto's highrise buildings. It was on the way to a native sun dance ceremony that the part-Swede, part-aboriginal met a man who cleaned windows for a living.

'That was the pivotal point that brought me into the joy of this business,' he says. He is sometimes afraid, but mostly he enjoys the thrill of being up so high. And the money is good. He tells me a beginner who works fast can usually make around $50 000 a year.

'It's great to be paid to go out there, have a little danger and have some fun,' he says. 'I've always wanted adventure, excitement, physical danger.'

Maple spends his days speeding up elevators with 250 feet of ropes draped over his shoulders, then lowering the rope down the side of buildings and **repelling** on a small plywood seat, holding a couple of squeegees, a suction cup to help him keep close to the windows and a five-gallon bucket filled with water and dish soap.

It's great exercise, especially pulling the ropes up at the end of the day – 'From a fitness standpoint, you've got a lot of **reps**,' he explains.

Instead of feeling trapped within the walls of a crowded city, he feels liberated in scaling them.

'I love the peace out there – on the outside of the building. You're not inside the fishbowl.'

By Carolyn Morris, *Metro Toronto*

Vocabulary

repelling (and reps): rappelling, a climbing technique for lowering yourself on a rope

5 This text is from a newspaper, but what kind of report is it? For example, is it breaking news? How does the following sentence help you answer this question?

> For the past two and a half years, the 24-year-old with long, blond hair pulled back in a ponytail has washed the windows of Toronto's highrise buildings.

6 Comment on what the following tells you about the form of the passage.

> 'That was the pivotal point that brought me into the joy of this business,' he says. He is sometimes afraid, but mostly he enjoys the thrill of being up so high. And the money is good. He tells me a beginner who works fast can usually make around $50 000 a year.

Apply the skills

7 Both this report and the ballooning account describe dangerous physical activities. Despite this similarity, their purposes are different. Explain how.

8 Now write one of the following:
- a report in the form of the *Metro Toronto* article but about Richard Branson's ballooning
- an account of the dangers of high-rise window-cleaning based on information in the *Metro Toronto* report, but in the same form as the ballooning account.

Deducing the audience

You will analyse and evaluate a text more effectively if you understand how its content and style are aimed at a particular audience. This will also help you respond to the text in your own directed writing.

Explore the skills

Texts are usually written with a target audience in mind – sometimes a very specific one.

1. What target audience do you think you fit into based on the type of things you read? Rank the following factors according to their importance:

   - where you live
   - how old you are
   - how much you have to spend
   - your gender
   - your level of education
   - your special interests or pastimes
   - your existing knowledge of a subject.

Build the skills

A writer will think about the target audience and make choices based on this audience that determine the content (what it is about) and the style and language of a piece of writing.

2. What can you deduce about the target audience of these sentences from their content, style and language?

   a) At a time when global warming is already creating havoc in the natural world, it's down to people like you and me to save the planet.

   b) Grange Park has something for everyone – wild water rides for adventurous teens, bouncy castles for the kiddies and relaxing gardens for Mum and Dad.

   c) Your Rebel T5i 700D offers a wide range of shooting options, from Scene Intelligent Auto to fully manual control of lens aperture, shutter speed and ISO.

3 Read the following review opening and make notes on any clues you find about its target audience.

J Hus – Common Sense

On his debut album, the man of many voices provides the sound of now

If any single artist embodies the boundary-trouncing **cross-pollination** that's making hip-hop so exciting right now, it's 20-year-old London rapper J Hus. He's a total vocal chameleon, capable of convincingly switching flows – switching nationality, even – depending on what the track requires. A single verse can find J scrolling through the **louche** grind of Jamaican dancehall, the autotuned bounce of Ghanian hiplife, the **aggy** energy of London grime and the **zoned-out** drawl of Atlanta rap. It's a dizzying, dazzling trick.

J Hus's **prodigious** genre-hopping means that – despite containing only four brief guest spots –

his 17-track debut album remains energised and entertainingly unpredictable from end to end.

From 'J Hus "Common Sense" Review' by Joe Madden, *New Musical Express*

Look closely at the following two quotations from the extract.

- 'the louche grind of Jamaican dancehall, the autotuned bounce of Ghanian hiplife, the aggy energy of London grime and the zoned-out drawl of Atlanta rap'
- 'energised and entertainingly unpredictable'

4 a) What kind of specialist knowledge in the target audience does the first sentence suggest?

b) What do the descriptive phrases in the first sentence suggest that the writer is trying to do for the benefit of the audience, and how would this help them?

c) How does the phrase 'energised and entertainingly unpredictable' make a judgement that might appeal to the target audience?

5 Which words in the Vocabulary box above are examples of informal 'street' language? Which are likely to be used by quite well-educated readers? What does this combination tell you about the target audience?

> ### Vocabulary
>
> **cross-pollination:** mixing of influences
>
> **louche:** disreputable, not respectable
>
> **aggy:** agitated, nervy
>
> **zoned-out:** not thinking, as if hypnotised
>
> **prodigious:** impressive in size or extent

Develop the skills

Now read the end of the J Hus review.

This is very much a post-Stormzy, post-Skepta, post-Drake-going-roadman album, and an important stepping stone along the path to the UK establishing itself as a bona fide world-beater at beats and rhymes.

With his attention-grabbing skills and knack for sculpting hooks, J Hus could crack the US with a single feature on some hot rapper's hit track. But honestly, with our homegrown scene so exciting right now, why not simply stay basking in that local adulation?

6   How does this ending reflect what the writer thinks the target audience will know about and care about?

7   What assumptions does the writer make about the audience in the final sentence?

8   The purpose of a text is closely linked to its target audience. For example, a review gives the writer's assessment of something – such as a play, concert or music album.

   a)   What would a reader hope to get out of reading a music review?

   b)   What kind of reader would therefore be interested in reading the J Hus review?

Apply the skills

Read the following article from *The Times* on page 49, aimed at a different type of reader. As you read, make notes on its target audience and purpose.

9   How does this article reflect its target audience? Consider how:

- the content relates to readers' interests
- the language relates to level of education
- the occasional informality (for example, 'flogs it') reflects its purpose
- the final sentence reflects why its readers might find it especially interesting.

Restoration of a king's art is long overdue

There is a moral case for the **Louvre** and other galleries to give us back masterpieces sold off by Cromwell.

A **cabal** of armed revolutionaries starts a civil war, overthrows the government, executes the ruler, confiscates his art collection and flogs it to buy guns and pay off debts. A few years later the self-same plotters are themselves ousted, the old regime returns, and wants its paintings back.

There is a strong case for **restitution** here. Under accepted modern mores, the rightful owners of art objects seized in war, sold off or destroyed should be compensated. Museums around the world are under pressure to return art objects to wherever they came from, whether these have been paid for or not. Claims for art looted, bought or otherwise obtained during the Second World War continue to crop up in the courts, almost always resulting in the object returning to the original owner.

There is one such case that has never been adequately resolved, however. Charles I assembled the greatest collection of art ever seen in this country, including works by Raphael, Leonardo, Tintoretto, Titian, Correggio, Mantegna, Holbein the Younger and Bruegel the Elder. When Charles was executed in 1649, Cromwell's republican government sold off more than 1500 works

of art, dozens of priceless tapestries and 500 sculptures, often through shady middlemen, sometimes for a pittance.

The great art collection was dispersed. After the **Restoration** in 1660, Charles II managed to reassemble perhaps three quarters of his father's great hoard, forming the core of the Royal Collection. But many of the best paintings never came back from Paris, Madrid or Vienna.

Some of those artworks are returning to Britain for the first time in 350 years, on temporary loan from the European galleries where they ended up, for a blockbuster exhibition at the Royal Academy next year entitled *Charles I: King and Collector*.

From 'Restoration of a King's Art is Long Overdue' by Ben Macintyre in *The Times*

---

10 Write a brief that the editor of either a music magazine for young people or a national newspaper might write for a young journalist wanting to write similar features to those in this section for either publication. Explain how to appeal to the appropriate target audience. You could include phrases from either text as examples.

Vocabulary

Louvre: Parisian art gallery
cabal: gang
restitution: compensation
Restoration: reinstatement of the monarchy

Check your progress

Sound progress

- I can usually locate suitable words or phrases to answer a question, and show that I understand their effects on the reader.
- I can locate some words with implicit meaning and begin to explain their effects.
- I can locate a fair amount of information from across a whole text or texts, and use it in an orderly and effective way.
- I can select some emotive words and phrases, and begin to explain their effects and why the writer has used them.
- I can identify the effect of sensory language and begin to explain how it is achieved.
- I can identify facts and opinions.
- I can analyse facts and begin to evaluate arguments.
- I can understand what factors determine audience, and how audience influences content.

Excellent progress

- I can locate a wide range of the correct words or phrases needed to answer a question, and show that I fully understand their meaning and purpose.
- I can locate a wide range of words with implicit meaning, and explain their effects and purpose.
- I can locate a range of information from across a whole text or texts, and use it in an extremely orderly and effective way, always including supporting detail.
- I can select a wide range of emotive words and phrases and evaluate their effects with reference to the reader and the writer's intention.
- I can analyse the different possible effects of sensory language and explain clearly how it is achieved.
- I can identify implied facts and opinions, and detect possible bias.
- I can analyse opinions and convincingly evaluate arguments.
- I can identify the link between audience and purpose, and show how audience influences style and language.

Key technical skills

In this chapter, you will develop a range of fundamental technical skills that you can use throughout your Cambridge IGCSE course.

You will learn how to:

- understand the functions of different types of words
- understand and use different types of sentences
- use tenses in your writing
- use sentence punctuation accurately and effectively
- use punctuation in reported and direct speech
- use paragraphs to organise ideas effectively and cohesively
- proofread your writing
- use formal and informal language effectively
- write in a variety of voices and roles.

On their own, some of the skills may seem simple, but remember that they are building blocks to completing larger and more complex tasks later on. For example:

- Tasks that ask you to write for specific audiences will require you to understand and cater for the needs of different audiences in your writing.
- Questions that ask you to write in role draw on your ability to create distinctive voices.
- Tasks that require you to structure pieces of work to present information, arguments, narrative or descriptions will draw on your ability to use paragraphs effectively.
- All writing tasks will require you to pay close attention to your word choice, drawing on a wide range of vocabulary.

Links to other chapters:

Chapter 5: Comprehension

Chapter 8: Extended response to reading and directed writing

Chapter 9: Composition

Chapter 10: Approaching written coursework

Vocabulary and word classes

It is useful to know the terms for and functions of particular words in English. This is true both when you explore writers' skills and when considering the effects you can create in your own writing.

Explore the skills

There are eight word classes: nouns, verbs, adjectives, adverbs, pronouns, prepositions, conjunctions and determiners. Each class performs a different job in a sentence.

Determiner	Adjective	Noun	Verb	Adverb
the	furious	wind	blew	strongly
a	gentle	breeze	wafted	down

In most cases, you can only replace words in a sentence with others from the same class.

Nouns

There are two types of **noun**: common nouns and proper nouns.

	Common nouns	Proper nouns
Physical objects or 'things'	table, car, computer, bread	*The Hunger Games, Pride and Prejudice*
Abstract concepts, emotions, ideas or ideals	peace, religion, anger	Judaism
Living creatures	cat, soldier, doctor	Sooty, Shaheed, Dr Jones
Places	beach, town	Malaysia, Paris

Key terms

noun: a word for a person, thing or idea

pronoun: a word that takes the place of a noun, for example, *it, she, something*

- Nouns have a plural form, often marked by an 's': *tables, cats, beaches*.
- Nouns combine with determiners such as: *the, a, that* and *some*: *the cat, some cheese*.
- Nouns and noun phrases can be replaced by a **pronoun**.

Shaheed was in the middle of explaining when suddenly he raced out of the room.

— proper noun
— pronoun

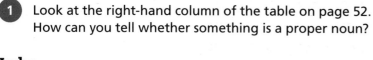

The black cat was about to cross the road when it stopped suddenly. — noun phrase — pronoun

1 Look at the right-hand column of the table on page 52. How can you tell whether something is a proper noun?

Verbs

There are three different types of **verb**:

- **Main verbs** express an action, process or state: *I **think**, we are **going**, they would have **loved** it.*
- **Auxiliary verbs** help create the tense: *we **are** leaving, they **have** eaten it all.*
- **Modal verbs** (a type of auxiliary verb) tell us how definite, likely or possible something is: *I **must** do that now, we **could** say that.*

Verbs are **conjugated** to make them agree with a subject (the noun or pronoun that is 'doing' the verb).

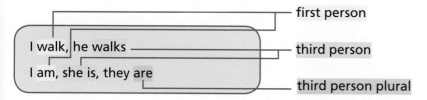

first person — third person — third person plural

I walk, he walks
I am, she is, they are

Verbs are also conjugated to make different **tenses**. For example:

I **am**, I **walk** (present tense)

I **was**, I **walked** (past tense)

Adjectives and adverbs

Adjectives and adverbs are used to modify other words. They are particularly useful when you need to describe people, places or experiences in detail.

Adjectives can describe or modify a noun:

The **timid** mouse

The tiger was **dangerous**.

Adverbs can modify or intensify a verb or adjective:

I **really** hope she's ready.

She was **incredibly busy**.

2 How many adjectives and adverbs can you think of in two minutes to fit these sentences?

a) The... woman/tree/car. b) That film/book/game was... c) I am... tired.

Top tip

Being able to spot proper nouns can be useful in comprehension and short-answer questions, as it may help you to identify certain information when skimming, scanning and selecting.

Top tip

Main verbs are essential – every full sentence must have one. Auxiliary verbs, including modals, are used with a main verb.

Key terms

verb: a word that expresses an action (*go*) or a state (*feel, like*)

conjugated: when verbs change form, usually taking on a different ending

tenses: forms verbs take to show the time of an action

Build the skills

Pronouns, prepositions, conjunctions and determiners

Pronouns, **determiners** and **prepositions** can ensure that your informative writing, such as articles and reports, is clear and accurate.

Pronouns and possessive pronouns replace a noun, to avoid repetition. You should use them only when it is clear exactly what you are talking about:

> I gave **it** to **him**.　　I want **that**.　　**That** bike is **mine**.

An exception to this is if you deliberately want to create mystery – for example, in the first sentence of a story:

> All morning I paced about the room, waiting for **it** to arrive.

Prepositions indicate a relationship between people or things, usually in space or time: *before*, *on*, *to*, *by*, *under*, and so on.

Determiners specify a noun: *a film; **this** cup; **my** cat*.

Conjunctions link two words, phrases or clauses together: *and*, *because*, *although*, *but*.

3　Look at this sentence. Which words are prepositions, determiners and pronouns?

> I'll meet Taylor at the entrance to the railway station at 6 o'clock with the secret plans.

Develop the skills

Vocabulary can also differ in other ways, for example, when you want to create a particular effect.

- **Emotive words** can convey or produce powerful feelings: *desperation, incredible, joyous, golden, shadowy, abandoned*.
- **Technical terms** or **phrases** are used for information writing: *species, habitat, migration, plumage*.

4　Read this short text, which uses emotive and technical vocabulary. Identify examples of each.

> Playing my first gig was a fantastic experience. As soon as I strapped on my shiny new electric guitar I felt a shiver of expectation run through me. My heart raced wildly as I strummed the opening chords of the 12-bar blues, and I faltered momentarily as Roxy's vocals kicked in.

Key terms

determiners: words that specify nouns

prepositions: words that describe the relationship between people, things or places

Conjunctions: words that join two words, phrases or clauses in a sentence

If you are writing about a particular topic, avoid repeating the same words or phrases. For example, a police officer might warn people about the **serious** *situation following the fire*, but they could also say *grave, important, worrying* or *drastic*.

5 How strong is each of these choices? How do they differ in meaning?

You might also choose longer, powerful words or phrases to replace more common ones.

6 Copy the following text, replacing the highlighted words with more powerful vocabulary.

> The storm in the desert was very bad. The sand was thrown up in the air and got into our ears, eyes and mouths. The wind made a loud noise and it was very hard to walk.

You can also use vocabulary to be more precise and to add further information. For example:

> The wind uprooted the trees in the park.

could become:

> The tornado uprooted the tall, slender cedars around the battered stadium.

- specific type of wind
- adjectives add visual detail
- precise type of tree
- preposition tells reader location
- adjective and precise noun provide even more detail

7 Rewrite this paragraph about the storm, adding your own details in the same way.

> The... (adjective) waves crashed down on the... (adjective), ... (adjective) ... (noun) ... (preposition) the... (adjective) beach. The... (adjective) hulk of the... (adjective) ship lay on its side, while the... (adjective) rain battered the... (adjective) ... (noun).

Apply the skills

8 Write 100–125 words describing your view of a deep cave in the side of a mountain as night falls. Remember:

- Do not tell a story: stick to the description of the cave and what can be seen, heard or felt.

- Select 4–5 specific things and describe them in precise detail, using well-chosen vocabulary.

- Use a range of word classes to accurately convey what can be experienced.

Accurate sentences

In all your writing, you need to use a range of sentences appropriate to the situation or audience you are writing for.

Explore the skills

The best writing:

- uses sentences accurately so that the meaning is clear
- uses a range of sentences for effect and impact.

Remember that sentences begin with a capital letter and end with a **full stop (.)**, **question mark (?)** or **exclamation mark (!)**. These punctuation marks point towards the different **functions** of a sentence.

Declarative (for statements or suggestions) • Maybe we could go for a swim later. • The crowd clapped enthusiastically.	**Interrogative** (for questions, requests or queries) • How does this work? • Is someone following us? • Do you honestly expect us to believe that?
Exclamatory (for stressing a point or showing strength of feeling) • How beautiful that dress is! • What a shame!	**Imperative** (for instructions, orders or commands) • Press the button now! • Turn left by the station.

1 Copy and complete this table. Write at least one sentence for each function that is appropriate to the text.

Text	Sentence function	My sentence
A report of a visit to a sports or music show	declarative	The show took place at the Beach Hotel.
A story with a mysterious event	interrogative	
Instructions about how to get from your home to the nearest shop	imperative	
An email to a friend after you have met a favourite celebrity	exclamatory	

Build the skills

It is important to understand and use the three main sentence types in your writing.

The **subject** of a sentence is the person or thing that is doing the action or feeling the emotion. The **verb** is the act of *doing*, *being* or *feeling* something.

Simple sentences are usually short and contain one clause with a subject and a verb. They are useful for explanations and instructions. They can separate distinct ideas or give a sense of time slowing down or speeding up.

I sat in the exam room.
The clock ticked.
I had failed.

A **compound sentence** is usually longer. It contains two or more clauses of equal weight linked by conjunctions such as *or, and, yet, so, but, for* and *nor*.

Our team played well and the players showed all their skills.

A **complex sentence** can add further information, provide contrast, or show cause and effect. It contains a **main clause** and one or more **subordinate clauses**, often marked off by a comma or connective.

Although it was the middle of the night, the dog barked loudly.

 2   Identify the sentence types and functions in this paragraph.

> The River Nile was incredibly wide, and we saw crocodiles basking in the midday sun. They seemed to be smiling! Even though we were travelling light, we were dripping with sweat. Then, while the dusty old jeep clattered along the track, I noticed Clark's face beginning to turn pale. It was the start of his fever.

Develop the skills

Subordinate clauses are important for expanding ideas. They are secondary to the main clause and cannot stand on their own. For example:

> Although our guide had given us a detailed and comprehensive map, we were utterly lost.

The main clause here is 'we were utterly lost' – it can stand alone as a sentence. The subordinate clause adds supporting information. In many cases, subordinate clauses that start with a subordinating conjunction (*although*, *even though*, *because*, *in order that*) can be switched with the main clause.

3   Add a subordinate clause to each of these sentences.

    a) …, we insisted the driver stopped.

    b) We placed Clark under the shade of the only tree, …

    c) Finally, his fever began to subside, …

Key terms

subject: the 'do-er' of the verb action in a sentence or clause

main clause: the main part of a sentence that could stand as a sentence on its own

subordinate clauses: clauses that do not make sense on their own; not complete sentences

Apply the skills

4   Write a narrative account of a dangerous journey, with six or seven sentences. Use at least one simple, one compound and one complex sentence.

Tenses and verb agreement

Your use of verbs and tenses should be consistent. While tenses can and do change in texts, there are conventions that you must follow to avoid confusion.

Explore the skills

You must ensure that your subject agrees with the main verb. A singular subject must have a singular verb form. For example:

> The teacher [singular subject] shouts [singular verb form] loudly.
>
> The teachers [plural subject] shout [plural verb form] loudly.

This applies even when the action is in the past. For example:

> He **was** shouting loudly NOT He **were** shouting loudly
>
> They **were** shouting loudly NOT They **was** shouting loudly

Key term

regular verb: a verb that follows predictable patterns in forming tenses and agreeing with subjects

The table below shows how the main verb tenses are formed for **regular verbs**, such as *to walk* and *to jump*.

Tense	Example	Explanation
Simple present	I jump, he jumps	The ending of the main verb changes according to the tense and subject.
Simple past	I jumped, she jumped	
Present progressive	I am jumping, he is jumping	These tenses are created by an auxiliary verb and a *present participle* of the main verb (ending in '–ing').
Past progressive	I was jumping, she was jumping	
Present perfect	I have jumped, he has jumped	These tenses are created with an auxiliary verb and a *past participle* of the main verb (ending in '–ed').
Past perfect	I had jumped, she had jumped	

1 Correct this paragraph from a discursive text:

> Digital technologies transforms the way we lives. Now car park themselves; you can even drove them remotely.

Build the skills

Many **irregular verbs** do not follow this pattern. The table below shows some common irregular verbs.

Key term

irregular verbs: verbs that do not follow the standard patterns

	to be	to eat	to run	to think	to take	to go
Simple present	am, are, is	eat, eats	run, runs	think, thinks	take, takes	go, goes
Simple past	was, were	ate	ran	thought	took	went
Progressive form	was being	was eating	was running	was thinking	was taking	was going
Perfect form	had been	had eaten	had run	had thought	had taken	had gone

2 Copy and correct the following paragraph.

> I had ran home when Sadiq text me and asking what we has to do for homework. I told him the teacher taking our books in so we didn't had any.

Develop the skills

Modal verbs are a form of auxiliary verb. They provide information about the certainty, possibility or improbability of an action or situation. For example:

- *He **should** go* (it would be best if he did)
- *He **might** go* (it is uncertain but possible)
- *He **could** go* (he has the potential to)
- *He **would** go... **if**...* (he isn't going but if things change)
- *He **can** go* (it is possible, or he is allowed to)
- *He **will** go* (he has decided – he intends to do it)

3 Read this reply to an invitation.

> I would come if I was free, but I will be watching Rav in his tennis final.

    a) What is unlikely?

    b) What is definite?

Apply the skills

4 Write a short account (50–75 words) explaining what you did last weekend and what you intend to do next weekend.

Checklist for success

✔ Make sure that your subject and verbs agree.

✔ Use tenses correctly and consistently.

✔ Use at least two modal forms.

Sentence punctuation

You have already learned how sentences always start with a capital letter and end with a full stop, exclamation mark or a question mark. However, you must use the full range of punctuation to write effectively.

Explore the skills

Using commas and apostrophes correctly is a basic punctuation skill, which you must get right in all your writing.

Commas

Use commas to separate items in a list:

> I bought fajitas, tomato sauce, onions and fried chicken to prepare for the party.

Use commas to separate adverbs, clauses or phrases (often as a way of adding detail, prioritising information or organising your ideas):

> *Although I was angry, I didn't say anything.*
> (The comma separates the subordinate clause so that it is clearly the first clause in the sentence, emphasising the writer's anger.)
>
> *First of all, I'd like to deal with the problem of traffic in the city centre.*
> (The comma sets apart the sequence phrase – *first of all*, emphasising the order in which ideas will be presented.)
>
> *Jose, on the other hand, believes that the biggest problem is pedestrians.*
> (Here, the bracketing commas tell us more about Jose's feelings.)

The comma splice

A comma splice is a common error where two clauses that should have been split into separate sentences or organised using a linking word/phrase, are mistakenly separated by a comma. For example:

> I went to see the film, it was fantastic.

This could be rewritten in several ways:

> I went to see a film, which was fantastic.
>
> I went to see a film. It was fantastic.
>
> I went to see a film: it was fantastic.
>
> I went to see a film; it was fantastic.

Apostrophes

Use apostrophes to indicate possession.

If the owner is singular, the apostrophe goes before the 's': *Japan's government*, *my uncle's bald head*.

Watch out for names already ending in 's': *Dickens's novels*.

If the owner is plural, then the apostrophe comes after the 's': *managers' problems with their teams*, *footballers' wives*.

Get this wrong, and you can change the meaning. For example:

- *The boy's bikes were both stolen* = one boy had two bikes stolen
- *The boys' bikes were both stolen* = each boy's bike was stolen

There are exceptions for special plural words, such as *children's*, *men's*, *women's*.

You should also use apostrophes to show omission. The apostrophe goes where a letter, or series of letters, has been removed:

- *There isn't much you can do.* (is not)
- *You'll be lucky!* (you will)

1 Read the following text, then rewrite it, adding or removing commas and apostrophes as appropriate. If you need to change or add any words, then do so.

> Even though it was raining we all went to the park. Shamira brought bread cheese salad and iced tea. Alina however brought nothing which made us all mad. Id brought a snack and so had Shan. Alinas excuse was that shed not had time to go the shop. However it didnt matter. Tourists hats were getting blown off so we knew a storm was coming and left after ten minutes. Luckily on the way back we found a café, it was warm and welcoming.

Build the skills

Brackets and dashes

Brackets and dashes often work in a similar way to commas. They can be used to provide additional information or to make details stand out, such as when describing a situation or event, or adding a humorous comment:

> We didn't mind hanging around at the beach in the winter (despite the cold) as it was where all our friends went.
>
> Florent told us he'd bought a secondhand car – not too expensive – to replace his battered old Ford. It was secondhand – a Ferrari!

2 Where would you add brackets or dashes in these two examples?

a) The goal was the best I'd ever scored although it was disallowed and I remembered it for months.

b) Zandra yes, shy Zandra of all people won the talent show and the 1000 dollar prize!

Develop the skills

Other forms of punctuation can be used more subtly for different effects. They can be especially useful in certain forms of writing.

Colons and semi-colons

A colon can introduce a list, following a general statement, like this:

> We can be proud of last year: increased sales, more customers and higher profits.

It can also introduce a clause that explains the first clause:

> She was overjoyed: the bag was exactly what she wanted.

Semi-colons are useful for contrasts and comparisons, to link two clauses of equal importance. For example:

> Rajesh likes table tennis; Irina prefers hockey.

Semi-colons can also be used when listing items that take more than a single word. For example:

> I watched all my favourite Bond films again last week – *Live and Let Die*; *Quantum of Solace*; *Skyfall.*

3 Correct or add colons or semi-colons to these sentences. Add any other punctuation they need, such as commas.

  a) My phone has lots of things wrong with it broken screen no audio dead battery.

  b) Grime is my favourite type of music Sasha has always loved techno.

  c) Javed carefully opened the box it was completely empty

4 Read this short article from a school website. Rewrite it, adding colons or semi-colons as appropriate.

> The new library is wonderful more shelf space an internet zone and comfy chairs for relaxing with a favourite book. The internet zone is already popular the computers are booked up every day. Some students come in early to do homework on them others use them once lessons have ended.

Apply the skills

Your main goal is to ensure that your use of punctuation is accurate.

5 Write the opening two paragraphs of an article in which you argue that exams are bad for students' health. Try to use the full range of punctuation (except speech marks, unless you include an interview). Check your work as you go along – and afterwards. You could:

- start with a question (for example, *Do you remember the first time that…?*)
- contrast two ideas with a semi-colon
- make a point and use bracketed text or dashes to give extra information or a humorous aside
- use a colon to introduce a list.

Top tip

Make use of colons in analytical or report writing to help provide clear explanations. Be careful not to overuse semi-colons. Use them sparingly and only when you are sure it is correct to do so.

Reported and direct speech

You will need to use speech punctuation in your narrative writing, but you may also need it to quote someone's words in an article or speech.

Explore the skills

The example below sets out the main conventions of speech marks (sometimes called inverted commas).

'How are you feeling?' asked my father.

'He looks pale,' said my mother.

I replied, 'I don't want to do it, but I guess I'll have to.'

'In that case,' said my father, helping me into my coat, 'you need to hurry, or you'll miss the bus.'

'I wish my mathematics exam was over,' I said. 'Can't I just pretend I'm ill?'

speech marks around actual words spoken, including any punctuation

new line for each new speaker

comma goes before the closing speech mark when the speech is not a question or exclamation

comma after the speaker and the speech inside speech marks, if the speaker comes first

speaker can be mentioned mid-sentence; if the speech continues, the first word does not have a capital letter

where the speaker is mentioned between two separate sentences, use a full stop and then a capital letter to start the next part

sentences containing speech begin with a capital letter and end with a full stop

1 Copy the sentences below and add the correct punctuation (you may also need to correct the use of capital letters).

a) Oh no! I dropped my phone in the swimming pool cried Natasha.

b) I'm sorry but it just doesn't fit you said Rita's mum you'll have to take it back.

c) A huge fan next to me asked who do you support sonny?

Build the skills

In reported speech, you do not need speech marks. Reported speech can be used to create distance or a sense of authority – for example, in reports where the narrator is less important than the facts being recounted.

Direct speech:

'Will you let me in?' I asked the doorman.

'Sorry. You're too late,' he replied.

Reported speech:

I asked the doorman if he'd let me in but he told me that I was too late.

— no speech marks

— direct form of address – 'you' changed to 'he'

— relative pronoun used to introduce what was said

— 'you' (said by doorman) changed to 'I'

— 'told' replaces 'said' where you are the subject

2 Change these direct speech examples to reported speech.

  a) 'The fire's still burning so you'll need to keep back,' said the police officer.

    The police officer told...

  b) 'I am delighted with the outcome of the meeting,' said the President.

    The President said...

Develop the skills

Inverted commas may also be used for titles of poems and short stories. Or, they can be used if you want to quote a word or phrase in an essay or other report. For example:

It is clear Wordsworth is struck by the beauty of the daffodils 'fluttering and dancing in the breeze'.

3 Copy and correct these sentences.

  a) Tidy your room first was all she would say when I asked her if I could go round to Ben's.

  b) When Wordsworth writes I wandered lonely as a cloud we get a vivid picture of him strolling through the mountains.

Apply the skills

4 Continue the dialogue below, between a boy who is late for school and his teacher.

I ran up the corridor towards the exam room. Out of breath, I turned the handle and burst in.

'You're late!' hissed my teacher.

Accurate use of paragraphs

Paragraphs help you organise your ideas and guide your reader through your writing.

Explore the skills

You should use a new paragraph:

- to change focus or switch to a new topic or perspective
- to signal a change in time (for example, a day later)
- to indicate a change of scene or place
- in speech, when a new person is introduced or starts to speak.

Writers often use topic sentences to help signal the key focus of the paragraph. Read this example. The topic sentences are highlighted.

> Cruise holidays may suit some people, but they are not for me. I couldn't stand the thought of being stuck with the same people for weeks on end, unable to escape except for the odd trip ashore. It is my idea of a nightmare.
>
> Yet I accept that they are increasingly popular, especially amongst older and retired people. Everything is done for you, and if you wish to make friends then you cannot help doing so. It's very good for socialising, that's for sure!

opening paragraph establishes writer's view or perspective

second paragraph switches to an alternative viewpoint

1 Read the paragraphs below, from the same text.

> Take my cruise trip with my parents last year. It was a disaster from the first day when I realised there was no one my own age on the ship. Who was I going to spend time with?
>
> Two weeks later, we came to the end of the most boring trip of my life. We docked at the harbour in Miami – dry land, I thought. At last!

a) What is the purpose of each paragraph?

b) What 'change' is signalled by each topic sentence?

Build the skills

Paragraphs can vary in style and function, according to when and where they are used.

Introductory or opening paragraphs	In texts *exploring* a subject (such as cruise ships) or *arguing a point of view*, these provide the context or the main viewpoint.
	In *descriptive* or *narrative* texts, these give background information, set the scene, but also plunge in, grabbing the reader's attention with an exciting moment.
Body paragraphs	*Longer paragraphs* can *build or expand* on the opening information, or *offer contrast* by way of new ideas or a change of pace. *Short paragraphs* might be used for shock or emphasis.
Concluding paragraphs	These might *sum up* key viewpoints, or *look to the future*. In stories, they might *resolve a mystery* or *leave things uncertain* for the reader to contemplate.

2 Where in this story about a sea voyage could the following paragraphs come? Why?

> 'You go on ahead,' I called to Chen as we queued to get off the ship. 'I'll meet you at the hotel.' I watched his slight figure fade into the swarming streets and disappear into the crowds.
>
> How was I to know that I would not see him again for six months?

3 How has the single-sentence paragraph been used for effect?

Develop the skills

The follow-up sentences in paragraphs after topic sentences are also useful.

> The popularity of cruises is indisputable. That is to say a significant number of people claim to enjoy them. In our small town, according to a recent survey, at least one member of every family has taken one. This is astonishing given that they are by no means cheap. It is one reason why we get so many ads for them on TV and online.

- topic sentence
- the idea is refined or redefined
- evidence is offered
- comment from writer
- consequences explored

4 Write one further sentence to develop each of these topic sentences.

   a) Social media is incredibly addictive.

   b) Extreme weather seems to be on the rise.

Apply the skills

5 Write two paragraphs of a text about cruise ships. You can either write about your views on cruises, or write paragraphs from a story set on one. Try to build several sentences to follow the topic sentence.

Paragraph cohesion

You can help guide the reader through your text by selecting words or phrases to link paragraphs together, or to introduce new information.

Explore the skills

Read how this student describes the build-up to a holiday.

> I had been looking forward to our holiday for weeks. Each day I crossed off a date on the calendar. I mooched around the kitchen getting under mum's feet. I sat and stared out of the window at our street. The hours dragged by, but eventually it was time for us to go. I crossed off the last day on the calendar and went to bed even though I couldn't sleep.
>
> The next morning, the bus ride to the airport was dreadful: we had roadworks, a demonstration and even a herd of cattle that wouldn't move! I thought we weren't going to make it.
>
> Finally, we made it to the check-in desk. As we queued up, I could see the look of relief on Dad's face.
>
> At the desk, the assistant looked at us blankly when we handed over our passports and ticket printout. 'Your flight is tomorrow, not today,' she said, pointing to the date on our tickets.

- topic sentence introduces idea that this is about holidays and writer's feelings
- details within the paragraph develop the topic
- linking phrase (connective) relating to time
- topic sentence introduces terrible bus ride
- sequence word (connective) relating to feelings and time
- topic sentence introduces where this part of narrative takes place

1. Note down how this text is held together by **cohesion**. Consider:

   - the different topics or information in each paragraph
   - how time or sequence phrases help
   - how the content is organised – for example, why is 'airport' not mentioned again once 'check-in' appears in paragraph 3?

Build the skills

2. Add a further paragraph to the text. Use one of the following ideas on page 69 and a topic sentence to make the situation clear. Make sure that you use a linking phrase to introduce your paragraph.

Key term

cohesion: how a paragraph is knitted together and linked to other paragraphs around it. Topic sentences, connectives and linking phrases all help to make a text cohesive

- The ride back in the bus
- Mum and Dad arguing back at the flat
- The next morning

Develop the skills

Different types of connective can help you link your ideas both within and between paragraphs. These include:

- chronological/time sequence ordering: *at first, next, later that day*
- simple ordering of events or actions: *first, second, finally*
- logical ordering (often related to cause and effect): *therefore, consequently, as a result*
- contrasting: *on the other hand, in contrast, however, although*
- developing ideas: *what is more, in addition, moreover, furthermore.*

3 Add appropriate connectives to the following email written by the check-in assistant to her boss, who was ill and away from the airport for the day.

| To: |
| From: |

… (time) was incredibly busy at the airport. …(cause/effect) there were long queues up to my desk. Apparently, the traffic in the city was terrible. …(development) there was a student demonstration, which closed the main road.

… (contrast) most passengers made it on time, …(contrast) one family, poor things, had a nasty shock when they handed me their tickets. They'd got the wrong day!

Apply the skills

4 Here is student's plan for a descriptive piece of writing called 'My Perfect Holiday'. Decide which paragraph to begin with, then write the text.

- Things I would like to do on my perfect holiday
- Terrible holidays I have had in the past
- The sort of place/country/location I would like to go
- Who, if anyone, I would take with me

Checklist for success

✔ Use a topic sentence to state the main idea of each paragraph.

✔ Link paragraphs with connectives.

✔ Use connectives within paragraphs to link sentences.

Proofreading

You can improve your performance by checking or proofreading your work, both while you write and after you have finished.

Explore the skills

Read these stages for proofreading your work.

Stage 1: checking for 'sense'. This means as you write (perhaps after each paragraph) and when you have finished, you read through your work to check that it *makes sense.* Can you follow the argument or story? Have you remembered who the reader or audience is? Is the purpose clear throughout? Or do you get confused at any point? Look out for:

- missing words or phrases
- consistency of tenses
- punctuation that helps the reader follow the viewpoint or plot, for example.

Stage 2: checking for detail. This means a line-by-line read-through looking for simple errors. These may or may not affect the overall sense, but they can stand out and draw attention away from what you are trying to say. Such errors can affect the meaning, too. Check for:

- spelling errors, such as words you often misspell, spellings of names, **homophones** (*bare/bear, your/you're; their/they're/there*), capital letters.
- punctuation, especially commas – have you used them where you should have used a conjunction or started a new sentence?
- apostrophes: incorrect apostrophes can be very irritating to a reader. In particular, do not confuse those meant for possession (*Saj's bike*) and those for omission (*It's a great bike!*).

1 Take 75–100 words from any recent piece of work you have completed. Follow the two stages above, highlighting any errors or omissions.

Key term

homophones: words spelled differently but which sound the same

Build the skills

The final stage is making corrections. In reality, you will probably do this as you make your checks, rather than afterwards, but there is no point identifying errors if you do not tackle them.

Stage 3: making corrections. If you need to cross out or add words or phrases, do so neatly and clearly:

- Put a simple straight line through the word or words. Write the replacement word above it, if there is room, or in the margin.

- Use the ^ mark between words to indicate a word or phrase that you want to add.

2 Copy out and then correct the short extract below, using the guidance above.

> *Theres no point in denying the influence social media. Know evryone knows youre buisness. Id rather have sum privacy.*

Develop the skills

The time you spend proofreading will depend on the type of task you are working on, and the context.

- For longer written responses, such as composition tasks, allow at least five minutes at the end of the task for proofreading.

- For coursework, you will have more time to write a first draft of your work, correct it and then write final copies, so the proofreading may happen more frequently and take longer.

3 Go back and look at any previous extended text you have written, and which you know you did not proofread correctly. Go through the three stages and redraft the text.

Apply the skills

4 This is the opening paragraph from one student's narrative story. Follow the stages as outlined above and rewrite the opening. (There are approximately 14 errors here.)

My fathers watch was a delicate item but it had a torn strap, it had scratches on the face. I placed it on the desk and tryed to read it's maker's label. But unfortunately, It was to faint, so I couldn't make it out. I picked it up and let it rest for a moment in the palm of my hand: it was surprisingly heavy. Then from an angle I was able to read the maker's name: wright and sons, London 1888. Wow – it was old. Later that day, my phone rung. Caller unknown. I answered and herd a strange voice on the line. 'Is that Sunil? it asked. 'Yes,' I replied carefully. 'You don't know me' the voice continued, But I know you.'

I had a sudden omen. Something bad is going to happen all because of that watch.

Audience and levels of formality

Choosing the right level of formality is important when speaking or writing. You need to be able to judge what is appropriate language for the audience or reader.

Explore the skills

At a basic level, we all adapt our vocabulary according to our audience and purpose. For example:

> School teacher to parent: 'Would you and Rita be able to attend the school production of *Romeo and Juliet* next week?'
>
> School teacher to small child: 'Can you and Mummy come to the school play next week?'

1 What vocabulary has been adapted by the teacher when speaking to the small child? Why?

We also adapt our language according according to context. For example, what is the difference between *formal* and *informal* language? Consider the way you might speak or write to your close friends about everyday things. Then contrast this with how you might communicate with an adult in authority about a more serious subject.

> **Formal:**
>
> Excuse me, Mr Bosingwa, what would be the best time to attend the job interview?
>
> **Informal**
>
> Hey, Frankie, what's the best time for me to turn up for this chat, then?

- more impersonal (less friendly, a sort of studied politeness) with 'distance' between the writer and recipient
- uses few if any, abbreviations, slang or exclamation marks
- formal vocabulary or conventions to match the context or audience: *attend* rather than *turn up for*
- generally adopts a close and personal tone
- informal vocabulary and abbreviations to match the context or audience
- uses the sentence tag *then*

2 Look carefully at examples A and B below. Make notes to identify the formal and informal elements in each.

A

> Well, you wouldn't believe it, Carlos, but there's me, kicking a ball around in our backyard when Utd's boss trots by!

B

> *Dear Mr Perez,*
>
> *I was very surprised by your kind invitation to attend a training session with Green Bay United on Monday, 23 March. I would be delighted to come and would like to thank you for noticing my skills when you passed by our house last week.*
>
> *Yours sincerely,*
> *Didier Brillianti*

Build the skills

Formality in forms such as letters means beginning and ending in specific ways that you would not use in an email to a friend, for example.

Imagine that your head teacher has written a letter inviting you to give a speech to new students about your positive experiences at the school. A formal reply might look something like this.

> Dear Mrs De Witt,
>
> I am writing in reply to your letter of the 17 May, inviting me to speak to new students at the school. I am extremely honoured to be asked and would like to thank you for offering me this opportunity.
>
> I would be delighted to accept the invitation and will arrange to meet with you at a mutually convenient time, as requested.
>
> Yours sincerely,
> Sinitta Long

- standard opening for a formal letter
- refers back to Mrs De Witt's letter
- reminds reader of the subject
- polite tone
- response to the request
- next action
- standard closing when a name is used in the opening
- full name

The order of information is a natural and logical one: *subject, thanks for the invitation, acceptance, further action, close of letter.*

3 Imagine that you are related to the head teacher and know her well. Write a more informal reply to the invitation. Start…

Dear Auntie Tanya,

How are you? Thanks so much for…

Top tip

Be careful that your informal letters do not come across as rude. Make sure that you are confident about how the recipient will react to this style and tone. Formal language can also seem comic or rude if exaggerated or used in the wrong situation. For example, you would not ask someone to move on a bus by saying: *Excuse me, my good man, could I trouble you to shift your position so that my bodily form can be located alongside yours?*

Develop the skills

Some formal texts require an *impersonal tone*, especially when an authoritative or factual account is needed.

4 Read the text below. Note down how the objective, impersonal tone is achieved. Look carefully at:

- the way the verbs are used
- who is speaking or writing.

> The shark was observed at 7:00 a.m. breaking the surface of the water approximately one kilometre from the shore. Local coastguards were alerted and the shark was guided out to sea to safer areas before any harm was done.

5 Now read this eye-witness account of the same event. What differences do you notice?

> I saw the shark at around seven this morning in the sea, I guess about one kilometre or so out. I called the coastguards and they guided it out to sea before it could do any damage.

If you are still not sure how the different tone is achieved, consider the verbs in the following examples, then go back to the task above.

> **Active form:** *I noticed the fire starting in the factory and called the police.*
>
> The subject of the sentence (*I*) is present and 'does' the action (noticing the fire/calling police).
>
> **Passive form:** *The start of the fire was noticed and the police were called.*
>
> The subject (person who noticed the fire) is missing, so the text seems more objective and 'distant'.

The passive, impersonal style is particularly useful for news reports or accounts by someone who wishes the text to have authority.

6 Turn this short account into a formal news report by changing the active forms to the passive where possible.

> I discovered the shipwreck yesterday as our fishing boat returned in the evening. I saw the hull shining deep down, then dived in. While underwater, I took photographs with my waterproof camera and returned to the surface where I passed them to the captain who sent them using a mobile phone to a local newspaper.

You will need to change the 'I' of the text to 'he' or 'she'. Begin with:

> The shipwreck was discovered yesterday by a local fisherman as his…

Apply the skills

Correctly handled, informality can be useful when establishing a convincing voice in a dialogue or in conversation in a narrative.

> So, Olga, you're saying 'last night's movie was the best film ever', right? Because it's not in my book. No way.

Other distinctive features of informal dialogue are contractions, tags and **idioms**. Here are examples from the speech above:

- **contraction:** *you're = you are; it's = it is*
- **tag:** *right?*
- **idiom:** *not in my book* does not mean that the speaker has a book of favourite films; it is a turn of phrase meaning 'in my view'.

Idioms appear in both formal and informal language, but they are more likely to be used conversationally. They can make the voice of your speakers sound convincing, but they do need to be used carefully and only when appropriate: for example, in informal speech between two close friends.

 7 Draft a dialogue between a bank manager and a teenage boy who wants to open a savings account. Use informal usages, like contractions and tags, for the boy to establish his voice and a more formal style for the bank manager. You could start as follows:

> 'So, Mr Ferrer, you have expressed interest in opening an account with us. Do you have any proof of identity?'
>
> The manager stared at Ray over her glasses.
>
> 'Well, yeah – I've got this pic of me with my mates. Look…'

Key term

idiom: a typical phrase common to a language: for example, *dead funny* meaning 'really funny'; *a right laugh* meaning 'a lot of fun'

Voice and role

Spoken and directed writing tasks often require you to write in role. You need to show that you have understood this and do not simply write as yourself. To be convincing, your writing voice may need to be adapted to match the person you are supposed to be.

Explore the skills

As individuals, we all have different views of the same situation. We therefore express things in different ways.

- **Voice** is the particular, personal expression and language that an individual uses (for example, chatty or serious, anxious or optimistic).

- **Role** is the particular part, profession or identity that someone has (for example, a ten-year-old child, schoolteacher or angry neighbour). The role adopted may affect voice and the content of what is said.

1   Here are two extracts written by different people. What roles do you think they have? How would you describe the two different voices?

> Oh no, I thought! Not my lovely dress! Just before the wedding… gone in a flash. Just my luck! I slumped on the bed and sobbed, tears streaking my face. What would I do?

> I observed the window had been forced. The wardrobe was open, and it was empty. The victim was sitting on the bed crying, but I tried to reassure her we would find the culprit.

Build the skills

Now, consider how you could 'get into' a role so that you can write in an appropriate style, as above. You need to:

- understand the role you have been placed in

- think about what a person in this role would spend their time doing and what is important to this type of person

- consider how they might feel about the topic you are writing about – their role will affect their viewpoint and attitude

- decide whether they have a particular type of character (for example, nervy and anxious, calm and collected) and if so, how that might be shown in a short piece of writing.

Put yourself in the role of a student called Poppy. You have just taken part in a spelling tournament against other students from around the country. Here is your diary entry for the morning of the competition.

> ### Day 1: preparing for the competition
>
> Got up at 8:00 a.m. and went down to join all the other students for breakfast. I'd made a sort of friend with a girl called Sonya last night – at least I thought I had, but this morning she ignored me and spent all breakfast with her nose in a dictionary. This made me laugh. If you don't know the spellings by now, then you never will. Mind you, I was so nervous I couldn't eat anyway. Breakfast just made me think of cooking-related spellings: 'restaurant' (remember the 'au'!), 'lasagne', 'cucumber' (not 'queue cumber'!!) and 'temperature' all kept on going through my head. Am I going mad? Is it all worth it? I was about to text Mum and Dad, but then in came the organiser – a thin, severe-looking man in a grey suit – and told us Round 1 was going to start in 10 minutes in the main hall.

2 Based on this text, create a stick figure version of Poppy like the one opposite. Add feelings, thoughts/attitudes around the figure.

Develop the skills

Now you need to create an effective voice. This means conveying a character's personality and emotions through the language and vocabulary used. You need to consider:

- Poppy's character
- formal or informal language, especially vocabulary choices (see Topic 2.9)
- how you might use sentences and punctuation to convey what she feels or thinks.

For example, you could say that Poppy is:

- nervous (about the competition)
- quite witty
- close to her mum and dad
- friendly, but competitive
- observant.

3 How might these characteristics be reflected in her writing? Write her next diary entry. Use what you know about her already, including:

- questions that show her doubting her abilities
- references to her parents
- possibly comical observations about other competitors or the organisers.

Maintain Poppy's voice in the diary. For example, she mixes present-tense observations and past-tense recollections. You could start:

Day 2: late morning – Round 1

After breakfast we all made our way to the Main Hall. My tum was rumbling and suddenly I felt hungry. Typical! ('al' or 'le'…?) Anyway, that Sonya was just in front of me, looking like…

> **Top tip**
>
> To help maintain the voice of a character, try imagining what they would say and do in different situations. Do they have a favourite phrase or two, for example?

If the type of text you are writing changes, then your voice will need to adapt. For example, imagine that Poppy's teacher has asked her to give a speech to her year group entitled 'Why taking part in competitions is good for you'.

4 Make some brief notes on the following questions.

a) How is the *purpose* of this task different from the diary entry?

b) How will the *form* and *style* of the text be different from the diary form?

c) In what way will you need to be selective about the details you include and leave out in your speech?

d) What elements of Poppy's voice will you continue using in the speech?

5   Read two sample speeches below, written in Poppy's voice, and make notes on how well each one:

- makes use of information about Poppy and what happens to her (for example, which one provides more detail about the events?)

- shows Poppy's feelings through the style and tone (for example, which uses variety of sentences and punctuation?)

- focuses on the purpose of the speech, rather than the diary (for example, which one shows the positive aspects of taking part?)

- uses the right style for a speech. (See Topic 3.1 for more on the conventions of speeches.)

A

Well, it all started when we got there. I wanted to win the competition really badly and made friends with this girl. But she wasn't very nice and just wanted to revise for the test. I was nervous so I tried to call my mum and dad. The competition was really scary and the organiser wasn't exactly friendly. I don't know why I did it, really.

B

This weekend I have been at a spelling competition. You may think I'm an idiot (no, don't answer that!) after all, who actually likes spelling? But from the moment I arrived, representing our school, I knew it was good for me. Yes, I was nervous. Yes, I had to face people who smiled to my face one evening, then ignored me at breakfast, but I had to grow up fast. I didn't care if I beat the snooty girl from breakfast (well, ok – I did a bit) – it was more about competing with myself, my nerves and being on my own away from home. And – I did it!

Apply the skills

6   Write two entries from the diary of the other girl, Sonya. In fact, she is shy and nervous and thinks that Poppy and the others are really confident. She does not have many friends at school, but English is her favourite subject.

- Use the diary conventions from Poppy's entry.

- Convey Sonya's character, feelings and observations through her voice.

Check your progress

Sound progress

- I understand the different word classes and how they can alter meaning.
- I can use simple and compound sentences effectively, and some complex sentences.
- I understand how different tenses work and can usually keep them consistent.
- I can write in clear sentences using a reasonably accurate range of punctuation.
- I understand punctuation in direct and reported speech.
- I use paragraphs to organise my work.
- I understand the proofreading process and can use it to check my work when I have finished.
- I understand the differences between formal and informal forms of expression.
- I can take on a role with a reasonably appropriate voice.

Excellent progress

- My vocabulary is varied and I use word classes confidently for a range of effects and purposes.
- I can use a full range and variety of sentence types and functions for effect.
- I can use a range of different tenses, keeping their use consistent throughout.
- I use a wide range of punctuation accurately for deliberate effects.
- I understand direct and reported speech and can punctuate them accurately.
- My paragraphs are well constructed and logically ordered with a clear sense of the task's purpose and effect.
- I use the proofreading process both to check my work as I go along and after I have finished.
- I can apply knowledge of formal and informal language to match audience or reader.
- I can adapt voice and role thoughtfully depending on the task and the purpose.

Key writing forms

3

In this chapter, you are going to develop a range of fundamental writing skills that you will use throughout your Cambridge IGCSE course.

You will learn how to write in the following forms:

- speeches and talks
- interviews
- diaries and journals
- reports
- news reports and magazine articles
- letters.

On their own, some of the skills may seem simple, but remember that they are building blocks to completing larger and more complex tasks later, which may ask you to write in specific forms. These will require you to understand the structural and stylistic conventions of those forms.

Links to other chapters:

Chapter 4: Writing for purpose

Chapter 8: Extended response to reading and directed writing

Chapter 10: Approaching written coursework

Conventions of speeches and talks

Speeches are usually formal spoken presentations for a particular purpose – often to persuade an audience to support an idea, or to explain or describe an interesting topic or past event. When you compose a speech, you need to think about:

- how you will engage your audience's interest as you begin to speak
- how you can structure your speech to retain their interest and make your points effectively.

Explore the skills

Have you ever given a speech? If so, what was the topic? Was it at school or at a family event? What do you think is the biggest challenge for someone giving a speech to an audience?

1 Try talking (without preparation) for two minutes on a topic you feel strongly about to a partner: how easy or difficult was it? Were you able to keep them interested?

Read the following extract from a speech given by the actress Angelina Jolie on World Refugee Day in 2009.

We're here today to talk about millions of desperate families – families so cut-off from civilization that they don't even know that a day like this exists on their behalf. Millions. And numbers can illuminate but they can also obscure. So I am here today to say that refugees are not numbers.	sets out the context for why she is speaking

repetition to stress a point

use of personal pronouns connects with the audience directly |
| They're not even just refugees. They are mothers and daughters and fathers and sons – they are farmers, teachers, doctors, engineers, they are individuals all. And most of all they are survivors – each one with a remarkable story that tells of resilience in the face of great loss. They are the most impressive people I have ever met and they are also some of the world's most vulnerable. Stripped of home and country, refugees are buffeted from every ill wind that blows across this planet. | repetition of 'They are' punches home message

provides reasons why she is speaking |
| I remember meeting a pregnant [...] woman in a completely abandoned camp. [...] She couldn't travel when everyone else | personal anecdote engages interest |

was relocated because she was too late in her pregnancy. She was alone with her two children and another woman. There was nothing for miles around the camp – not a single tree, no other people in sight. So when they asked me to come in for tea I said I didn't feel it necessary. But [...] they take pride in how they treat their guests so they insisted and they guided me into a small dirt house with no roof to keep out the scorching heat, and they dusted off the two old mats that they ate, slept and prayed on. And we sat and we talked and they were just the loveliest women. And then with a few twigs and a single tin cup of water, they made the last of their tea and insisted on me to enjoy it.

pattern of three details creates rhetorical impact

vivid descriptive images build picture

Since before the **parable of the Widow's Mite** it has been known that those who have the least will give the most. Most refugee families will offer you the only food they have and pretend they're not hungry. And the generosity of the poor applies not only to refugees. We should never forget that more than 80% of refugees are hosted and have been for years and years in the poorest developing countries.

develops and provides further detail on the speech's purpose

From http://speakola.com

2 Read the speech again, this time aloud. Are there any obvious changes in tone or focus? If so, where are they? How might they affect how the speech is given?

Vocabulary

parable of the Widows' Mite: a Bible story in which a very poor woman gives a few small coins to the local government

Build the skills

Part of the speech's overall effect comes from the way that Angelina Jolie:

- connects with her audience through her voice and style
- creates an emotional impact with her language
- paints vivid pictures to describe what she has experienced.

3 How does Jolie draw attention to herself and her audience? Note down:

a) how she refers to herself and her audience

b) the purpose for the speech

c) her own personal experiences.

4 What particularly emotive language does she use to

a) describe the families at the start of the speech

b) describe the way in which refugees are mistreated all over the world by misfortune?

Key term

rhetorical: designed to have a powerful effect on a reader; rhetorical questions are intended to create impact rather than elicit information (for example: *Should we simply forget the awful suffering and hardship?*)

5 What is the rhetorical impact of the single word 'Millions'?

6 How does she use descriptive/sensory details to convey her message? Think about the references to:

- the mats
- the making of the tea.

Develop the skills

The structure of the speech is also important. How exactly does Jolie's speech work?

7 Copy and complete the table below to sum up the focus of each section.

Section	Purpose	Key language or feature	Effect
Paragraph 1	to introduce the purpose of the speech	'We're here...' 'I am here' 'Millions.'	draws audience in; states her own commitment; shock and surprise
Paragraph 2	to get across message that refugees are individuals	'Mothers and daughters' 'each one with a remarkable story'	creates image of...?
Paragraph 3			
Paragraph 4			

8 How are the paragraphs linked? Think about:

- how the second paragraph elaborates or builds upon the first
- how the third and fourth paragraphs are connected by the Widow's Mite
- how they all contribute to the overall message.

In summary, any speech you give will need a structure with:

- an **opening** that engages the audience and makes the purpose clear (perhaps through personal references, shocking or interesting facts or something similar)

- **middle sections** that provide specific examples or further detail so that the tone is not too abstract or general (perhaps further personal experiences or, at the very least, vivid details of actual events or examples)

- a **conclusion** that links back to previous points or examples and enhances the overall effect.

Apply the skills

9 Look at this speech task.

> Write a speech for your classmates, persuading them to do more physical exercise and/or sport.
>
> Decide:
>
> - who the audience is
> - what the purpose is.
>
> Draft your opening two paragraphs (up to 75 words).

Top tip

Make each of your points clearly, using rhetorical language or an anecdote to strengthen your view not to take you off course.

Try out your opening on a partner. How well did you do?

If you wish, complete your speech, building on what you have learned and remembering to show a clear, well thought-out structure.

Checklist for success

✔ Make sure that your voice or viewpoint is lively, strong and engaging.

✔ Structure your speech so your listeners are immediately interested.

✔ Keep their attention with new points or ideas, and finish strongly.

✔ Speak directly to the audience by using inclusive pronouns (*you*, *we*) and rhetorical devices.

✔ Use appropriate language for your audience and vary sentences to change pace or tone.

✔ Use personal references (such as reference to your own experiences) and emotive language.

Conventions of interviews

Interviews have their own conventions. How do interviews usually start and end? Who tends to say more – the interviewer or the 'guest'?

Interviews: conversations in which one person asks the other questions on a topic or aspect of their life

Explore the skills

Read the bullet points below about the Siberian tiger, which come from a conservation website.

- Only 350–400 tigers left
- Used to be in north-east China, Mongolia and Korean Peninsula
- Poaching and cutting down trees for logs are main problems; need vast forests to survive
- Body parts used in traditional medicine

1 Now read the interview in which a conservation expert discusses these issues with a reporter. As you read, make notes about the different roles of each speaker, and how this is represented by the way they speak.

Reporter:	I'm here to talk to Dr Sandra Cappello, a consultant for animal charity Save Our Species.
Expert:	Good evening.
Reporter:	So, Dr Cappello – with just under 500 tigers still in the wild, it seems like conservation efforts have failed, haven't they?
Expert:	Well, it's true that numbers have dwindled. There were once many more tigers in China, Mongolia and Korea. Places such as the Eastern Himalayas were ideal for them but it's a fragile landscape.
Reporter:	(interrupts) You haven't answered my question. Have efforts failed? I have been reporting for years on this issue and it's just not improving.
Expert:	There are so many problems – we can't do everything. Many, many organisations are committed to protecting different tiger species, but it's a monumental task.
Reporter:	So, what would you say is the biggest threat to them?

— speakers' names/roles on left

questions directed personally to the 'expert'

reply to question – or part of it.

Expert:	It's difficult to single one out – but loss of habitat is clearly a huge issue. Once hunting grounds have disappeared, it can take literally hundreds of years to recover them.
Reporter:	Right – I get it. No trees, no tigers.
Expert:	It's not quite as simple as that, but broadly speaking that is the situation.
Reporter:	Thank you, Dr Cappello. That's all we have time for.

— specialist language of expert

— punchy, informal summing up

Build the skills

2 Write brief answers to these questions.

a) How are the roles of the reporter and expert different?

b) Where have synonyms or **paraphrases** been used?

c) In what way is this obviously an interview?

d) What information from the website was not used in the interview?

Key term

paraphrases: rewording of things that have been said or written

Develop the skills

Look at this list from a tiger charity's website, which offers some solutions for saving the tiger.

- Identify high-priority tiger populations – larger areas are better, as tigers need 1000 square kilometres free of human activity.
- Enforcement officers and guards to protect tigers from poachers.
- Develop local community-based conservation programmes.
- Continue well-managed captive breeding (for instance, in game parks) for the most at-risk tigers.

3 In pairs, carry out a brief role-play of an interview between the manager of the charity and a reporter. Use some of the content above. Make sure that:

- the reporter continues to speak in the same style
- the charity manager is forceful and tries to get his or her message across about what needs to be done.

Apply the skills

4 Write up your own version of the interview using the conventions of the written interview.

Conventions of diaries and journals

A diary or journal is a personal record of things that have happened to the writer. It can also record the writer's thoughts or feelings.

Explore the skills

1   Read this diary extract. Who do you think is writing?

Monday, 11 March

What a day it's been! I overslept and missed the school bus and then, when I finally arrived, I found out the whole class was on a science trip and they had already left. I felt such a fool. I had to sit on my own outside the head teacher's office all day. It was so boring!

I'm back home now, sitting in my room. I haven't told Mum or Dad I missed the trip. If I do, they'll go mad. Dad's home. I'd better pretend I'm asleep.

— date of entry

— use of the first person and past tense

— recounts events that have happened that day

— reference to time/sequence

— personal feelings

— present tense gives sense of things happening now

— future tense shows worries

Build the skills

Diaries and journals give a sense of the writer's personality and explain his or her changing emotions. They focus on key moments or incidents in the writer's world and (usually) provide a sense of time or sequence.

2   Make notes on the following.

*   **Content:** What incident made this student record his thoughts? Identify three different emotions felt at different times of the day.

*   **Structure:** How does the structure reveal what he feels about the situation?

*   **Style:** How does the style of the writing match the likely age of the person writing?

Develop the skills

Your diary entries should aim to develop and extend ideas fully.

3 How does the following diary entry do this? It is written by Tanya Saunders, a woman who lives in Kenya, East Africa.

Yesterday, it was cloudy and rainy all day, the crocodiles starved of any sunlight and barely any warmth [...] then today we awoke to a totally different morning: back to the scorching heat and the crocodiles returning in droves to bask on the sandbanks, while the Goliath Heron, too hot even to finish washing, just sat down in the river and stayed there (and who could blame it?) I had to take a cold shower at midday, just to fortify myself for the onslaught of the afternoon heat.

Tonight, as might be expected, the thunder and lightning are raging again, huge storm clouds fomented in the heat of the day, now towering overhead [...] and the rain continues, and the bugs multiply, and the flowers prepare to launch into their reproductive cycles once again [...] the tiny pretty blue commelina flowers are already blooming everywhere you look (including on our **nascent** lawn) and the **sansevieria** we transplanted into our garden (both on the balcony and outside) are sending up a proliferation of shoots, the new spikes breaking the surface of the earth like spiky aliens, and reaching up towards the light.

From the blog 'Tales from Kulafumbi: The Diary of a Nature Lover'

4 Answer these questions.

a) What does the writer focus on? Is this like the student's diary? Why/why not?

b) How does she use words or phrases related to time and sequence to structure her entry?

c) How are tenses used in different sections to show what has happened and is happening?

d) How does she use detailed description of the natural world to develop a vivid picture of the weather, and the flowers and plants in the garden?

Apply the skills

5 From reading Tanya Saunders' diary entry, what picture do you get of the writer and her interests?

6 Reread the diary entry in Task 3. Write the beginning of the entry for the next day in which you:

• refer to the time(s) of day and how the weather affects you

• give a detailed and well-developed observation of some aspect of nature.

Vocabulary

nascent: starting to grow

sansevieria: type of flowering plant with tongue-like leaves

Conventions of reports

At many times in your life you may find you need to report on situations. Reports usually tell the reader about an event that has taken place, using factual detail. The writer may analyse or observe these events, or offer a more personal perspective.

Explore the skills

Reports are always written for a particular audience. They must be clear and sound convincing.

1 Read this short extract from a report. Then make brief notes on the following:

a) What is the subject or topic?

b) Who is the likely audience?

c) Why is the report split into two paragraphs?

d) What sort of report is it?

e) Where might you read it?

f) Does the report sound convincing?

> The school fundraising day was a great success, thanks to you all. Three things made the day such a success: the weather, your hard work and the generosity of visitors and parents.
>
> The day began well, with clear blue skies, but it wasn't too hot. As our families arrived, it began to get really busy. I was working on a stall selling cold drinks. We soon ran out and needed more supplies desperately! I must thank Kiki in particular, who cycled all the way to the shop and back with baskets full of lemonade and soda. She's been my best friend since Grade 2 and now you all know why. In fact, just as we restocked, the Mayor appeared and we were able to serve him a wonderfully cool drink.

Build the skills

Understanding your audience will make your report sound realistic. For this, choose the right content, style and structure.

2 Copy and complete the table below, based on the extract above.

Report to classmates in school magazine about charity day	
content	It gives clear information, but also covers…
structure	It could be in time sequence, but could also jump around to topics such as the weather, money raised and number of people there.
style	

Develop the skills

Read this longer report, then answer the questions below.

> Getting students to give to charity is one of our school's biggest challenges, and it's time we and readers of this magazine did something about it.
>
> Recent research I have carried out shows that one in five students has given to charity, although slightly more (two out of five) have been directly involved in some form of fundraising. As our head teacher Mr Marquez said, 'Getting good results and working hard is, of course, vital. But if we are to show that we are a caring community, we must do more, right now, for those less fortunate than ourselves.'
>
> The good news is that since the start of the year, we have raised over $2000 for charity, so we can do it. But is it enough? Surely we can do more.
>
> Tomorrow at 3 p.m. there will be a meeting in the school hall for any teachers and students who wish to organise fundraising events in the coming term. Let's hope it is well attended. Watch this space!

3 Content:

    a) What is the purpose of this report? How do you know?

    b) What evidence is there of statistics, expert comment, and so on, to support this purpose?

4 Structure:

    a) How effectively does the report use paragraphs?

    b) Does it have a strong beginning and ending? Why/why not?

5 Style:

    a) Is it clear who the report is for?

    b) How formal or informal is it?

    c) Does it use detail to make events clear?

    d) Does it use a variety of sentences to engage listeners?

Apply the skills

6 Imagine that the meeting has taken place. Write a follow-up report of at least 100 words including:

- facts or statistics about who and how many attended
- the outcome of the meeting and your views on this, good or bad.

Top tip

Put different points into separate paragraphs for clarity. Write a strong opening and a powerful conclusion to draw points together.

Conventions of news reports and magazine articles

News reports and articles, whether online or in newspapers or magazines, are vital sources of information. They usually fall into two types. Those that report the main facts or information about very recent specific incidents are news reports. Those that discuss, analyse or investigate a topic are called feature articles. Feature articles are often, but not always, in magazines.

Explore the skills

Sometimes the headings give clues about what sort of report or article the text is. Look at these headings:

> **Temperatures dip to −30 ° for coldest night on record**
>
> **Why are our winters getting colder?**
>
> *Ice causes chaos on motorways*
>
> **Snow go – 36 hours stuck on train**
>
> *How to predict cold winters*

news article: it is a specific single happening that has just occurred

Top tip

Succinct vocabulary in headlines can capture an idea immediately.

1 Try to identify which of the headings belong to news reports and which to feature articles.

Build the skills

This news report has a very clear structure, which is indicated in the annotations. Read the article, and then answer the questions below it.

> # Mountain Goat Kills Hiker
>
> *by Alex Robinson*
>
> ROBERT BOARDMAN, 63, was hiking with his wife and friend in Olympic National Park on Monday when he was attacked and killed by a mountain goat. The trio was

simple headline sums up what happened

main event/news

hiking up a popular switchback trail and decided to stop for lunch when the goat approached them and started acting aggressively.

Boardman tried to scare the goat off, but instead of running away, it charged him goring him badly in the leg. More hikers came to try to help Boardman, but the goat stood over the man's body and wouldn't let any other hikers come to his aid.

An hour after the attack, rescuers finally arrived at the scene but Boardman died from his injuries. Park officials eventually shot and killed the goat.

Apparently, that specific goat had shown aggressive tendencies in the past. 'It has shown aggressive behaviour, however, nothing led us to believe it was appropriate to take the next level of removal,' park spokeswoman Barb Maynes told the Associated Press. 'This is highly unusual. There's no record of anything similar in this park. It's a tragedy. We are taking it extremely seriously and doing our best to learn as much as we can.'

The goat is being examined by scientists to see if it had any diseases that could have caused it to act so aggressively.

From www.outdoorlife.com

how the incident happened and what led up to it

how the incident ended

'expert' comment, often with direct quotation

current situation and what is happening next

2 Content and structure (what is in the article):

a) News reports often have the 'who, what, where and when' at the start of the story. Is this the case here? If so, note down each aspect. For example, 'who' is Robert Boardman?

b) Expert or witness comments in direct speech are often included to give weight to a story. What do we find out from Barb Maynes? Why wouldn't this be the first paragraph of the report?

c) What does the final paragraph focus on?

3 Style (how it is written):

a) To make the report sound objective, writers of news articles tend not to use 'I'. Is this the case here?

b) News reports often report events in sequence: what happened, what happened next. Identify any time connectives in the article (for example, *first*, *later*, *finally*).

c) Most verbs about what happened are in the past tense (for example, *goat **approached** them*), but what do you notice about the headline and the last paragraph? Why do you think these are different?

Develop the skills

Feature/magazine articles are often more complex than news reports. They:

- are often personal (the writer refers to himself or herself)
- cover wider ground or more complex ideas
- offer a distinct viewpoint
- explore ideas more deeply.

Read this feature article, then answer questions 4 and 5.

First, catch your *feral* kitten. then call in the experts.

article title explains the topic

My neighbourhood is inundated with **feral** cats, scraggy wild things that cadge food from animal lovers in winter and cadge baby blackbirds and robins from their nests each spring. Typically, I've moaned about this without taking any responsibility – until last week, when I became so exasperated, I set a humane trap.

opening sentence is about problem/issue

I bought a wire cage to see if I could catch a squirrel or rat to show my animal-mad daughter, Esme. Luckily she was at school when the door slammed on an adorable kitten. Clueless about what I should actually do, for the first time in my life I called the **RSPCA**. Rather like the first time I needed a hospital and was astounded by the brilliance of the doctors and nurses, the RSPCA was amazing.

descriptive detail paints picture of cat

The charity knew all about my street's cat problem and had caught 20 feral cats so far. I was asked to take "21" to meet an RSPCA officer at a nearby vet, where the kitten was checked (cats are assessed and adults scanned for microchips to ensure they are not pets) and pronounced a feral tomcat.

personal involvement of writer

Because 21 is only eight weeks old, he will be found a home as a pet. Adults are neutered and released wherever they came from, which my neighbourhood blackbirds won't welcome, but feral cats have hard lives and only survive for a couple of years.

The RSPCA has now lent me a better trap so I can join other neighbours in helping feral cats and other wildlife, at no expense to the taxpayer. Bravo for the **big** (cat) **society.** One problem remains: Esme is tearfully begging to keep the next catch.

writer ends with a dilemma

From 'First catch your feral kitten' by Patrick Barkham, *The Guardian*

4   Structure and content:

    a) Is this feature article about a news event that has just happened? Check the opening paragraph and see whether it describes a particular incident.

    b) Compare the mountain goat news report with this one. How is the structure different? For example, think about how the report recounts information about the event.

5   Style:

    a) What is it about the headline that suggest this is a feature article rather than a news report?

    b) What can you infer about the viewpoint of the writer based on the language he uses? For example: what can you learn from the adjectives *humane*, and *adorable* and the reference to cats' *hard lives*?

> ### Vocabulary
>
> **feral:** wild, undomesticated
>
> **RSPCA:** Royal Society for the Prevention of Cruelty to Animals (in the UK)
>
> **big society:** a political idea in the UK related to helping others

Apply the skills

6   Write your own feature article about animals that are not normally seen as problematic, but which can cause issues or be dangerous.

- Use some of the ideas or facts from the goat report and feral cat article.

- Give a clear viewpoint: whether you think all animals should be treated as 'wild' or 'dangerous'.

You could start with the goat attack but do not make it the whole focus. For example, you could begin:

> The recent death of a hiker, gored by a mountain goat, might make us think that all animals, however 'cuddly', are a real danger to humans and other wildlife…

Conventions of letters

In some areas of life, written letters are still very important.

Explore the skills

When writing letters, make sure that you:

- think about the audience (this will change your style)
- focus on purpose (why you are writing)
- match your style to both (how formal or informal).

1 Here are two short letters. Compare their style, tone and structure. What is similar and different about them?

14 Jacaranda Street
Hightown
HK1 3BS

7th June 2017

Dear Jo,

I'm so sorry it's been so long since I contacted you. We don't have a computer here and I can't get a signal on my phone. Anyway, I just wanted to say that the new house is ok. Only four rooms so I have to sleep with Leila, who still sucks her thumb and snores! I miss you so much. I can't write more now as I have to catch the post before it goes. I'll try to phone you or send something longer when I have time.

Love to you and the rest of the gang.

Davina

Sharp's Stores
23 Willow Avenue
Hightown
HK1 3BS

7th June 2017

Re: Post of shop assistant

Dear Mrs Sharp,

Thank you for your letter of 1st June, in which you kindly offered me the post of shop assistant, I am writing to inform you that I would be delighted to accept and look forward to working with you.

Yours sincerely,
Davina Khan

Build the skills

2 What do you notice in particular about the different styles used in the letters? Consider:

- choice of vocabulary
- abbreviations and sentence types
- punctuation
- openings and closings.

Develop the skills

Unfortunately, Davina makes a poor start when dealing with a customer. The customer has now written a letter of complaint.

> Dear Mrs Sharp,
>
> I'm writing to complain about the unsatisfactory level of service I received when I visited your store yesterday.
>
> As you are aware, I am a regular customer and expect high levels of courtesy and advice from your staff.
>
> Unfortunately, your new assistant, Miss Khan, did not meet my expectations in either regard.
>
> Firstly, it was extremely disappointing that when I approached the counter...

— makes the reason for writing clear

— develops and begins to explain in what areas the shop failed

— links to and develops the previous point, beginning to specify the bad service she received

The customer then explains:

- the first specific problem with Davina
- the second specific problem
- what action the customer would like Mrs Sharp to take.

3 Note down some ideas you could use if you were the customer writing the letter.

Apply the skills

4 Now complete the customer's letter of complaint, developing the points in the plan into full paragraphs. Make sure that you write with an appropriate level of formality.

Check your progress

Sound progress

- I understand and can use some of the key conventions of a speech.
- I can use some of the main conventions of interviews in a clear way.
- I can compose a diary text using the main conventions.
- I can write a clear report or article with a sense of the reader/audience.
- I understand the key conventions of formal and informal letters.

Excellent progress

- I understand the variety of ways a speech can be effective and can apply them skillfully to my own work.
- I understand the different conventions of interviews and develop them fully in my own work.
- I can use the main conventions of diaries or journals to express feelings and convey information clearly and effectively.
- I can adapt the style and content of a report or article to effectively engage and interest a given audience.
- I can apply my knowledge of different letter forms according to task, audience and purpose.

Writing for purpose

In this chapter, you are going to develop a range of fundamental writing skills that you will use throughout your Cambridge IGCSE course.

You will learn how to write for a range of purposes:

- to inform and explain

- to persuade

- to argue

- to explore and discuss

- to describe

- to narrate.

Learning about the conventions of these kinds of texts will help you to complete larger and more complex tasks later that may ask you to write for a specific purpose and audience, using a specific form. These will require you to understand how the purpose can affect the style and structure of your writing.

Links to other chapters:

Chapter 3: Key writing forms

Chapter 7: Analysing language

Chapter 8: Extended response to reading and directed writing

Chapter 9: Composition

Chapter 10: Approaching written coursework

Writing to inform and explain

Informative or explanatory texts, such as articles or reports, should be clear and provide information in a logical, structured way. The features listed in the box also apply when you include informative writing in other texts, such as argument texts (see Topic 4.5).

Explore the skills

Read the opening two paragraphs from an article about grey wolves.

> There are many reasons why humans view wolves harshly. For a start, fairy tales such as the Brothers Grimm's *Little Red Cap* from 1812 often feature the wolf as an evil beast. Then there's the fact that wolves are a genuine threat to livestock, especially as their natural prey in the wild declines. Finally, there is their pack mentality – the idea of wolves being prepared to act together to get what they want.
>
> So, have fairy stories and myths always represented the wolf as a malignant force? Not exactly. For example, the formation of the city of Rome is said in myth to have been achieved after twin brothers were saved from death and suckled by a she-wolf. One of them, Romulus, gave his name to the city. Such a myth dates back to the 3rd century BC, but for whatever reason this image of the wolf as caring parent has not continued.

— topic sentence

Features of informative writing:

- clear and concise sentences
- connectives to explain processes or make things clear
- precise vocabulary
- data and statistics, diagrams, tables, illustrations
- subheadings or different categories of information
- a general statement and introduction
- both past and present tenses
- references, quotations or citations.

1. The text opens with a general statement in the form of a topic sentence. What is the focus of the text as a whole?

2. In what way is factual information used in the second and third sentences?

3. Is the information presented logically? For example, could the final sentence be swapped with the first – or does it have to go at the end?

4. The opening paragraph presents the general picture. In what way is the second paragraph more focused and detailed?

Build the skills

The topic sentence often comes at the beginning of a paragraph, as in the example above, but it does not have to. Read this later paragraph from the same article.

> They have strong jaws with sharp canine teeth for tearing and chewing meat. Add to this their swimming prowess and their ability to travel up to 50 kilometres a day to hunt. All in all, they seem to be the ultimate hunting beast.

5 Which is the topic sentence in this paragraph? How do you know?

Develop the skills

The way you link sentences together is also important. In the examples on page 100 and above, the **connectives** *For a start*, and *Add to this* link the sentences in the following ways.

- *For a start* introduces a first example to show the reader what the writer means.

- *Add to this* introduces another example to provide even more information.

Read these further details about the grey wolf.

> - Usually hunt in family packs of 3–30 wolves.
> - Packs useful for killing larger animals such as deer.
> - Packs usually led by an 'alpha' male and female (whose offspring comprise the pack).

6 What is the common thread or focus in each of these statements? How does this information link to the original paragraphs?

Key term

connectives: words or phrases used to link sentences

Apply the skills

7 Write a paragraph of three or four sentences, using the bullet points above. Include either a topic sentence that introduces these specific details or a concluding sentence that sums them up.

Use some of the connectives and prompts from the word bank below to help organise your paragraph.

What is more	Also	For example	In fact	So	Wolf packs

Structuring informative writing

You can use paragraphs and tenses to order your texts logically.

Explore the skills

Read this short article about a different type of predator.

Falconry is a centuries-old activity, and it is still revered today. It is the act of hunting animals in their natural habitat through the use of a trained bird of prey.

The process of training hawks is highly skilled. It begins with 'manning' – that is, getting the hawk used to your presence. Once the hawk trusts you and will feed calmly on your gloved fist, training can begin. The hawk now has to learn to come to you for food. First, it needs to be attached to a line – called a 'creance' – and placed on a post or an assistant's hand. Then, you hold a piece of meat in your gloved fist so the hawk can see it. To start with, it will probably only come for a very short distance, but after a few days you can increase the distance to about 50–100 metres. When the hawk comes this far without hesitation, you are ready to let it fly freely. Then, using a 'lure' (a line with meat at the end) you can train it to follow or come to you.

These specialised words go back many, many years. In fact, back in the 16th century, Shakespeare wrote a speech in his play *The Taming of the Shrew* in which the main character, Petruchio, talked about how he was going to tame his wife as if she were a hawk!

Nowadays, falconry is used for more pleasant purposes. People hire displays for fairs, exhibitions and even weddings. But, don't forget the ancient skills or training that go into it as you watch such a display this summer.

1 What is the main focus or purpose of each paragraph? Check for:

- a topic sentence (often, but not always, at the start of the paragraph)
- the particular content (the facts or specific details covered in each paragraph).

Build the skills

2 The second paragraph explains a process.

a) What main tense does it use?

b) What words or phrases does the writer use to explain the order of events? (Look for time-markers such as *Once*.)

Develop the skills

3 Now think about the article overall.

a) Would the four paragraphs make sense in any order? Why, or why not?

b) How are the paragraphs themselves linked? (Look at the first sentences of the third and fourth paragraphs.)

Imagine that you have been asked to write an article about whaling for a magazine. First, read these three columns of information on the subject.

The past/history	The process	The situation today
• Whaling dates back to 3000 BC • First organised whaling fleets in 17th century • In late 1930s, more than 50 000 whales killed annually • The 1986 International Whaling Commission banned commercial whaling • Not all countries signed up to it	• Many different types of whaling, for example, Norway catches Minke whales by firing harpoons from cannons on bow of boat; follow up with rifles if not killed immediately • Hunters have to take safety classes and proficiency exam to prove that they know how to use weapons • Other methods include beaching whales by driving them onto land	• Some countries have continued so-called 'scientific-research' whaling • They believe that whale stocks are now at a level where whaling could start again • Many arguments over whaling, including who should decide whether it is legal, whether the data about stocks is correct, and so on

4 How would you order the information? Create a paragraph plan.

Apply the skills

5 Now, write your article. Make sure that you:

- explain the history of whaling
- give information about what whaling is
- explain what the situation is in the present day.

Checklist for success

✔ Decide what the function of each of your paragraphs will be (for example, to give the history or to explain a process).

✔ Think about the tenses you will use.

✔ Decide which connectives of time or sequence will help you organise the information.

✔ Consider what the topic sentence for each paragraph might be and where it should go.

Writing to persuade

When you write to persuade, you aim to change someone's beliefs or point of view. To achieve this, the information you include must be carefully selected to justify your own point of view. In addition, you will need to apply various other persuasive techniques.

Explore the skills

There are three key elements to bear in mind when writing to persuade:

- **A:** ideas – the points you choose to make and the evidence you use to support these points
- **B:** language – the vocabulary or other techniques you use to influence how your reader thinks
- **C:** structure – the way you present and order your points so that they have the greatest effect.

Look at this opening to an article about 'driverless' cars.

> I cannot see a future for driverless cars. The idea of robotic machines with minds of their own ferrying passengers from A to B appals me: technology is just too unreliable.
>
> A key problem is hacking. What happens if the computer that drives the car is affected by a virus or some other nasty attack? It would be absolute chaos!

1 What other powerful uses of language can you identify here?

2 The structure of this text is logical because the first paragraph introduces the general view and the second paragraph develops it. In what ways does the second paragraph develop the first?

Features of persuasive writing:

- strong, single-minded viewpoint
- personal tone expressed in the first person
- direct appeals to the reader/listener (*you*)
- rhetorical questions: *Do you really think that climate change is a myth?*
- emotive images or other language (*dying gulls slicked with oil on a trash-covered beach*)
- patterns of three (*the Antarctic will soon be a myth, a memory, an extinct continent*)
- counter-arguments acknowledged and demolished
- a 'call to action'.

Element A: clear statement of viewpoint and evidence

Element B: strong, negative language

Build the skills

You can use vocabulary and persuasive devices to make an emotional appeal to your reader and to make a 'call to action'. Read this extract from a parent to a head teacher.

3 Write down answers to these questions.

    a) What does the parent want to happen?

    b) What 'happy picture' does the parent paint?

> Just picture the street by our school if you were to ask the council to ban cars: instead of huge metal monsters belching out smoke, grinding their gears and skidding to a halt with a screech of brakes, all you would hear would be the happy chatter of little children and their parents. After all, what could be more important than the safety and well-being of our precious children?

Develop the skills

How do you achieve such emotional appeal? Look at this table.

Method	Example	Effect
powerful or **emotive** vocabulary	*huge metal monsters*	suggests that they are enormous beasts, threatening children
rhetorical question	*After all, what could be more important than the safety and well-being of our precious children?*	emotional appeal: makes the point unanswerable – no one is likely to disagree!
pattern of three	*belching out smoke, grinding their gears and skidding to a halt*	has a rhythmic emphasis that hammers home the message

4 Which verbs in the table have a particularly powerful impact? What comes to mind when you read them?

5 Why is the opening sentence of the letter especially effective?

Key term

emotive: likely to make people feel strong emotions

Apply the skills

6 Reread the extract about driverless cars. Below is the start of a paragraph that is *in favour of* driverless cars. Continue the paragraph.

- Add one supporting sentence with evidence or reasons to back up your view.
- Include language that has emotional power (use the table to help you).

> Driverless cars are a great idea! Just think of …

Structuring persuasion

When writing to persuade, you need to make sure that the arguments or ideas you include, and the way that you organise them, are as effective as possible.

Explore the skills

- **Content:** You need strong arguments supported by persuasive *evidence* or *examples*.
- **Structure:** You need sentences or paragraphs *sequenced* in a logical way to have maximum impact.

Read this paragraph, which effectively presents an argument on the topic of parking outside school. Note how it *builds* the argument.

> One benefit of a traffic-free zone outside school is clear. Recent research has shown that when cars are banned, up to 70% of parents walk their children to school, which would be incredibly beneficial to our children's health. Furthermore, it might be good for parents too – we all need that extra bit of exercise.

clear topic sentence to introduce the point

factual evidence to support the point

specific benefit from the evidence

1 What additional point does the final sentence make?

2 Is this the only logical place for this sentence to be positioned in the paragraph? Why, or why not?

Build the skills

It is vital to decide what your key arguments are and plan how you will present them before you start writing.

3 What other points can you think of to support the proposal to ban cars outside the school? Consider:

- the social benefits to children – and parents – from walking to school
- the financial benefits or savings
- the impact on the environment in and around school.

Top tip

Develop your key points fully. Just mentioning a fact without saying what it shows does not help your persuasive argument.

Develop the skills

The tone you use in persuasive texts is also important. It is tempting to get angry and demand changes – 'Ban cars now!' – but it is usually more effective to show the effects of a particular course of action, using modal verbs and 'if' clauses.

Modal form	Condition	Example (in an 'if' clause)
will, would	probable or, in theory, likely	If you *ban* cars, you *will* improve air quality. If you *banned* cars, you *would* improve air quality.
might, could, may	outcome unsure	If you *ban* cars, you *might* improve air quality.
would have	not possible (too late)	If you *had banned* cars, you *would have* improved air quality.

4 Look back at the paragraph about parking outside school.

  a) What modal forms have been used?

  b) Which of the two points being made is more certain or likely, according to the writer?

5 Complete the following 'if' clauses:

  a) If parents had used their cars less, they ....

  b) If the children are exposed to car fumes, they ....

Apply the skills

6 Write a further two paragraphs about the traffic-free zone. Explain:
  • what you want to happen
  • the further benefits or advantages of the proposed traffic-free zone.

Checklist for success
···
✔ Structure your paragraphs to build an argument, adding evidence and further ideas.

✔ Use modal forms to show the benefits of acting or the problems that might arise if no action is taken.

✔ Use emotive language where appropriate.

Writing to argue

Persuasive texts tend to be one-sided. When you write an argument text, however, you need to consider both sides of an issue.

Explore the skills

There are different ways of organising argument texts. For example, consider how you could approach this topic:

> Bike rental schemes: should they be introduced into your local town or city?

The simplest structure is:

- Paragraph 1: introduction – the issue: what bike rental schemes are
- Paragraphs 2–4: points for bike rental schemes in your town
- Paragraphs 5–7: points against bike rental schemes
- Paragraph 8: conclusion: weigh up the points and give your opinion.

1 Do you think this would be an effective structure to use? Why, or why not?

2 What alternative ways of structuring the essay can you think of?

Build the skills

Evidence can come in different forms. For example, it could be:

- facts or statistics
- 'expert' or witness comments
- personal experience (from the writer).

3 Read the following response to the bike-rental scheme topic on page 109. Which of the three forms of evidence have been used?

Features of argumentative writing:

- a less personal tone than persuasive writing
- considers the facts and ideas on both sides of an issue
- supports points with evidence (for or against), but also **rebuts counter-arguments**
- use of counter-balancing linking words or phrases (*on the other hand...*)
- works logically towards a conclusion that states the writer's viewpoint.

Key terms

counter-argument: the opposite or contrasting viewpoint

rebut: to 'knock down' a counter-argument

Bike rental schemes are very popular right now, but are they really worth it? After all, it costs a lot of money to build the **docking stations**, create and plan signage and run the schemes. However, think of the income generated. In London in 2011, a bike scheme raised over nine million dollars in one year, which seems good value to me.

Some critics claim that you need to be earning a lot of money to hire a bike, but consider the alternatives. As **commuter** Jon Devani says, 'I used to have to pay to park my car at the station and then for my rail ticket – now I'm paying less for the bike and I'm getting fitter too.'

4 What 'personal experience' could be added to the argument? Remember – it needs to be related to the advantages of using a bike to get to work.

Develop the skills

The structure of the response above is slightly different to the simple structure outlined at the start of this topic.

5 Look at the structure of the response above.

a) *Where* are the counter-arguments placed in the extract? Do they appear in different paragraphs?

b) *What* are these counter-arguments and *how* have they been rebutted?

This approach can be summarised as follows:

- Paragraph 1: introduction – the issue
- Paragraph 2: point 1 plus counter-argument
- Paragraphs 3–4: points 2 and 3, with counter-arguments alongside
- Paragraph 5: further points to strengthen the main view but which do not have counter-arguments
- Paragraph 6: conclusion – summing up the evidence.

Vocabulary

bike rental schemes: many cities have schemes where you rent bicycles from docking stations and cycle them to others

docking stations: the places the bikes are kept

commuter: someone who travels to work by car or public transport

Apply the skills

6 Write the third paragraph of this argument. Use the 'counter-argument' structure:

- Start with a new problem (for example, you live too far away to cycle all the way to work).
- Suggest the solution (it could be to take the bus to a certain place, then pick up a bike).
- Finish the paragraph with a short, impactful sentence or a rhetorical question.

Structuring paragraphs in argument texts

Cohesive devices can help you structure your paragraphs to present arguments and counter-arguments clearly. They can also help you develop and expand on a point of view.

Explore the skills

When you write to argue a point of view, you should use a variety of connecting words and phrases to make your ideas and evidence clear.

Look at this example.

Tidal energy is plentiful **and** can generate significant power.

first idea

conjunction *and* gives additional information to support the first idea

second idea

Now look at this second example.

Tidal energy is plentiful, yet it can be difficult to harness.

1. Which is the **conjunction** in the second example? (Remind yourself about conjunctions by looking back to Topics 2.1 and 2.2.)

2. What is its function? (Is it supporting the first idea or doing something else?)

3. Conjunctions can be used for different purposes. Match each conjunction to its purpose. One has been done for you.

Conjunction	Purpose
idea + *and* + idea	to offer an alternative
idea + *so* + idea	to give additional information
idea + *but* + idea	to give a reason
idea + *or* + idea	to show a result or consequence
idea + *because* + idea	to give a contrast, indicate difference or problem

Key terms

conjunction: a word used to join clauses or words in the same clause or sentence, for example, *and, but, or*

conjunctive adverbs: a conjunctive adverb links independent clauses in a sentence, or links ideas between two sentences – for example, *finally, therefore, moreover,* to show cause and effect

Some adverbs act in a similar way to conjunctions, linking ideas or actions, or suggesting causes or sequences. These **conjunctive adverbs** include words or phrases such as *however*, *finally* and *immediately*. Both conjunctions and conjunctive adverbs are sometimes referred to collectively as connectives.

4 What is the purpose of each conjunction and conjunctive adverb in the passage below?

> Tidal energy is plentiful, yet can be difficult to harness. We need to invest in research in order to find out how practical it is. However, this is not straightforward as research costs a lot of money.

— conjunction
— conjunctive adverb

Build the skills

You need to know how to construct paragraphs that use conjunctions or conjunctive adverbs to build arguments. Look at this opening to a speech about wind turbines.

> Every drive or train journey along a major road or route now reveals a wonderful phenomenon – wind turbines. These inspiring structures, sprouting like giants from the landscape, are huge and beautiful. They attract the eye like wonderful visitors from another planet. People even divert their journeys in order to experience the thrill of seeing them up close. Indeed, I love them because of their other-worldly appearance, and, furthermore, I'd be happy to have one of them stand guard over my own house.

topic sentence introduces the subject of the speech

follow-up sentences give supporting detail to the argument about wind turbines

5 What viewpoint is expressed here? How do you know this from the very first sentence?

6 Write down the conjunctions or adverbs used to:

   a) add further information or evidence (that is, one idea plus another one)

   b) strengthen an idea

   c) present the outcome or consequence of something.

7 Note down any other language that supports the argument (for example, the choice of adjectives or noun phrases).

8 Write an opening paragraph in the same style but arguing *against* wind turbines. Use conjunctions or conjunctive adverbs to add information, strengthen ideas and to show the outcome of a course of action. You could start:

> Every drive or train journey along a major road or route in the UK now reveals a dreadful spectacle – wind turbines. These...

Develop the skills

When you want to present points in a straightforward way, you can use conjunctive adverbs such as *Firstly, Secondly* and *Finally* to sequence ideas. However, weighing up or contrasting the ideas or argument requires a different approach.

Read this extract from an article about fracking – a controversial means of getting gas from the ground. As you read, think about how the article sets up the debate and then introduces the arguments for and against fracking.

Hailed as a game changer and the harbinger of cheap energy or as an ecological disaster, the cause of earthquakes and pollution, fracking's entrance into our lives has been colourful. The fundamentals are clear. Fracking is a method of extracting gas from rock formations by using high-pressure water and chemicals.

It enables us to extract from places that were hitherto uneconomic, but it's not cheap and is only cost-effective because of the high price of energy. Nevertheless, in the USA, it has transformed costs and is rapidly replacing coal as a source of generation. Dirty coal produces higher emissions, so fracked gas cuts American pollution and allows the country to claim to be fighting climate change. However, gas, like coal, is a fossil fuel. Its emissions are significant and, in the absence of carbon capture and storage, still contribute hugely to global warming.

From 'Fracking: the pros and cons' by Lord Deben and Emma Hughes, *Country Life* magazine website

9 According to the article, what are the arguments for and against fracking?

10 How are the different ideas presented? Copy and complete the table below to track the progress of the argument of the debate.

Sentence	Conjunction or conjunctive adverb used	Effect (To contrast? To show an outcome?)
Hailed as... colourful.	or	presents the positive and negative sides
It enables us... price of energy.		
Nevertheless... generation.		
Dirty coal... climate change.		
However,... fuel.		
Its emissions... global warming.		

Read the following task and think about how you would answer it.

> You have learned that a wind farm is to be built very close to your village or town. The council has invited people to come to a public meeting to express their views and you have been asked to make a speech arguing against wind turbines. Write your speech.
>
> Here are some arguments you could include:
>
> - It spoils the natural beauty of landscape.
> - It costs too much: currently wind energy is not as efficient as fossil fuel or nuclear energy; farms are expensive to build.
> - Noise pollution: some people living close to turbines claim low-level noise causes stress-related illness.

11 Add some ideas of your own to this list. For example, consider issues such as: birds or wildlife; TV, computer and radio reception; military defence.

12 How would you organise these points? Note down the order in which you would present your ideas.

Top tip

Look back at Topic 3.1 to remind yourself about the conventions of speeches.

Apply the skills

13 Write your speech.

Checklist for success

✔ Begin with a paragraph that 'sets up' the argument (look again at the first 'pro-turbine' example).

✔ Link ideas *in* your paragraphs by using conjunctions and conjunctive adverbs you have come across in this unit. Here are some others you could use: *in order that, since, unless, until, whenever, while, similarly, likewise, nonetheless, furthermore, accordingly, otherwise, in fact.*

✔ Use these connectives to give reasons, strengthen points, suggest outcomes or present the other side of the case in order to knock it down.

Writing to explore and discuss

If you are asked to *discuss* or *explore* a topic, you need to show that you have thought about it in depth by taking into account different viewpoints.

Features of discursive writing:

- engages the reader in the opening paragraph, perhaps by using an anecdote or by giving unusual or surprising information
- has a *measured tone* – although it can still be personal
- provides a *clear explanation* of an issue, often by reference to *facts or statistics*
- explores *different viewpoints* about an issue
- comes to some sort of *conclusion*, although this may not be strong or forcefully expressed.

Explore the skills

Read the following article.

Last week I was taken to a local restaurant by a friend, and was surprised to see on the menu such things as 'yarrow flower shortbread' and 'nettle soup'. Such items represent a new craze around here – food that has been 'foraged', or gathered in the wild. So, is it worth all the fuss?

My friend believes foraged food is the future. 'It's natural, it's unusual, and it tastes great!' he says. It seems local people agree: there are now three restaurants in our town (including the one we visited) that serve strange-sounding things that you would normally regard as weeds or wild plants.

However, is it such a good thing? For example, it is often the most expensive restaurants that feature foraged food, such as Danish restaurant Noma, voted the best in the world in 2014. This leads some to say that it is a fad and just an excuse for restaurants to charge a lot for weird-sounding dishes.

Yet the popularity is not just down to a celebrated restaurant or two. At a time when more and more people are rejecting fast food, which is often unhealthy, the idea of going back to nature seems very appealing. While foraged food is free and close to hand, it seems likely to remain popular, even if not everyone is convinced.

1.
  a) What issue is being discussed?

  b) What is the writer's viewpoint, if any?

  c) What statements, if any, suggest this?

Build the skills

2. Reread the article. Which features from the list at the start of this topic can you identify?

Develop the skills

One of the ways that you can identify the 'exploratory' nature of the text is through its tone. Look at how the final sentence might have been written:

> Because foraged food is free and close at hand I am convinced it is an absolutely wonderful innovation!

— use of first person

— powerful verb of personal belief

— emphatic noun phrase

— exclamation mark

3. Look at the final sentence in the article. How is it more measured than the example above? Consider:

- the use of the first person

- the effect of the verb *seems*

- the final subordinate clause after the comma.

Apply the skills

4. Here is another paragraph on a similar topic. Rewrite it so that is has a more measured tone by replacing the underlined sections.

> I am utterly appalled by the way restaurants want to make food look like art. I hate the idea of my meal looking like a painting, but like everyone I just want something nutritious, tasty and filling.

Start: *It seems slightly...*

End: *... even though...*

Structuring content in discursive writing

It is important to have a clear structure for your discursive writing. Just because you are 'exploring' a topic, this does not mean that you should lose sight of the focus of the task.

Explore the skills

In Topic 4.7, you read an article about foraging. The tone of the article was key, but the structure was equally important:

- Introductory paragraph: anecdote of personal experience
- Second paragraph: developing point made in first paragraph
- Third paragraph: introduces alternative viewpoint
- Fourth (concluding) paragraph: weighing up both sides.

In a directed writing task, you may be given some information on which to base your writing. Below is some information about a different food topic: chocolate and what is good/ bad about it. The information includes comments from an expert and the writer.

> 100 g dark chocolate per day could reduce the risk of a heart attack or stroke by 21%. (*British Medical Journal* research)
>
> Chocolate usually contains large quantities of antioxidants (chemicals that can prevent the build-up of harmful pollutants in the body and lower blood pressure).
>
> 'I bought a large bar of chocolate recently and finished it all in one go, and I felt really guilty, especially when the dentist told me a week later that I needed two fillings.'
>
> Contains caffeine which can help make you more alert.
>
> Too much caffeine can lead to disturbed sleep.
>
> Typical ingredients in a chocolate bar: butter, sugar, cream or milk, lots of calories that can make you put on weight.
>
> 'Eating chocolate is fine, provided it is in moderation and you stick to dark chocolate.' (Dr Miles Better)
>
> Chocolate can be a pleasant reward, from time to time.

1. How would you organise the information into a structure similar to the one used in the foraging article? You may need more than four paragraphs.

2. Come up with an alternative structure that addresses some of the pros and cons within the same paragraphs. For example:

    *   First paragraph: anecdote – visit to the dentist
    *   Second paragraph: problem of calories/weight versus benefit of antioxidants
    *   Third paragraph: …

Build the skills

An overall structure such as this allows you to balance the different arguments, but it also helps you to build ideas across your paragraph.

Look again at the final paragraph from the foraging article.

> Yet the popularity is not just down to a celebrated restaurant or two. At a time when more and more people are rejecting fast food, which is often unhealthy, the idea of going back to nature seems very appealing. While foraged food is free and close to hand, it seems likely to remain popular, even if not everyone is convinced.

topic sentence introduces point

second sentence provides supporting information

final complex sentence sums up writer's view

3. Write a paragraph about the benefits of chocolate. Start with the topic sentence below, then:

    *   add any supporting information
    *   finish with a summary point.

> Some believe that chocolate has a role to play in our physical health. For example…

Develop the skills

Another important feature in effective discursive writing is how you link and connect ideas *within* paragraphs. The words and phrases you use to link or explore ideas are sometimes called 'discourse markers'.

Time or sequence markers	Cause and effect markers	Comparison markers	Contrast markers	Development markers
This morning, that day	As a result	In the same way	On the other hand	Moreover
Earlier,	Thus	Similarly	In contrast	Furthermore
Afterwards	Therefore	Likewise	However	Additionally
Once,	Following this	As	Yet	What is more
Finally	Because	Both	But	Also
Subsequently	In this way	Also	Although	In addition
	As can be seen			For example

Read this opening to an article on the benefits of chocolate. It uses a slightly different anecdote from the notes in 'Explore the skills'.

> This morning at break time, I noticed hundreds of students tucking into their favourite chocolate bar. Perhaps they were rewarding themselves with a quick snack, which is often something sweet, or perhaps they felt they needed the energy from a sudden sugar rush. However, I wondered if they really understood the effect that chocolate is having on them.

adverbial of time specifies the moment

relative clause adds extra bit of information

coordinating conjunction offers alternative possibility

adverb signals writer's personal question

All these discourse markers and phrases allow the writer to explain, explore and suggest. These things help create the measured tone needed for discursive writing.

4 Here is another paragraph. Choose an appropriate joining word or phrase for each space from the word bank on page 119 to create the same sort of measured tone.

> _____ , sugar is known as a contributory factor to weight gain, _____ can lead to heart disease. _____ , chocolate usually contains large quantities of antioxidants (chemicals that can prevent the build-up of harmful pollutants in the body and lower blood-pressure)._____ , 100 g dark chocolate per day could reduce the risk of a heart attack or stroke by 21%. _____ , we are talking about relatively small portions of dark chocolate.

Key terms

adverbial of time: a word or phrase expressing when something happened

relative clause: part of a sentence which usually explains or adds detail to a preceding noun

| yesterday | that | who | which | at the present time |
| yet | so | as | nevertheless | as a result |

Now consider this additional information that you could use in a discursive article about the benefits or drawbacks of chocolate:

- retail sales of chocolate worldwide = 101 billion US dollars
- sales of M&M's in the USA = 616.5 million US dollars
- some producers of chocolate are household names, such as Mars, Nestlé and Lindt
- chocolate plays a part in festive and religious celebrations, for example, Easter, Christmas and Hanukkah. In Mexico, chocolate is used to make offerings during El Día de los Muertos (the Day of the Dead festival).

5 What links all these items of information?

a) popularity of chocolate

b) sales of chocolate

c) consumption of chocolate

6 Where would this sort of information work best in your article (beginning, middle or end)? Why?

Apply the skills

7 Write an article exploring the role that chocolate plays in people's lives and whether it does harm or good.

Checklist for success

✔ Begin with an anecdote, personal experience and/or background information to the topic.

✔ Continue with a range of viewpoints.

✔ Link your ideas carefully, using appropriate connective words and phrases.

✔ Keep a measured, balanced tone throughout.

✔ End with a conclusion that provides some idea of your own viewpoint.

Top tip

Look back at Topic 3.5 to remind yourself about the conventions of articles.

Descriptive writing

What makes a description effective? Whether the description is part of a story or whether the place or experience being described is the focus of the writing, there are several key techniques for creating good description.

Explore the skills

When you write to describe, your main purpose is to give the reader a vivid or accurate sense of the person, object or experience. To do this well, writers often:

- use specific vocabulary (for example, *dinghy* rather than *boat*)
- choose vivid **imagery** such as **similes**, **metaphors** or symbols to make their descriptions original (*arrowing through the water*)
- use the senses to provide a memorable picture or impression (*icy wind chilling the bones*)
- use language techniques such as **personification**
- create an overall mood or atmosphere
- use a variety of sentences and paragraph structure to create different perspectives or viewpoints.

Read this description of a remote place.

> The long, dangling tendrils of the huge tree fell to the damp soil. Like the hair of a giant monster, they swayed and rolled as the weather began to worsen. Under them, sparkling raindrops danced on the forest floor. A tiny tree frog on one tendril gulped twice. Its orange eye swivelled. Then, it leapt off into space. The tendrils continued to shift and shake to the rhythm of the rain.

Key terms

imagery: words or comparisons that create a mental picture

simile: a vivid comparison of two things or ideas using *as* or *like* – for example, *the hoarse voice sounded out like sandpaper on a broken brick*

metaphor: a powerful image in which two different things or ideas are compared without using *as* or *like* – for example, *my fingers were tiny splinters of ice*

personification: when a thing or idea is described as if it has human qualities (*the storm bared its teeth and roared with anger*)

1 Which of the features listed in the bulleted list above can you identify in this description?

2 What is the paragraph *as a whole* describing? Consider each of these possibilities:

- the tendrils of the tree
- the raindrops
- the tree frog.

3 What different things are described in order to create the whole picture?

4 Are there any descriptive details that particularly stand out? Are all five senses used by the writer? If so, how?

If you are going to describe a particular person, place or experience, you need to think about *what* you describe. For example, the student who wrote the paragraph on page 120 made these notes:

> Remote place – no people; tropical forest or river? Both?
>
> When? Before, during and after a storm – sun's rays disappearing; rain hitting ground.
>
> What? Plants and trees – branches, roots etc.; earth/soil; forest creatures – red ants, python, tree frog.

5 What ideas from the notes has the student *not* used yet?

Build the skills

It is important to have a wide vocabulary to use in your descriptive writing. Having a variety of words and phrases at your fingertips means that you are less likely to repeat yourself and, more importantly, you will be able to choose the most appropriate or powerful word or phrase.

Do not just use the first word that comes to your mind. Many words have **synonyms** – some of which might be better than your first choice. For example, consider the sun's rays: they can …

Key term

synonym: a word that is identical, or very close in meaning, to another word

(shine) (glow) (sparkle) (shimmer)

(dazzle) (glitter) (beam) (flicker)

6 What is the difference in meaning between each of these verbs?

7 Which would be best for describing the rays coming through the branches or trees? Write a sentence or two describing the rays, using the word (or words) you have chosen.

In the description of the forest, the student uses a number of closely related words to describe the movement of the tendrils: *swayed, rolled, shift, shake.* The tendrils are likened to the *hair of a giant monster.*

8 What synonyms or related words can you find for the following words?

a) hair

b) monster

c) shake

It can also be helpful to think in terms of the **semantic field** when describing. This is a good way of making sure that you have enough to describe in relation to a particular experience or setting. Look at the table below, which contains some words connected to various features of the rainforest setting.

Key term

semantic field: vocabulary or set of terms closely linked by subject or usage

Storm	Forest	Creatures	River
thunder	tendrils	red ants	muddy banks
raindrops	roots	python	
disappearing sun	canopy	tree frog	
darkness, gloom	leaves		
oppression			

9 Copy and complete the table, adding further nouns to each semantic field. You could create an additional table with a set of related verbs – for example, to describe the movement of a river you could add *swirl* or *flow*.

10 Choose one of the words or phrases from the table (not one used in the original extract) and write one or two sentences using it.

Develop the skills

Descriptions can be structured in a range of ways. One effective way of planning is to select the key elements from the overall scene or place you are describing and allow a paragraph for each one. If you can, go one step further, and break down each paragraph into further details.

Paragraph	Overall focus	Elements	Up close
1	tree and its tendrils in the storm	tendrils and how they move, tree frog on tendrils, raindrops	eye of the tree frog
2	tree canopy		
3	banks of river		
4			
5			

11 Copy and complete the table, adding your own ideas to each row.

Apply the skills

You might be asked to describe a person rather than a place, but you can take the same approach to this description. Look at this start of a student's plan for a task about seeing a lonely person.

1. Bench with a homeless woman – clothing/face – old newspapers

2. A child stopping …

3.

4.

5.

Here is the first paragraph.

The old woman lay on the wooden bench fast asleep. Wrapped in several layers of tattered brown coats she seemed cocooned from the busy workers who rushed by. Her wrinkled face lay on its side, propped up on a bundle of old newspapers with frayed, greying edges.

12 Finish or rewrite the plan, using a structure like the one in the table in Task 11. Come up with your own ideas.

13 Write another paragraph from the plan.

Checklist for success
✔ Have a general overview or idea of what you are describing in the paragraph.

✔ Describe several elements using vocabulary to create a vivid picture.

✔ Zoom in on a specific detail or feature.

Narrative writing

A story is a type of writing built around events and their effect on the people involved. So, what makes a good story?

Explore the skills

Some basic guidance is useful for all short narratives:

- Stick to a limited number of main/developed characters (usually just one or two, although others can be mentioned in passing).
- Have one main plot and avoid too many actions, time spans or events.
- Develop a convincing voice or style for your main character(s).
- Make their story memorable through its structure and language (such as unusual imagery or lively dialogue).
- Capture the reader's attention from the start.

1 Look closely at the points above. What further guidance or points would you add, based on good stories you have read?

The way you structure your story is very important. You need to know what will become of your main character, even if this is something you do not reveal until the end.

It can be useful to plan your plot in five stages:

1. **Introduction:** the reader finds out about the situation and usually the main character.

2. **Development:** something happens or changes that affects the main character.

3. **Complication:** a problem or obstacle faces the main character and creates rising tension – the reader wonders what will happen.

4. **Climax:** the most dramatic or emotional point of the story.

5. **Resolution:** the tension drops and loose ends are tied up (for better or for worse).

Top tip

This is just one useful plan for stories, but it can be varied. For example, you could add more stages or have more than one complication or problem.

Read this short story plan by a student based on a fictional or autobiographical account of a disappointing experience.

- The reader finds out about six school friends, their names, what they're like.
- A school talent contest is announced.
- There is not much time to rehearse.
- The night of the talent show; none of them win.
- They meet in a cafe the next day and agree to enter next year.

2 How effective is this as a story structure? Consider the following:

   a) Does it follow the five-stage sequence in the order suggested above?

   b) Does it reflect the guidance given in the bullet points in 'Explore the skills'?

3 Try to improve the plot and the details. What would you change? Note down your ideas.

Build the skills

The overall plot is very important, but as you have seen, it is the individual ingredients that make the story work. After the plot, perhaps the most important element of a story is the choice of character. Here are four possible main characters for the story 'A Disappointing Night'.

Jake	Michelle	Priya	Marco
A popular and confident boy who is good at most subjects and sport. He usually wins prizes in competitions or rewards for his work.	A newcomer to the school, she appears a tough person who rarely reveals her feelings, but in fact has a heart of gold.	A talented musician but not good at English, Maths or Science. She longs to leave school and make her living as a performer.	Shy and small for his age. Marco prefers fiddling around writing software or mending laptops to school subjects.

4 Which of these would you choose as your main character? Consider which character:

- you can visualise best in your mind
- you can imagine speaking or thinking
- you think would fit best with any ideas you have for 'A Disappointing Night'.

5 Come up with an alternative main character. It does not have to be a student.

Develop the skills

Whether you write in detail about a character or mention people in passing, **characterisation** needs to be convincing. Characterisation is built by providing the reader with details such as:

- how someone behaves
- how they speak
- what they look like
- what others say about them.

6 Which of the factors listed above can you identify in the following extract?

> Marco scurried, like a mouse in a hurry, into the computer suite. He hopped up on to the stool, peered through his glasses at the laptop and rapidly tapped in a code. A voice suddenly interrupted his train of thought.
>
> 'Ah, Marco. Aren't you supposed to be in Science now?'
>
> It was the head teacher. Marco gulped, and turned around guiltily.

Key term

characterisation: how an author presents a particular character

7 How do you think Marco would reply? Write a sentence of speech that fits with his character.

It can help to consider the character's journey. Sometimes, this is literal – they go from one place to another. More important, however, is their personal or emotional journey – how they develop as a person, or how events change them over time. For example, look at these notes a student has made when planning a story:

Introduction	Marco likes messing around with computers; we find out he lacks confidence in other subjects, and doesn't have many friends.
Development	He misses a lesson because another student has bullied him into fixing his laptop.
Complication	He is caught by the head teacher and given detention. The head teacher gives him a letter for his parents asking them to come in to see him. At detention are some other students. They want to enter the talent show but they need some good backing music…
Climax	
Resolution	

8 Marco's emotional journey begins with him lacking confidence and friends. What could happen to Marco? How might it change or help him? Copy and complete the table, adding your own ideas.

Finally, where you set your story is important. There is more information about settings in Topic 1.7. Good locations can even make you think of good plots! Here are five different settings:

- a subway covered in graffiti in a dark, remote part of a city
- an ultra-modern office at the top of a tower block with huge glass windows and a white desk
- a pond full of still, slimy water in the middle of a dark forest
- a pretty walled garden with roses climbing the sides, and colourful birds singing
- a storeroom in a school in which old pieces of computer equipment are dumped.

9 What stories come to mind when you consider these locations? Make some basic notes on:

- characters you might see or associate with the locations – or perhaps someone who would be out of place there
- story ideas based on what might happen or have happened in these locations.

Top tip

Beginning in an atmospheric location can really engage your reader, especially if it is linked directly to the events of your story. Stories can work well in everyday places, too, but the characters or events have to be especially interesting in that case. See Chapter 9 for more information about story openings.

Apply the skills

10 Using what you have learned, write a fictional or autobiographical account of a dangerous experience or time in someone's life.

- Decide on a main character and location (or locations) – this might be you, if the account is true!
- Use the five-stage plot structure to help you.

You can use any of the ideas you have worked on or encountered in this topic. You do not need to go on and write the whole story, but if you wish to you could try writing the opening paragraph or two.

Check your progress

Sound progress

- I can identify some of the key features of informative and explanatory writing.
- I can structure an informative text in a logical way, using tenses to clarify ideas.
- I can write a text which uses some persuasive techniques effectively.
- I can structure a paragraph so that it presents my point of view clearly.
- I can write a sequence of paragraphs that clearly sets out my arguments.
- I can explore different aspects of an issue using some evidence to support what I say.
- I can state a viewpoint clearly.
- I can use a range of descriptive details and create a particular atmosphere through some use of senses, imagery and sentence variety.
- I can plan and write a simple, clear story with one or two main characters.

Excellent progress

- I understand and apply a wide range of elements of writing that informs and explains.,
- I can carefully structure an informative text so it is logical, and can use tenses to clarify and expand my ideas.
- I can write a text which uses a wide range of persuasive techniques for impact.
- I can structure a paragraph in different ways for a range of effects.
- I can write and adapt a sequence of paragraphs that clearly sets out my arguments.
- I can explore a wide range of aspects of an issue using well-chosen evidence to support what I say.
- I can state a viewpoint powerfully using a range of language and structural devices.
- I can use a wide range of descriptive details and create atmosphere through thoughtful use of senses, imagery and sentence variety.
- I can plan and write an interesting story with engaging characters and plot.

Comprehension

5

Some reading tasks require you to respond to a series of comprehension questions based on a text.

To answer this type of question, you will need to:

- demonstrate understanding of explicit meanings (R1)
- demonstrate understanding of implicit meanings and attitudes (R2)
- select and use information for specific purposes (R5).

You may come across different types of question in comprehension tasks. Closed questions tend to focus on the literal meaning of words and what this suggests. Open questions ask you to explore the subtler meanings of a word or phrase – what it might be suggesting about a person, place or attitude.

Links to earlier chapter:

Chapter 1: Key readings skills

Locating and selecting information

You will often be asked to read passages and answer brief comprehension questions that test whether or not you have understood the basic facts and ideas that the texts contain. Skimming and scanning skills will help you to identify facts, opinions and details related to a specific topic or idea.

Explore the skills

Skimming is used to gain a quick, general understanding of a text, while scanning is used to find specific information without having to reread the whole text. You will probably not come across questions about what you discover from your first skim-read. However, it will still be helpful to both skim and scan a text.

1 Skim the following article about a national park in Cambodia, then answer the questions.

Top tip

Look back at Topics 1.1 and 1.2 to remind yourself about skimming and scanning skills.

Vocabulary

acolytes: followers or servants

Kirirom National Park

All that remains of the king's palace is the fireplace. Twenty feet tall, it was built in the 1940s by the king and his **acolytes**. It stands on a flattened mountain top. The view is of
5   Cambodia's only high-altitude pine forest, in Kirirom national park – two hours' drive southwest of Phnom Penh. The scenery is almost alpine, the skinny pines saluting the sun, the air aromatic and fresh. [During a
10 period of unrest] the palace [was smashed] along with 150 surrounding villas that once made up the king's "Happy Mountain" resort. Some buildings are intact – more deserted than ruined.

Today, Kirirom is popular among locals but often overlooked by foreign visitors. Away from the hot chaos of the capital, there are   15
peaceful treks, mountain biking and dips in waterfalls. A stay at Kirirom Mountain Lodge (doubles from US$35; from $60 on weekend),   20
a converted 1940s villa near Oamrei Phong village in the centre of the park, Moroccan chef Bouchaib serves flatbread, honey-dripped and dotted with raisins. Guests can eat while surveying the green expanse of   25
cardamom forests below.

From 'Undiscovered South-East Asia'
by Nathan Thomson, *The Guardian*

a) Is this text fiction or non-fiction?

b) What is the purpose of the text?

c) Who do you think the writer's intended audience is for the text?

d) Is it all fact-based or does the text also include description?

e) How is the focus of the first paragraph different to that of the second paragraph?

2   Now scan the text to answer the following questions.

a) What nationality is the chef at the Kirirom Mountain Lodge?

b) In which decade was the king's palace built?

c) How far is the national park from Phnom Penh?

d) What is the only remaining feature of the king's palace?

e) What is the starting price for a weekend double room at the Kirirom Mountain Lodge?

3   Note down the techniques that you used when scanning the text for the answers to Task 2.

Top tip

When scanning, think about *key words* that relate to the kind of information you have been asked to select.

Build the skills

When scanning a text, you should be able to tell the difference between factual information and opinion. A comprehension question may ask you to identify several facts or opinions.

A fact is something that can be proven – it is based on evidence and may be linked to a specific statistic:

'The fireplace at the king's palace is 20 feet tall.'

An opinion is someone's perception – what they think or feel about a subject:

'Kirirom national park has the most beautiful scenery in Cambodia.'

4 Skim the paragraph below and decide what it is about. Then scan the paragraph and note down two facts and two opinions.

There are different types of chocolate, defined by the amount of cocoa solids used. All chocolate is delicious but I particularly like dark chocolate which contains 70–85% cocoa solids. Milk chocolate uses fewer cocoa solids and was first sold as a bar in 1875. White chocolate was first launched in the 1930s and is a pale yellow or ivory colour. It contains more sugar and no cocoa solids so it tastes a bit too sweet; however, the additional vanilla flavour is nice. Producers of chocolate include Cadbury, Hershey, and Lindt.

Develop the skills

Sometimes you will need to scan a text for information about a specific **theme** or idea. To do this, you will need to scan for *key words* instead of facts or opinions. For example, in an article about a workplace, you might be asked to find two things that workers feel about their job. You could therefore scan for words linked to positive or negative emotions, or look for points where the workers' speech is quoted.

5 Reread the passage about chocolate. Locate and select two ways in which white chocolate is different from other chocolate.

6 Why would the following answers *not* have been correct?

a) White chocolate contains more cocoa solids.

b) Lindt makes white chocolate.

c) It tastes too sweet.

d) White chocolate was launched in the 1930s.

e) The vanilla flavour is nice.

Apply the skills

7 Read the text on page 130 about the Kirirom national park again. Use your skimming and scanning skills, and your understanding of facts, opinions and information related to a specific theme, to answer the following questions.

a) Give two facts about the king's palace, according to the text.

b) Give two examples of things that you can do in Kirirom national park, according to the text.

c) Give two features of the natural landscape in Kirirom national park, according to the text.

Checklist for success

✔ Quickly skim the text to remind yourself what it is about.

✔ Think about the type of information that the question is asking you to locate.

✔ Use your scanning skills to help you select appropriate information.

Key term

theme: a recurring idea within a piece of writing

Top tip

Underline key phrases or make quick annotations at the side of the text to help you identify facts and opinions.

Check your progress:

I can locate the main topic or idea in a text.

I can locate a range of information in a text.

Literal and inferred meanings

In a comprehension task, you will be expected to identify both literal and inferred meanings and to explain what these meanings suggest. When writing your explanation, it is important to use your own words.

Explore the skills

Read the paragraph below about a journey by river.

> We travelled down the river by canoe. This was particularly exciting as the current was fierce, forming many rapids that threatened to **pitch** us into foaming waters. The river itself was very wide and the safety of the grassy bank seemed far away. If we capsized, all we would have to grab onto would be the razor-sharp rocks that jutted now and again from the river's surface.

Vocabulary

pitch: throw hard

If you were asked to explain what the rocks are like, you would scan the paragraph and locate the phrase 'razor-sharp rocks that jutted now and again from the river's surface'. The trick then is *putting it into your own words*.

Start by thinking about the key words that you must avoid using:

> razor-sharp rocks that jutted now and again from the river's surface

Then you can start thinking about alternatives. For example:

> razor-sharp > jagged
>
> jutted > stuck out
>
> now and again > occasionally
>
> river's surface > the water

You can then put these words together to form a sentence, such as:

> Jagged rocks occasionally stuck out of the waters.

1 Put the following phrases into your own words.

  a) the current was fierce

  b) threatened to pitch us into the foaming waters

  c) the safety of the grassy bank seemed far away

Build the skills

You may not understand all the language in a text, which can make it difficult to explain what a phrase means in your own words. It can help to identify the *context* – read around the word or phrase in order to work it out.

Read the article below about a town in Malaysia.

Taiping town

Penang and Ipoh are now hot tourist destinations in Malaysia. But the road between them is strewn with small towns, each with their own charms and history. Taiping is perhaps the most
5 storied of them all: once a wealthy tin mining hub, it saw bloody feuds and rapid development in the 19th century. British colonialists set up base here, leaving behind churches, gardens and neoclassical buildings.

10 These days, Taiping defies its eventful past, settled in the sleepy yet steadfast rhythms of a market town. But what a market it is: two magnificent wooden arcades, dating back over 130 years, host fruit sellers by day and
15 hawkers by night. Food is cheap and delicious: try local dishes such as kuay teow goreng (wok fried noodles with fishballs) and chee cheong fun (rice noodles drenched in spicy sauce and sesame seeds).

On the fringes of town, the Lake Gardens attract 20 joggers and cyclists to sprawling green grounds, lined with ancient rain trees. You can rent a bike to find the most scenic spots. But for wilder nature, head just a bit further towards the jungle and take a dip in the waterfall at Burmese pool. 25 If you're staying more than a day, hike up Bukit Larut, also known as Maxwell Hill.

To get to Taiping, take the ETS train from Kuala Lumpur Sentral. The three-hour journey passes through beautifully rugged, limestone 30 landscapes. Louis Hotel offers mid-range hotel rooms in the town centre from £20 [$25] a night.

From 'Undiscovered South-East Asia' by Ling Low, *The Guardian*

In a comprehension task, you may be asked what the writer means by a specific word. For example:

> What does the writer mean when she refers to the towns of Penang and Ipoh as 'hot' in line 1?

To answer this, you will need to consider the word's context.

2 **a)** What is the adjective 'hot' being used to describe in this sentence?

b) What does the word 'now' suggest about Penang being hot?

c) What other phrase in the sentence gives a clue about the context in which the towns are being discussed?

d) If the word 'hot' is not describing the temperature of the town, what do you think it is describing?

3 By putting the following words or phrases in their context, explain what they mean.

a) 'sleepy'

b) 'Taiping is perhaps the most storied of them all'

c) 'Taiping defies its eventful past'

Top tip

Remember, when you explain what something means you are being literal; when you explain what something suggests you are inferring.

Develop the skills

In some comprehension tasks, you may be asked to explain the different things that a text suggests.

Read the paragraph below.

> The sun was blazing by the time we reached the crowded beach. Hundreds of children were happily playing games, running back and forth, jumping up and down, their smiling faces brightening the scene. The ice cream vendor had sold
> 5 out and people were queuing for glasses of iced water. We scanned the beach, searching for a spot where the four of us might be able to sit. I imagined this place was once paradise but tourism had spoiled the peace and beauty.

'the sun was blazing'

'the crowded beach'

'children were happily playing games'

'smiling faces brightened the scene'

'people were queuing for glasses of iced water'

'searching for a spot'

'this place was once paradise'

'tourism had spoiled the peace and beauty'

4 Copy and complete the following table, using the quotations from the box in the margin. For each statement, choose one piece of evidence that has literal meaning and one that implies meaning.

Statement about the text	Quotation with literal meaning	Quotation with implied meaning
The weather is hot.	'the sun was blazing'	
The beach is busy.		'searching for a spot'
The children are happy.		
The writer feels that tourists have ruined the beach.		

5 Look at your list of quotations with implied meanings. Underline the specific words or phrases in those quotations that suggest meaning.

You may also be asked to infer someone's attitude towards an aspect of the article. For example, you might be asked to explain, in your own words, what the writer feels about the beach. The writer says he feels that tourism has spoiled the beach's peace and beauty; however, it would be incorrect to phrase your answer like this, as it copies the writer's words.

6 a) Which words in the statement: *The writer feels that tourism has spoiled the beach's peace and beauty* do you need to alter?

b) What alternatives can you think of for each of the words you need to change?

c) Rephrase the statement so it is in your own words.

7 Use the information in the table from Task 4 to complete the following.

a) In your own words, identify two things that show the beach is popular.

b) In your own words, explain why some people might not enjoy visiting the beach.

Apply the skills

8 Look back at the passage on page 135 about Taiping town in Malaysia. Using your skills of explanation and exploring literal and inferred meanings, answer the following questions.

a) Using your own words, explain what the text means by 'drenched' (line 18) and 'On the fringes of town' (line 20).

b) Using your own words, identify two things that people might do at the Lake Gardens.

c) Using your own words, give one negative aspect of visiting Taiping or the Lake Gardens that might put off tourists.

d) Using your own words, explain why people might visit Taiping town.

Checklist for success

✔ Identify literal meanings.

✔ Explore words and phrases in order to uncover inferred meanings.

✔ Use your own words in order to prove full understanding.

Check your progress:

⬆⬆ I can usually explain the literal meanings of phrases.

I can infer and explain meanings.

⬆⬆ I can explain the literal meanings of complex phrases.

I can infer and explain a range of complex meanings.

Practice questions and sample responses

- Locate information in a text.
- Explain the literal meanings of phrases.
- Infer and explain meanings with some complexity.
- Use synonyms to explain ideas in your own words.

Your task

Read the following text about the Cambodian town of Kratié and its surroundings, then read the 'Checklist for success' before answering the questions that follow.

Kratié town and its surrounds

Few tourists stray into Cambodia's "wild east" where, beyond Kampong Cham, the main roads are dirt tracks or just poorly surfaced. Yet this sparsely populated region offers a
5 quintessential slice of Cambodian rural life largely unaffected by the world beyond.

Kratié is a little market town 216 miles north-east of Phnom Penh. A spattering of tourist-friendly cafes and hotels has sprung up near the
10 central market place or facing the Mekong river. An evening stroll is the ideal time to absorb the spectacle of sunset. It's like watching a giant blood orange fall from a tree in slow motion. As the sun dips behind the treeline it turns the sky
15 a dazzling vermilion, tinting purple the French colonial villas, traditional wooden stilt houses and Wat Roka Kandal – a beautiful temple that dates back to the 19th century.

The nearby river island of Koh Trong boasts the alluring possibility of seeing Cantor's giant 20 soft-shell turtles in the wild. After a short ferry ride from an unsheltered wharf, the Preah Soramarith Quay (preceded by a long, hot wait), visitors enter a bucolic world of fruit plantations and rice paddies still tilled by Cambodia's iconic 25 white cows, the humped zebu.

The local community office advertises rural homestays organised by NGOs, bicycle hire and ox cart tours. The 8.5-mile perimeter route takes you right around the island's edge. 30 It's unchallenging and climaxes with the sight of a floating Vietnamese village buoyed-up just off the south-west tip of the island. The Vietnamese are a recognised ethnic minority in Cambodia and this community 35 lives offshore, though they've established a Vietnamese-style temple on the island. An

unexpected treat after a hard day's pedalling is Rajabori Villa Resort in the north-east of
40 the island, where it's possible to cool off in the pool for just $5 (doubles from $65 a night).

The route north out of Kratié is so breathtakingly scenic one almost forgives the dismal quality of the roads. It's a necessarily bumpy tuk-tuk ride in
45 order to take in Kratié's rare ecological treasures. In Phnom Sambor, 22 miles north of Kratié, visitors are guaranteed a sight of the soft-shell turtles. In the hallowed grounds of the Pagoda of One Hundred Columns, a small breeding
50 centre aims to return the turtles to the river.

Closer to Kratié the fishing village of Kampie offers boat trips to view Kratié's other aquatic marvel, the Irrawaddy dolphins. Though locals have long revered the dolphins,
55 believing them to be half human, half fish, their numbers have diminished in recent years due to electric rods and explosives used for fishing. Don't expect any flipper-style antics, these retiring creatures only surface
60 to breathe.

From 'Undiscovered South-East Asia'
by Thomas Bird, *The Guardian*

1 Give **two** facts about Kratié according to the second paragraph.

2 Using your own words, explain what the text means by:

a) 'climaxes with the sight' (paragraph 4)

b) 'breathtakingly scenic' (paragraph 5)

3 Reread paragraph 3. Give two reasons why people might visit the island of Koh Trong.

4 Reread paragraphs 2 and 6.

a) Identify **two** things that tourists can enjoy in the town of Kratié.

b) Explain some of the different attitudes displayed towards dolphins.

5 Using your own words, explain why some people may find visiting Kratié and its surroundings too challenging.

Checklist for success

✔ Use your scanning skills to help you select appropriate information.

✔ Identify literal and implied meanings.

✔ Use your own words in order to prove full understanding.

Exploring responses

Read the following response.

Response 1

1   The Wat Roka Kandal is a beautiful 19th-century temple.

Kratié is in the east of Cambodia.

2 a) The village you see is really impressive

   b) The scenery is nice

3   The chance to see giant soft-shell turtles in their natural habitat.

The ferry ride is short.

4 a) Go shopping in the market and watch a giant blood orange fall from a tree.

   b) The writer is really impressed by the dolphins. The locals kill the dolphins with explosives because they think they are half-human, half-fish. They like the dolphins because they can make money by taking tourists to see them.

5   People might find visiting Kratié too challenging because it is dirty and the roads are poorly surfaced. This makes any journeys really bumpy. It's also really hot and sometimes there is nowhere to take shelter. The temples sound boring and it would be really tiring having to cycle everywhere.

Feedback

1 Although the first point contains a fact, the response also includes an opinion. The second point is a good fact about Kratié but it comes from the first paragraph, not the second paragraph.

2 Both explanations show a general understanding of the quoted statement. However, the first explanation doesn't consider the meaning of 'climax' while the second explanation fails to express the full meaning of 'breathtaking' and scenic/scenery are a little too close to be considered the student's own words.

3 Only the first comment is a reason for visiting the island.

4 a) The first point is accurate but the second point is based on an incorrectly literal interpretation of a simile.

   b) The first point is accurate and the last point is a perceptive interpretation. However, the second point is a confused misreading of different attitudes towards the dolphins.

5 The response makes some good points about why visiting Kratié might be considered too challenging. However, it is sometimes badly expressed and the writer includes their own – irrelevant – opinions. There is also some misreading of details from the text. Too often the writer uses words directly from the texts rather than choosing his or her own.

6 For each question above, identify one thing in the sample response that could be improved. Use the 'Excellent progress' points on page 142 to help you.

Now read this second sample response.

Top tip

It is very important to choose your own words, rather than using words directly form the text.

Response 2

1 It is 348 kilometres away from Phnom Penh.

Its Wat Roka Kandal temple dates back to the 19th century.

2 a) The most impressive view comes at the end of the tour.

b) The landscape is strikingly beautiful.

3 The plantations and paddies are peaceful and attractive.

The humped zebu are a classic feature of Cambodia.

4 a) The beautiful sunset and the different styles of architecture.

b) The writer thinks the dolphins are impressive. The locals share this opinion and respect the dolphins due to the mythical belief that they are half-human. However, fishermen don't appear to care about the dolphins as their fishing methods have caused many of the creatures to die.

5 People might find the visit too challenging because it is a countryside area that seems cut off from civilisation and modern conveniences. The roads are badly constructed and this makes journeys very uncomfortable. Some of the places to visit can only be reached by a long bike ride which some might find exhausting. People might also find the weather too warm, especially in places where there is little shade.

Feedback

1 Two appropriate facts about Kratié' have been selected from the second paragraph.

2 The quoted statements are explained clearly and precisely.

3 Despite the difficult language in the text ('bucolic' and 'iconic'), the student provides two clear reasons why tourists might visit Koh Trong.

4 a) Two accurate points.

b) Three clear attitudes towards dolphins that are presented in the text.

5 This is a full answer, gathering details from across the text to suggest why the trip could be considered too challenging for some travellers. The student has used their own words throughout the response.

7 Using the responses and feedback in this topic, and the 'Excellent progress' points on page 142, evaluate your own responses and improve them where you can.

Check your progress

Sound progress

- I can use skimming and scanning skills to identify examples in a text.
- I can explain literal meanings, usually using my own words.
- I can infer more subtle meanings.
- I can identify attitudes in a text.
- I understand how information is used for different purposes.

Excellent progress

- I can use skimming, scanning and selecting skills to identify a variety of examples in a text.
- I can explain literal meanings clearly using my own words.
- I can infer and explain complex subtle meanings in a text.
- I can identify and explain attitudes in a text.
- I can select and use information for different purposes.

Summary writing

6

During your course, you may be asked to write a selective summary of a particular passage of text.

To answer this type of question, you will need to:

- demonstrate understanding of explicit meanings (R1)
- demonstrate understanding of implicit meanings and attitudes (R2)
- select and use information for specific purposes (R5)
- organise and structure ideas and opinions for deliberate effect (W2)
- use a range of vocabulary and sentence structures appropriate to context (W3)
- make accurate use of spelling, punctuation and grammar (W5).

Links to other chapters:

Chapter 1: Key reading skills

Chapter 2: Key technical skills

Chapter 5: Comprehension

Identifying and selecting according to the question focus

If you are asked to summarise one or two aspects of a passage, your first task is to identify the focus – what information is the question seeking?

Explore the skills

Look at this question about a passage written by a retired professional footballer:

> According to the author, how has football changed since the start of his career?

1. Which phrase in the question above tells you that the focus is not the overall history of football?

2. Now imagine that the points below all appear in the text. Which are relevant to the focus?

   a) The author disliked rugby.

   b) Players become millionaires.

   c) Players used to represent their home town.

   d) The author's family was poor.

   e) Football has become highly commercial.

3. Rewrite the question in your own words retaining its key ideas. For example, find a synonym for 'changed'.

Build the skills

Read the passage below about Malakhara wrestlers in Pakistan.

Vocabulary

sacrosanct: time-honoured and therefore important

The wrestlers wore the baggy trousers of their *shalwar kameez*, with the bottom of the trousers pulled up and tucked into the waist, looking like short baggy bloomers which ballooned from their bottoms. They [...] wore a turban on their heads. Before the fight, they carried out a **sacrosanct** ritual particular to this sport. Each took his *sundhro*, which is a very long piece of green material, and with the help of his opponent twisted it into a long rope. Then each wrestler wrapped his *sundhro* round his waist and tied it securely.

From *A Game of Polo with a Headless Goat* by Emma Levine

4 What two aspects of Malakhara wrestling are described?

5 Imagine the question asked *what* the wrestlers do and *why* they do it.

   a) Which points in the passage would be relevant?

   b) Which would be irrelevant?

Develop the skills

Read how the account continues.

> The rule of this form of wrestling, which is quite unique, is for each man to aim to get his hand inside the back of his opponent's *sundhro*, and then throw him to the ground from that position. (Some believe that this is the origin of *sumo*.) Other than this move, the arms may not be used to perform any type of wrestling grip, the legs being more important and used to trip and overbalance the opponent and eventually floor him. [...]
>
> They darted, each trying to grab at the other's waist, snatching their necks, trying to spin them round to overbalance them. The pair nearest to me grabbed each other's arms, trying to fling each other around, legs kicking in a kind of clumsy waltz; after a few minutes of this, one eventually got his hand in the other's *sundhro*, grabbed it, pulled it and flung his opponent on his back. He hit the ground with a tremendous wallop.
>
> Such force meant that the fallen wrestler suffered not only defeat, but also it seemed to me severe concussion. He lay motionless on the ground with no one overly concerned except me. The victor went over, slapped him around to revive him and poured water over his face, so if he didn't die by knock-out it would probably be through drowning.

6 Jot down the rules and aims of Malakhara wrestling. Be selective. For example, do not include what happens to defeated wrestlers.

Apply the skills

7 Make notes on:

   a) what happens to a defeated wrestler

   b) what the author's attitude to this is.

Check your progress:

I understand what is meant by 'focus'.

I can identify the focus of some questions.

I can sift out irrelevant information.

I can identify the focus of most questions.

I understand implied meaning.

I can distinguish separate aspects of a passage.

Selecting and ordering main points

When writing a summary, you will need to identify the *main points* in the text relating to the question focus, excluding details and examples. You must also organise these main points to show that you understand the passage as a whole.

Explore the skills

Read the passage below from a travel account.

The Italian Lakes are a little slice of paradise. Generations of travellers from the north, descending wearily from the chilly Alpine passes, have come into this Mediterranean vision of figs and palms, **bougainvillea** and lemon blossom, and been lost for words. Elegant ribbons of blue water stretch out ahead, folded into the sun-baked foothills: after the **rigours** of the high Alps, the abundance of fine food and wine must have been a revelation. Warming, awe-inspiring and graced with natural beauty, the lakes are still a place to draw breath and wonder.

These days, of course, mass tourism has found the lakes, and the shoreside roads that link every town can be as packed as the ferries that chug to and fro. But the chief reason to visit the area – its spectacular landscapes – remains compelling, and there are plenty of ways to avoid the crowds.

The lakes – deep, slender fjords gouged by glaciers – are sublime. All are oriented north–south, ringed by characterful old villages often wedged onto narrow beaches between rugged cliffs and the water. And those classic lakes images of flower-bedecked balconies, Baroque gardens and splendid waterside villas can be found here in abundance.

From *The Rough Guide to The Italian Lakes*

Vocabulary

bougainvillea: a flowering shrub with pink or purple foliage

rigours: hardships

Remember:

- A *main point* is essential information, which often reflects the purpose of the text.

- A *detail* enhances the main point, but is non-essential information.

- An *explanation* usually develops a main point, often for information or emphasis, but can sometimes be a main point in itself if it is important.

- An *opinion* expresses the writer's point of view on the topic, and could be regarded as a main point if you are asked about the writer's views.

Imagine that you have to summarise the following:

> What would attract visitors to the Italian Lakes area?

Which of these do you think is a main point?

- Travellers have descended 'wearily from the chilly Alpine passes'.
- They found 'figs and palms, bougainvillea and lemon blossom'.
- Newcomers to the area have found it delightful.

The answer is the last bullet point. The statement would be true even if the travellers were not weary and encountered roses and bananas rather than figs and palms!

It can sometimes be difficult to distinguish essential information (main points) from non-essential information (details or explanations). Punctuation may provide a clue. For example, the commas around the subordinate clause 'descending wearily from the chilly Alpine passes' suggests that this is non-essential information.

1 Look at the start of the third paragraph. If you were summarising what would attract visitors to the Italian Lakes area, what piece of information here is non-essential?

2 In the second sentence of paragraph 3, which piece of information is relevant to the focus of the question?

Build the skills

Now read the continuation of the passage below.

> Dotted around and between the lakes are some of Italy's finest art cities. Milan is pre-eminent, while Verona, Bergamo, Mantua and others display – in their architecture as well as their art – a civilized, urban vision that stands in marked contrast to the wild, largely rural character of the lakeside **hinterlands**. Italy only became a unified state in 1861 and, as a result, people often feel more loyalty to their home town than to the nation as a whole – a feeling manifest in the multitude of cuisines, dialects and outlooks that span the region.
>
> Geography, of course, doesn't adhere to political boundaries: the lakes are intimately connected in culture and landscape with the southernmost, Italian-speaking extremities of Switzerland. Lakes Maggiore and Lugano have shorelines in two countries.

Individual details can often be summarised within a main point. For example, the details 'Mediterranean vision of figs and palms, bougainvillea and lemon blossom' could be summarised as 'exotic plants' or 'Mediterranean fauna'.

Vocabulary

hinterlands: nearby area

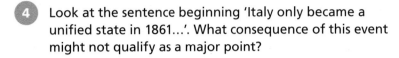

3 How could you summarise these details within main points?

   a) 'Verona, Bergamo, Mantua and others'

   b) 'the multitude of cuisines, dialects and outlooks that span the region'

Not all explanations are main points.

4 Look at the sentence beginning 'Italy only became a unified state in 1861...'. What consequence of this event might not qualify as a major point?

Develop the skills

When planning a summary, first list your selected points, then decide how best to order them. The order you choose may not be the same as in the text – it will depend on what aspects you have been asked to summarise.

In a summary, aim to demonstrate an overview – do not just summarise one bit at a time.

5 Below is a list of points summarising tourist attractions in the Italian Lakes. Which points could be grouped together to create a concise overview?

- lush vegetation
- lots of play areas
- good weather
- food and wine
- variety of watersports
- beautiful landscapes
- ferries
- theme parks
- possible to avoid crowds
- beautiful lakes
- interesting villages
- horse-riding and cycling routes through woodland
- art and architecture
- city–country contrast
- local variations.

6 Imagine that you are asked to summarise: 'What would make the Lakes region appeal to *families*?'. Reorder the list to answer this question.

Top tip

Do not include your own opinions in your summary.

Apply the skills

Read the text below, which is another introduction in a travel guide.

Welcome to Crete

There's something undeniably artistic in the way the Cretan landscape unfolds, from the sun-drenched beaches in the north to the rugged canyons spilling out at the cove-carved and cliff-lined southern coast. In between, valleys cradle moody villages, and round-shouldered hills are the overture to often snow-dabbed mountains. [...]

Crete's natural beauty is equalled only by the richness of its history. The island is the birthplace of the first advanced society on European soil, the Minoans, who ruled some 4000 years ago, and you'll find evocative vestiges all over, including the famous Palace of Knossos. At the crossroads of three continents, Crete has been coveted and occupied by consecutive invaders. History imbues Hania and Rethymno, where labyrinthine lanes – laid out by the Venetians – are lorded over by mighty fortresses, and where gorgeously restored Renaissance mansions rub rafters with mosques and Turkish bathhouses. The Byzantine influence stands in magnificent frescoed chapels, churches and monasteries.

If you're a foodie, you will be in heaven in Crete, where 'locavore' is not a trend but a way of life. Rural tavernas often produce their own meat, cheese, olive oil, *raki* and wine, and catch their own seafood. Follow a gourmet trail across the landscape and you'll delight in distinctive herbs and greens gathered from each hillside, cheeses made fresh with unique village- or household-specific recipes, and honey flavoured by mountain herbs. [...]

Crete's spirited people champion their unique culture and customs, and time-honoured traditions remain a dynamic part of the island's soul. Look for musicians striking up a free-form jam on local instruments, like the stringed *lyra*, or wedding celebrants weaving their time-honoured traditional regional dances. Meeting regular folk gossiping in *kafeneia* (coffee houses), preparing their Easter feast, tending to their sheep or celebrating during their many festivals is what makes a visit to Crete so special.

From *Welcome to Crete, 6th edition*

7 Select points to answer the following question:

According to the text, what makes Crete an enjoyable and interesting place to visit?

8 Use a mind map or spider diagram to order your points. (Hint: the question says 'enjoyable and interesting', so you might address each factor in turn.)

Check your progress:

 I can identify main points in a text.

I can combine details within a main point.

I can order points logically.

 I can identify main points relating to the question.

I can distinguish between essential information and non-essential information.

I can convey an overview.

Writing a summary

When writing a summary, your response should be concise, fluent and written in your own words as far as possible. You should also use accurate spelling, punctuation and grammar.

Explore the skills

Read the first part of a review of a documentary film.

Jillian Schlesinger's 'Maidentrip' [...] chronicles Dutch teen Laura Dekker's sail around the globe at age 14, a feat which would win her the title in 2012 of youngest person in history to make the voyage alone. Observant and unassuming, the documentary looks at the significance of Laura's trip not in terms of records, but as a rite of passage, and as a way for the teen to negotiate her past.

The film gets the ugly stuff out of the way first. Following Dekker's announcement to sail in 2009, she and her father were embroiled in a ten-month legal battle. Dutch authorities claimed that Laura needed a custody transfer, while the internet tossed words at her including 'arrogant', 'spoiled' and the particularly nasty sentiment: 'I hope she sinks.' After a year of warring with the courts and shouldering waves of media opinion, Laura was permitted to make her voyage, and to remain under her father's custody. This period in time Schlesinger keeps to an economical five-minute montage.

Indeed, 'Maidentrip' is pleasantly free from the hysteria that surrounded Laura Dekker for over a year, and instead presents her trip in a judgment-free manner. It neither suggests (as it understandably could) that 14 is an alarmingly young age to traverse the mightily unforgiving Pacific and Atlantic Oceans, nor takes a blindly positive 'Ra! Ra! Go Laura!' stance. [...]

Instead, Laura is portrayed as an independent outsider, at once open-hearted, enviably confident and a bit prickly, sick of what she sees as daily life in Holland (which she rounds up succinctly: 'Get money, get a house, get a husband, get a baby, then die'). She pines for a truly outsized adventure. While other young record-holding sailors completed the round-world trip without lengthy stops at ports, Laura gives herself two years for the excursion, so that she can soak in the land-bound culture of the different climes where she alights (among them French Polynesia, Australia, the Galapagos Islands and South Africa).

From *Indie Wire* website by Beth Hanna

You may need to work out the meaning of some words in the passage from their context (see Topic 1.5).

1 What is the correct meaning of 'embroiled' in line 8?

- cooked
- entangled
- found guilty

To summarise an aspect of a text you should:

- identify the main points
- write them out, using fewer words and paraphrasing if possible.

Read the following question.

> What do we learn about Laura Dekker's trip and what made it newsworthy in this passage?

Here are some possible points you could make in response:

- sailed round the globe at the age of 14
- youngest person in history to make the voyage alone
- embroiled in a ten-month legal battle before the trip
- internet tossed words at her including 'arrogant', 'spoiled' and 'I hope she sinks'
- gave herself two years for the excursion.

However, these notes are too close to the wording of the text to use in the summary. In addition, some of the points should be combined. For example:

At 14 Dekker became the youngest ever solo circumnavigator.

2 **a)** Identify the points that have been combined in this sentence.

b) What single word has been used to replace several?

Build the skills

3 Some details may be important, such as Laura's age, but others can be omitted. Which could be omitted or replaced with one word in the third bullet point?

Examples can be combined to save words:

> We ate apples, oranges and bananas. → We ate fruit.
>
> The British love rabbits, cats and hamsters. → The British love pets.

4 **a)** Rewrite the fourth bullet point more concisely by combining examples.

b) Find an even more concise way to say this, beginning, 'She received…'.

Develop the skills

The best way to write a concise and fluent summary is to aim for an overview rather than just using synonyms for individual words or even summarising one sentence at a time. Complex sentences will help you combine ideas. Compare the following:

- 'Maidentrip' is about a Dutch girl. She sailed round the world solo. Her name was Laura Dekker.
- 'Maidentrip' is about a Dutch girl, Laura Dekker. She sailed round the world solo.
- 'Maidentrip' is about Laura Dekker, a Dutch girl who sailed round the world solo.

The third version is the most fluent because it is a complex sentence, using a subordinate clause and punctuation to combine information.

Top tip

To achieve an overview, try writing your summary from your notes without looking back at the text.

5 Copy the line below, filling in the gaps with your own words to combine all the bullet points from Activity 1 in a single sentence that provides an overview.

> We learn that at 16, after overcoming... and spending two... Laura Dekker became...

Experiment with different wording until you think you have found one that includes all points fluently in your own words.

Apply the skills

Now read this continuation of the review of 'Maidentrip':

● ● ●　　　　　　　　　　　　　　　　C ⟳ Q 🏠

Dekker acts as her own camera operator and narrator, periodically filming herself throughout her trip, commenting on the winds, weather and whatever else might be on her mind.

Laura's camera proves **therapeutic** for the onset of loneliness that strikes her early in the expedition; the device is something to talk to. She comments on the silly and mundane, but also on the more profound experiences of being thousands of miles from land or another human. We hear her sniffling through tears as she films a pod of dolphins swimming alongside her boat, pleading with them to stay awhile and **assuage** her feelings of isolation.

Yet as time and the documentary go on we sense a change in Laura. She's relishing the days on end of alone time, and seemingly more attuned to the fluctuations of the ocean.

Vocabulary

therapeutic: describing something that has a healing effect or that makes you feel better

assuage: to relieve, or make something feel less unpleasant

6 Using both parts of the review, write a 100–150-word summary in response to the question:

> What do we learn about Laura Dekker?

Begin by listing your main points, remembering to focus on Laura herself. Write in your own words, using complex sentences to write fluently and concisely. Aim to demonstrate an overview.

Check your progress:

 I can rewrite sentences using my own words.
I can combine details in single ideas.
I can replace examples.

 I can rewrite sentences fluently and concisely to present an overview.
I can find synonyms for words from their context.
I can combine simple sentences into fluent complex ones.

Practice questions and sample responses

· ·

Key skills

You will need to show the following skills:

- locate the particular section of the passage that the task or question refers to
- understand the focus of the question
- understand the explicit meanings of words and phrases in the passage
- understand the implicit meanings and attitudes in the passage
- select, analyse and evaluate what is relevant to include
- write in an appropriate style for a summary, concisely and using your own words.

Your task

Read the following passage and the task that follows.

Exploring responses: summary questions

Read this newspaper report. Then read the 'Checklist for success' before answering the question that follows.

Lynx could return to Britain this year after absence of 1300 years

After an absence of 1300 years, the lynx could be back in UK forests by the end of 2017. The Lynx UK Trust has announced it will apply for a trial reintroduction for six lynx into the Kielder
5 forest, Northumberland, following a two-year consultation process with local stakeholders.

The secretive cat can grow to 1.5 m in length and feeds almost exclusively by ambushing deer. Attacks on humans are unknown, but it was
10 hunted to extinction for its fur in the UK. The Kielder forest was chosen by the trust from five possible sites, due to its abundance of deer, large forest area and the absence of major roads.

Sheep farmers and some locals are opposed to the reintroduction, but Dr Paul O'Donoghue, 15 chief scientific advisor to the Lynx UK Trust and expert adviser to the International Union for the Conservation of Nature (IUCN) believes there are good reasons for reintroducing the predator. 20

'Lynx belong here as much as hedgehogs, badgers, robins, blackbirds – they are an intrinsic part of the UK environment,' he told the Guardian. 'There is a moral obligation. We killed every single last one

25 of them for the fur trade, that's a wrong we have to right.'

Rural communities would also benefit from eco-tourism, O'Donoghue said: 'They will generate tens of millions of pounds for struggling rural UK

30 economies. Lynx have already been reintroduced in the Harz mountains in Germany. They have branded the whole area the 'kingdom of the lynx'. Now it is a thriving ecotourism destination and we thought we could do exactly the same for Kielder,'

35 he said.

Lynx would also boost the natural environment, said O'Donoghue, by reducing the overgrazing

of forests by deer, allowing other wildlife to flourish. 'We have a massive overpopulation of roe deer in the UK,' he said. 'We are one of the 40 most biodiversity poor countries in the world. We need the lynx, more than the lynx needs us.' [...]

If lynx are reintroduced, it would be very difficult for eco-tourists to see the mainly nocturnal animals, O'Donoghue said: 'Lynx are very secretive and 45 elusive, but that's completely irrelevant. It's a chance to walk in a forest where lynx live, a chance to see a lynx track, to see a lynx scratching post. And if you did see a lynx in the wild, it would be the wildlife encounter of a lifetime.' 50

From 'Lynx could return to Britain'
by Damian Carrington, *The Guardian*

According to the text, what plans are there for reintroducing the lynx, and what are the arguments in favour of this?

You must use continuous writing (not notes) and your own words as far as possible.

Your summary should not be more than 150 words.

Checklist for success

✔ Show an understanding of the passage.
✔ Stick to the focus of the question.
✔ Omit details or group them together as single points.
✔ Order the important points to show an overview.
✔ Write fluently, using your own words as far as possible.
✔ Try to use accurate spelling, punctuation and grammar.

Exploring responses

Now read the following response to the task, and the annotations.

Response 1

Lynx could be back in the UK by the end of 2017. The Lynx UK Trust is going to apply for a trial reintroduction of this beautiful creature in the Kielder Forest. This was chosen for its abundance of deer. They do not attack humans, they would probably attack sheep.

— unnecessary personal judgement

— not relevant to task and quotes passage directly

Lynx belong in the UK, like hedgehogs, badgers, robins and blackbirds. We morally should bring them back because we made them die out in the first place by hunting them unnecessarily for fur.

— better to group these together in one phrase

It would be great for tourism, like it is in Germany, which is now known as the 'kingdom of the lynx'. They would eat roe deer which would be good for forests. We need them more than they need us for our biodiversity. They are secretive and hard to see, but it would still be exciting to know they were there by seeing their tracks and scratching posts.

— unnecessary quotation, and used inaccurately

— some explanation needed for the point to make sense

Feedback

This response is broadly accurate, although there are two misunderstandings. It makes some effort to paraphrase and provide an overview, but it still uses the wording of the text too much and tends to summarise line by line rather than as a whole. It does not always stick to the focus of the task. The style would be more fluent if complex sentences were employed, along with better punctuation. The precise sense is not always clear.

1 Identify three things in the sample response that could be improved. Use the 'Excellent progress points' on page 158 to help you.

Now read this second sample response.

Response 2

The Lynx UK Trust hopes to reintroduce six lynx in the forests of Northumberland by the end of 2017, and have consulted carefully prior to doing this. According to Paul O'Donoghue, we have a moral duty to restore lynx because they are an indigenous species that was completely wiped out by human hunting. Their predation of the UK's excessive roe deer population would benefit the diversity of the ecosystem by reducing the deer's overgrazing and allowing other species to flourish. Lynx pose no threat to humans and would greatly benefit the local economy, as demonstrated by their successful reintroduction in Germany. For tourists, even finding evidence of lynx would be exciting, and actually seeing one would be truly memorable.

succinctly makes point with a phrase in place of a list

effective paraphrasing

concise vocabulary

complex sentence concisely combining points, correctly punctuated

Feedback

This response is accurate and concise. It shows evidence of an overview by reordering some points and making connections between ideas across the text. The student paraphrases succinctly and fluently, showing an understanding of the text, and of what is most important in it. Complex sentences are used for fluency and concision, and with helpful and correct punctuation.

2   Using the responses and feedback in this topic, and the 'Excellent progress points' on page 158, evaluate your own responses and improve them where you can.

Check your progress

Reading

Sound progress

- I can show a reasonable understanding of the focus of the summary.
- I can show understanding of some ideas in the text.
- I can work out the meaning of difficult words from their contexts.
- I can select some ideas that match the question focus.

Excellent progress

- I clearly understand the focus of the summary.
- I can show understanding of a wide range of ideas that match the question focus.
- My ideas are relevant at all times.
- I can select points carefully to demonstrate an overall grasp of the text and what it says about the topic in focus.

Writing

Sound progress

- I can usually express myself clearly and concisely .
- I do not speculate or give opinions.
- I can generally use my own words when writing my summary.
- My spelling, punctuation and grammar are often accurate.

Excellent progress

- I can write a clearly expressed response that is fluent and concise.
- I can structure my response logically in a way that makes it easy for the reader to follow.
- I can summarise in my own words, using precise synonyms and collective nouns.
- I can combine several pieces of information into complex sentences, using clauses.
- My spelling, punctuation and grammar are mostly accurate.

Analysing language

7

Some tasks will require you to consider the language used by writers and the effect that it has on the reader.

To answer this type of question, you will need to:

- demonstrate understanding of explicit meanings (R1)
- demonstrate understanding of implicit meanings and attitudes (R2)
- demonstrate understanding of how writers achieve effects and influence readers (R4).

Links to other chapters:

Chapter 1: Key reading skills

Chapter 5: Comprehension

Identifying synonyms and literal meanings

The first step in writing about language is to show your understanding of the meaning of words and phrases.

Explore the skills

In Chapter 5, you practised putting phrases into your own words. Synonyms are different words that have similar meanings. To show your understanding of the meanings in a text, you need to be able to find quotations that match a synonymous word or phrase that has been given to you.

Read the following paragraph.

> As soon as the ball was passed to him, Etebo headed for the goal. Constantly tapping the ball a few metres ahead of him, he raced down the pitch. Glancing backwards, he sped up as he saw three opposition players gaining on him. Dodging and weaving, he managed to pass two defenders.
> 5   One attempted a sliding tackle but Etebo jumped over him, met up with the ball again and continued determinedly towards the goal. Bearing down on the single keeper, Etebo paused momentarily to gather his strength and choose his angle. The side of his boot smashed against the centre of the ball, sending it hurtling through the air like a rocket and straight into the
> 10   back of the net.

1   Find a word or phrase in the final sentence that means *to hit with force*.

There are several ways to work out the meaning of a word, including:

- looking at the stem and thinking of words you know with a similar stem
- looking at the context of the word.

For example, you can work out the meaning of the word *dodging* by first placing it in the context of Etebo managing to *pass two defenders*. To clarify the meaning, you can then reduce *dodging* to the stem *dodge* and think about word stems with similar meanings such as *evade* or *avoid*. This would help you to work out that *dodging* means avoiding.

2   What is meant by the word *constantly*, at the start of the second sentence?

Top tip

Consider the words carefully. In this example, *hurtling* and *like a rocket* both suggest speed and power, but they do not mean that something has been hit.

Build the skills

3 For each statement below, select a word or phrase from the text that matches the underlined words.

a) Etebo <u>looked quickly behind</u> him.

b) Etebo headed towards the goal in a <u>purposeful</u> way.

c) Etebo <u>ran faster</u> when he saw the opposition getting nearer.

d) Etebo <u>stopped very quickly</u> to prepare his shot at the goal.

Develop the skills

Synonyms are also useful if you are asked to explain what words or phrases mean. You should do this as precisely as possible. For example, if you were asked to explain what the word *tapping* means in the phrase *constantly tapping the ball*, do not just write *kicking* or *hitting*. It would be more precise to explain the word as *kicked lightly*.

4 Look at the following question, then correct the responses below to make them more precise.

Explain the meaning of the underlined words or phrases.

a) He <u>managed to pass</u> two defenders.

b) Sending it <u>hurtling</u> through the air.

> a) He got away from the two defenders.
>
> b) The ball moved through the air.

Apply the skills

5 Using precise language, explain the underlined words or phrases from the passage.

a) <u>As soon as</u> the ball was passed to him.

b) He <u>raced</u> down the pitch.

c) <u>Bearing down</u> on the single keeper.

Check your progress:

 I can explain ideas in my own words.

I can make some use of synonyms to explore and express meaning.

I can use language with some precision.

 I can explain complex ideas in my own words.

I can make use of a range of synonyms to explore and express complex meanings.

I can use language precisely.

Explaining the suggestions that words can create

As well as showing that you understand the literal meaning of words and phrases, you need to be able to explore the ideas that phrases suggest.

Top tip

To remind yourself about how words carry implicit meanings, look back at Topics 1.6 and 1.7.

Explore the skills

Read this passage about a soccer match.

> The spectators followed the ball, open-mouthed, as it shot through air. When it hit the back of the net, the crowd erupted. With only one minute of the match remaining, they leapt to their feet and cheered excitedly. Looking around at the spectators, Etebo grinned widely and punched the air in triumph. His team mates ran towards him, throwing their
> 5   arms around his shoulders in congratulation. He basked in their attention, his heart warm at the idea of having scored the winning goal. Aware that there were still sixty seconds to play, the players quickly returned to their positions and Eteborefocused on the match, resolute that the opposition wouldn't manage a late equaliser.

A short-answer question might ask what the phrase *punched the air in triumph* shows about Etebo's feelings during the match. You might start by putting the phrase in its context (Etebo has just scored a goal), then break the phrase down. 'Triumph' means celebration, joy or pride. Punching the air suggests an expression of excitement or pleasure.

1. Put these ideas together to create an explanation in your own words, in a single sentence.

Build the skills

2. Here are two phrases from the text. Below each phrase are three explanations for what it suggests about Etebo during the soccer match. Decide which explanation is correct.

   a) 'refocused on the match':

   - The phrase shows that Etebo stopped thinking about his goal and returned his attention to the game.
   - The phrase suggests that Etebo hadn't been concentrating hard enough.

- The phrase suggests that Etebo didn't want his happiness about the goal to get in the way of winning, so he refocused on the match.

b) 'his heart warm':

- The phrase shows that Etebo felt hot.
- The phrase shows that Etebo felt pleased with himself for having scored the goal.
- The phrase shows that scoring the goal made Etebo feel warm inside.

Develop the skills

Top tip

Remember to keep using your own words to show your full understanding.

3 Look at the sixth sentence. What does the phrase 'basked in their attention' suggest about Etebo's feelings during the match?

- Think about what Etebo has just done and how his team mates have reacted (the context of the phrase).
- Consider the meaning of *attention* and *basked*, and what these words suggest Etebo is feeling.

4 What does the phrase 'resolute the opposition wouldn't manage' suggest about Etebo feelings during the match?

- Think about what the opposition are going to want to do (the context of the phrase).
- Consider the meaning of the words *resolute* and *manage*, and what these words suggest that Etebo is feeling.

Apply the skills

Top tip

When explaining a phrase, you do not need to explain each word. Focus on key words or consider what the phrase as a whole suggests.

5 Using your own words, explain what the underlined phrases suggest about the crowd during the soccer match.

a) The spectators <u>followed the ball, open-mouthed</u>, as it shot through air.

b) When it hit the back of the net, <u>the crowd erupted</u>.

c) With only one minute of the match remaining, they leapt to their feet and <u>cheered excitedly</u>.

Check your progress:

 I can use my own words.

I can work out the implied meanings of individual words and phrases and explain what these phrases suggest to the reader.

 I can use my own words with clarity and precision.

I can consider the specific effects of individual words and phrases and explore what they suggest to the reader.

Checklist for success

✔ Use your own words.

✔ Don't just say what words mean.

✔ Consider the precise effect of individual words – what do they suggest?

Identifying the writer's craft

Writers craft their work in order to achieve effects in an interesting and impactful way that is enjoyable to read. Most writers try to do three things:

- convey meaning/feelings/atmosphere
- create a sensory picture
- provoke an emotion.

They achieve this through careful selection of words that have literal and implicit meanings, which build an effect. Writers also achieve effects through a range of devices such as imagery, comparison and personification.

Explore the skills

Read the following extract from a novel.

> At first we walked along the beach, hoping to circle the coast, but the sand soon turned to jagged rocks, which turned to impassable cliffs and gorges. Then we tried the other end, wasting precious time while the sun rose in the sky, and found the same barrier. We were left with no choice but to try inland. The pass between the peaks was the obvious goal so we
> 5 slung our bin-liners over our shoulders and picked our way into the jungle.
>
> The first two or three hundred metres from the shore were the hardest. The spaces between the palm trees were covered in a strange rambling bush with tiny leaves that sliced like razors, and the only way past them was to push through. But as we got further inland and the ground began to rise, the palms became less common than another kind of
> 10 tree—trees like rusted, ivy-choked space rockets, with ten-foot roots that fanned from the trunk like stabilizer fins. With less sunlight coming through the canopy, the vegetation on the forest floor thinned out. Occasionally we were stopped by a dense spray of bamboo, but a short search would find an animal track or a path cleared by a fallen branch.
>
> After Zeph's description of the jungle, with Jurassic plants and strangely coloured birds,
> 15 I was vaguely disappointed by the reality. In many ways I felt like I was walking through an English forest, I'd just shrunk to a tenth of my normal size. But there were some things that felt suitably exotic. Several times we saw tiny brown monkeys scurrying up the trees, Tarzan-style **lianas** hung above us like stalactites—and there was the water: it dripped on our necks, flattened our hair, stuck our T-shirts to our chests. There was so much of it that our half-empty
> 20 canteens stopped being a worry. Standing under a branch and giving it a shake provided a couple of good gulps, as well as a quick shower. The irony of having kept my clothes dry over the swim, only to have them soaked when we turned inland, didn't escape me.
>
> From *The Beach* by Alex Garland

1 The writer has created a detailed sensory picture for the reader. How has he achieved this?

   a) Which nouns has the writer chosen for their precise literal meaning?

   b) Select adjectives and adverbs that help to create a sensory picture.

2 The writer has also conveyed the narrator's different thoughts and feelings. How have these been presented?

   a) Which verbs show that the narrator found the exploration of the island difficult?

   b) Which adjectives add to the impression that the narrator found the journey difficult?

3 Reread the first paragraph. Look at the list of paired words below. Considering what the words tell you about the narrator's feelings or experiences, decide which is the most powerful word in each pair.

   a) try   picked

   b) barrier   inland

   c) sky   precious

   d) goal   pass

Vocabulary

liana: a long, woody vine (often used by monkeys to swing from tree to tree)

Build the skills

Try to comment on any powerful imagery that you read in a text. This means that you should look out for any effective examples of:

* simile
* metaphor
* personification.

4 Look at the table below, which gives a definition, example and effect of the three types of imagery. Which type of imagery goes with which row in the table?

Top tip

When you are analysing the writer's craft, there is not one correct answer – all readers will have an individual response to a text. However, there *will* be wrong answers. Make sure that you can explain why your chosen words are interesting, powerful or impactful. If you can do this, your choices are correct.

Definition	Example	Example effect
a descriptive technique, giving human characteristics to an object or idea	'He gazed around at the bright fireworks of flowers with their petals of reds, blues, and yellows.'	This describes the sun as if it is angry or unwelcoming in order to convey the discomfort caused by its heat.
a descriptive comparison, using *like* or *as*	'The sun glared down from the cloudless sky.'	This captures the sparkling appearance of the water. By comparing it to diamonds, the writer also suggests how much the thirsty man values the water he has found.

Definition	Example	Example effect
a descriptive comparison, written as if one thing *is* something else (rather than it being *like* or *as*)	'The man looked thirstily at the pool of water as it glistened like diamonds in the sunlight.'	This makes the multicoloured flowers sound vibrant and in abundance, as well as suggesting that they were a striking sight.

Develop the skills

> **Top tip**
>
> Do not try to explore *all* the words in a quotation. Focus only on those that are powerful or interesting.

5 Consider the phrase 'trees like rusted, ivy-choked space rockets' from paragraph 2 of the extract on page 164. Make notes using the following prompts.

   a) What type of imagery is this phrase?

   b) What is the writer trying to convey by comparing the trees to space rockets? How does this make the trees sound? What might the narrator be feeling about the trees?

   c) Why does the writer describe them as *rusted*? How does this help the reader to imagine what the trees look and feel like?

   d) How is the ivy made to seem when it is described as *choking* the trees?

6 Reread the second paragraph of the extract on page 164, then copy and complete the table on page 167. Choose powerful phrases, apply subject terminology and consider what the phrase suggests about the narrator's feelings or experiences. Some examples have been given.

Chosen phrase	Subject terminology	Effect
'strange rambling bush'	noun phrase	This shows the vegetation is unusual which makes the narrator's journey more interesting and could suggest that something is wrong.
	simile	
		This shows that the journey was physically difficult but that the narrator was determined to continue.
'dense spray of bamboo'		

Apply the skills

 7 Reread the final paragraph of the extract. Choose the two individual words and the two phrases that you think are most effective in suggesting the narrator's emotions in the paragraph. Note them down, use subject terminology to identify the type of words and devices the writer has used and what they suggest.

Checklist for success

✔ Select interesting and powerful words and phrases from a text.

✔ Analyse the effects of language in a text.

✔ Use subject terminology.

Check your progress:

 I can select some interesting words and phrases from a text.

I can explain what my chosen words and phrases suggest to the reader.

I can apply some subject terminology to my chosen words and phrases.

 I can select a range of interesting or powerful words and phrase from a text.

I can analyse the effects of my chosen words and phrases.

I can apply a range of subject terminology to my chosen words and phrases.

Analysing the writer's craft

Once you have selected powerful words and phrases from a text, you need to explain how they are being used effectively by the writer.

Explore the skills

Reread the extract from *The Beach* on page 164. Then look at the example of analysis below.

> In the first sentence, the adjective 'jagged' is a powerful way to describe the texture of the rocks as it highlights how sharp they are. This makes the narrator's exploration of the island sound challenging as well as suggesting that this could be a dangerous place.

1. Annotate a copy of the analysis, identifying the following elements:

   a) evidence (reference to the text)

   b) use of subject terminology

   c) analysis of why the word is powerful

   d) further development of the explanation.

Build the skills

When writing about a text, it is important to focus on specific details, give clear and precise explanations and try to make use of subject terminology.

Look at the following two examples of analysis.

> In the second sentence, the writer uses the verb phrase 'wasting precious time' to convey the narrator's feelings when exploring the island. The verb 'wasting' suggests that he is getting frustrated by their inability to get across the island. The adjective 'precious' adds to this frustration by creating a mood of urgency: the narrator feels the hours of the day are quickly passing and they are running out of time. These examples of word choice clearly show his feelings.

Top tip

You can use the following steps to effectively analyse the writer's craft:

1. Point: make your point by stating the effect created.

2. Evidence: make reference to the text as evidence of your point.

3. Analysis: give your analysis, which may be:

   - literal meanings
   - associations (that is, the senses or emotions)
   - language devices.

4. Effect: restate the effect.

> The writer uses the words 'wasting precious time' when they are exploring the island and failing to find a way to get further inland. Despite wanting to explore, the narrator feels that the day is being 'wasted' and this word is a powerful way to show how he feels. The word 'precious' is also powerful as it describes the hours of the day. The text said the sun had already 'rose in the sky' which means that they are running out of time because they are spending so long trying to find a passable route around the island.

 2 Decide which response is the best and why. Which aspects of the less successful example need improvement?

Develop the skills

Look back at the information on imagery in Task 5, Topic 7.3. Consider again the phrase 'trees like rusted, ivy-choked space rockets' from paragraph 2 of the extract from *The Beach*.

3 Turn your notes into an explanation of why the phrase is effective. Remember to:

- make a clear reference to the text
- use subject terminology
- explain the effect of a specific word or device that you think is powerful or interesting
- develop your explanation by focusing on another specific aspect of your quotation.

Apply the skills

 4 Pick out three powerful words or phrases from the last paragraph of the extract on page 164. Include one example of imagery. Explain how each of your choices has been used effectively by the writer.

Checklist for success

✔ Write a concise yet detailed response.
✔ Use subject terminology.
✔ Include at least one example of simile, metaphor or personification.

Check your progress:

 I can respond to a text in some detail.

I can use some subject terminology in my response.

I can explain the effects of some descriptive devices.

 I can construct a concise and detailed response to a text.

I can include a range of subject terminology.

I can explore a range of descriptive devices.

Practice questions and sample responses

Key skills

You will need to show the following skills:

- locate and select relevant or appropriate words, phrases or language
- identify explicit and implicit meanings
- explain or analyse the effect of a writer's language choices using your own words
- explore the writer's craft, using terminology to comment on what makes a piece of writing powerful.

Your task

Read the following extract from Alex Garland's novel, *The Beach*. Then read the 'Checklist for success' on page 173 before answering the questions that follow.

After a long journey, the narrator has finally arrived at his hotel.

The first thing I did after shutting the door behind me was to go to the bathroom mirror and examine my face. I hadn't seen my reflection for a couple of days and wanted to check things were OK.

5   It was a bit of a shock. Being around lots of tanned skin I'd somehow assumed I was also tanned, but the ghost in the mirror corrected me. My whiteness was accentuated by my stubble, which, like my hair, is jet black. UV deprivation aside, I was in bad need of a shower. My T-shirt had the salty stiffness of material that has been sweated in, sun-dried, then sweated in again. I decided to head straight to the beach for a swim. I could kill two birds
10   with one stone—soak up a few rays and get clean.

Chaweng was a travel-brochure photo. Hammocks slung in the shade of curving palm trees, sand too bright to look at, jet-skis tracing white patterns like jet-planes in a clear sky. I ran down to the surf, partly because the sand was so hot and partly because I always run into the sea. When the water began to drag on my legs I jumped up, and the momentum
15   somersaulted me forwards. I landed on my back and sank to the bottom, exhaling. On the seabed I let myself rest, head tilted slightly forward to keep the air trapped in my nose, and listened to the soft clicks and rushes of underwater noise.

I'd been splashing around in the water for fifteen minutes or so when Étienne came down to join me. He also ran across the sand and somersaulted into the sea, but then leapt up
20   with a yelp.

'What's up?' I called.

Étienne shook his head, pushing backwards through the water away from where he'd landed. 'This! This animal! This... fish!'

I began wading towards him. 'What fish?'

25 'I do not know the English—Aaah! Aaah! There are more! Aaah! Stinging!'

'Oh,' I said as I reached him. 'Jellyfish! Great!'

I was pleased to see the pale shapes, floating in the water like drops of silvery oil. I loved their straightforward weirdness, the strange area they occupied between plant and animal life.

From *The Beach* by Alex Garland

1. Identify a word or phrase from the text which suggests the same idea as the words underlined:

   a) The narrator carefully inspects his face in the bathroom mirror.

   b) The narrator's dark hair emphasised the paleness of his skin.

   c) When Étienne is stung by a jellyfish he jumps from the water and cries out in pain.

   d) Because the white sand reflected the light, it was almost blinding.

2. Using your own words, explain what the writer means by each of the words underlined:

   > I was pleased to see the pale shapes, floating in the water like drops of silvery oil. I loved their straightforward weirdness, the strange area they occupied between plant and animal life.

3. Explain how the phrases underlined are used by the writer to suggest the narrator's responses to the jellyfish. Use your own words in your explanation.

   > I was pleased to see the pale shapes, floating in the water like drops of silvery oil. I loved their straightforward weirdness, the strange area they occupied between plant and animal life.

4. Reread paragraphs 2 and 3, describing the narrator's feelings about himself and the beach. Select four powerful words or phrases from each paragraph. Your choices should include imagery. Explain how each word or phrase is used effectively in the context. Write 200–300 words.

Exploring responses

Now read the following response to the questions, and the annotations.

Response 1

1 **a)** check

   b) shock

   c) 'Aaah! Stinging!'

   d) the sand was so hot

2 pleased – unlike Étienne, he isn't scared

   silvery – shining like silver

   weirdness – behaving like a freak

3 pleased to see – the narrator had seen the jellyfish before and wanted to see them again.

   like drops of silvery oil – the jellyfish were silver and oily looking

   I loved their straightforward weirdness – the narrator is fascinated by the jellyfish.

4 The word 'shock' is a powerful way to describe what the narrator feels when he looks in the mirror because he was expecting to look more tanned. The word 'sweated' is also powerful because it shows how hot it was. The phrase 'soak up a few rays' describes how he wants to go sunbathing.

   The palm tree is described as 'curving'. This is good because it sounds quite peaceful and graceful which matches the atmosphere on the beach. This is similar to the phrase 'the soft clicks and rushes' which is a powerful way to describe what he hears underwater. The word 'clicks' makes it sound unusual which is suitable because he's underwater and the word 'rushes' links to the movement of the sea over him. However, because he says 'soft' this makes it seem really gentle and relaxing because he's enjoying himself.

Feedback

1 None of these quotations fully match the question's underlined words and phrases, although 'check' comes close to 'examine'.

2 The first and third answers are inaccurate. The second answer is correct, but the writer does not fully use their own words.

3 The first comment is not precise enough: although it implies the narrator liked jellyfish, it also implies that he has seen the same jellyfish before. There is not enough use of own words in the second comment. The third comment is accurate but does not fully explain the second half of the underlined phrase.

4 There are some good choices from the text, including one example of imagery, but there is not a full range and not all the words selected are powerful. Other words and phrases that stand out in the extract have been omitted. There is some attempt to explore the different associations that words carry but, too often, the comments focus on literal rather than inferred meanings. The last example could be explored in a much more concise way. The explanations lack precision so fail to convey a full understanding of how language is used. Subject terminology could be applied.

5 Look back at the incorrect answers from Question 1. Can you work out why the student thought those quotations were correct and what they misunderstood or missed out?

6 a) Look at the response to Question 2. What different things are wrong with the first explanation?

b) How could the second explanation be altered to ensure that it is all in their own words?

c) What is wrong with the words 'behaving' and 'freak' in the third explanation?

7 For each of the points in the response to Question 3, identify what could be improved.

8 Consider the response to Question 4.

a) Which word or phrase choices would you cut from this answer?

b) What additional words or phrase could you add from the extract?

c) Make the final explanation more concise.

d) Apply subject terminology to the examples given.

> **Checklist for success**
> ....
> ✔ Make use of synonyms and explain ideas using your own words.
> ✔ Select interesting or powerful words and phrases.
> ✔ Consider the precise effects of language.
> ✔ Use subject terminology.

Now read this second sample response.

Response 2

1   **a)** examine

    b) accentuated

    c) leapt up with a yelp

    d) too bright to look at

2   pleased – happy and welcoming

    silvery – shimmering

    weirdness – being strange or unusual

3   pleased to see – the narrator likes jellyfish so he welcomed the sight of them.

    like drops of silvery oil – the jellyfish shimmered in the light and looked liquid rather than solid.

    I loved their straightforward weirdness – the narrator is fascinated by how strange yet simple the jellyfish look.

4   Salty stiffness' is an effective way of describing the disgusting texture of the narrator's t-shirt and this is highlighted by the sibilance. The 'stiffness' sounds uncomfortable and the 'salty' implies it feels grainy, as well as emphasising how much he's sweated and how unclean the journey has made him.

    The metaphor 'ghost in the mirror' is a powerful way to describe the narrator's pale appearance and emphasise how strangely white he looks, while also suggesting that he feels almost dead after his exhausting journey.

    The length of his journey is also captured in the hyperbolic phrase 'UV deprivation' which suggests he feels that he's been locked away like a prisoner without any sunlight. The idea of being deprived also shows how relieved he is to have finally reached the beach.

    The metaphor 'soak up a few rays' is a good way to describe sunbathing. The verb 'soak' suggests bathing by linking to water. It also sounds relaxing and pleasurable, with the word 'rays' making the sunlight seem like individual beams warming his body.

    The third paragraph opens with a good metaphor: 'Chaweng was a travel-brochure photo'. This implies that it looks perfect in an almost unbelievable way.

    The narrator continues to use idyllic images with the simile 'like jet-planes in a clear sky'. This makes the jet-skis seem miles away rather than close-up and noisy. Comparing the sea to the sky also makes the waters seem clean and still, which adds to the peaceful atmosphere.

    The narrator also seems relaxed when he describes the 'soft clicks and rushes'. This uses the senses of sound and touch to convey the strange yet soothing sensation of being underwater. 'Clicks' sounds unusual and helps the reader to imagine the exotic marine world, while 'rushes' suggests the calm movement of the water on his skin. This contrasts with 'the momentum somersaulted me forwards' which creates fun and excitement by linking to movement and speed. The verb 'somersaulted' suggests he feels exhilarated, like a gymnast, when he's knocked into the water.

Feedback

1 The three answers are accurate and show precise understanding.

2 The three answers are accurate, working out the correct meaning of the word in relation to its place in the extract.

3 The three explanations are accurate and the writer of the response makes use of their own words.

4 This response contains a range of well-selected words and phrases, including some imagery. The writer considers the different meanings and associations of the words being quoted. Writing is concise and precise, making good use of subject terminology; there is clear understanding of the effects achieved by language.

9 What is better about the answers here? Identify one improvement in each answer. Use the 'Excellent progress points' on page 176 to help you.

10 Using the responses and feedback in this topic, and the 'Excellent progress points' on page 176, evaluate your own responses and improve them where you can.

Check your progress

Sound progress

- I can understand most meanings in a text.
- I can explain most meanings of words and phrases.
- I can select some powerful words and phrases from a text.
- I can select some powerful imagery from a text.
- I can apply some subject terminology.
- I can explain some of the effects of words and phrases.

Excellent progress

- I can understand complex meanings in a text.
- I can explain the meanings of words and phrases precisely and concisely.
- I can select a range of powerful words and phrases from a text.
- I can select a range of powerful imagery from a text.
- I can apply a full range of subject terminology.
- I can explain the effects of words and phrases precisely and concisely.

Extended response to reading and directed writing

8

Sometimes you will need to read one or two texts, then select points and details from them to create a new piece of writing for a specified audience.

To respond to tasks like this, you will need to use both reading and writing skills.

Reading:
- demonstrate understanding of explicit meanings (R1)
- demonstrate understanding of implicit meanings and attitudes (R2)
- analyse, evaluate and develop facts, ideas and opinions, using appropriate support from the text (R3)
- select and use information for specific purposes (R5).

Writing:
- articulate experience and express what is thought, felt and imagined (W1)
- organise and structure ideas and opinions for deliberate effect (W2)
- use a range of vocabulary and sentence structures appropriate to context (W3)
- use register appropriate to context (W4)
- make accurate use of spelling, punctuation and grammar (W5).

Links to other chapters:

Chapter 2: Key technical skills

Chapter 3: Key writing forms

Chapter 4: Writing for purpose

Understanding extended response to reading questions

Sometimes you will be asked to write a new type of text, based on information given in another passage. You will need to demonstrate reading skills that show understanding of the passage. You will also need to make inferences from that information, drawing on the detail and expanding on it to create your own piece of writing.

Explore the skills

Look at this example task. The key features – those that would form the basis of a response – have been labelled. (This question refers to Text A on page 179, but you do not need to read this yet.)

the role you should write in

the material you should use in your writing

the purpose of your writing

You are Alfredo. You are hoping to organise guided tours, including a visit to a football game like the one in Text A. You need to persuade your business partner that this is a good idea, explaining:

the audience (in this case the reader) for your writing

- what it is like before the game
- the different ways to experience the match
- what tourists will learn or experience from going to one.

the key points you must include

the form of writing you must use

Write a letter to your business partner.

Base your letter on what you have read in Text A, but be careful to use your own words. Deal with each of the three bullet points.

a reminder to use material from the passage in your answer

Begin your letter: 'Dear Raul, I have had a great idea for our guided tours...'

the opening sentence you must use

Write about 250 to 350 words.

Up to 15 marks are available for the content of your answer, and up to 10 marks for the quality of your writing.

1 Look at the last two paragraphs in the task. Which two important bits of guidance have not been labelled here?

Develop the skills

2 Read Text A below. As you do so, note down:

a) whose perspective the text is from (for example, is it Alfredo's?)

b) what sort of text this is (for example, is it a letter?).

Text A

In this text, the author, from the USA, has been taken to a football match between El Salvador and Mexico by his friend Alfredo. **Touts** *are trying to sell them tickets.*

'Take your watch off,' he said. 'And your ring. Put them in
5 your pocket. Be very careful. Most of these people are thieves.
They will rob you.'

I did as I was told. 'What about the tickets? Shall we buy
some **Suns** from these boys?'

'No, I will buy **Shades**.'

10 'Are they expensive?'

'Of course, but this will be a great game. I could never see
such a game in Santa Ana. Anyway, the Shades will be
quieter.' Alfredo looked around. 'Hide over there by the
wall. I will get the tickets.'

15 Alfredo vanished into the conga line at a ticket window.
He appeared again at the middle of the line, jumped the
queue, elbowed forward and in a very short time had
fought his way to the window. Even his friends marvelled
at his speed. He came towards us smiling, waving the
20 tickets in triumph.

We were frisked at the entrance; we passed through a
tunnel and emerged at the end of the stadium. From the
outside it had looked like a kettle; inside, its shape was
more of a **salver**, a **tureen** filled with brown screeching
25 faces. In the centre was a pristine rectangle of green grass.

Vocabulary

Touts: people who sell tickets at high prices outside grounds

Suns: tickets for places in the sun

Shades: tickets for places under cover or out of the sun

salver: flat silver or metal tray

tureen: serving dish, often oval in shape

It was, those 45 000 people, a model of Salvadorean society.
Not only the half of the stadium where the Suns sat (and it
was jammed: not an empty seat was visible); or the better-
dressed and almost as crowded half of the Shades (at night,
30 in the dry season, there was no difference in the quality of
the seats: we sat on concrete steps, but ours, being more
expensive than the Suns, were less crowded); there was
a section that Alfredo had not mentioned: the Balconies.
Above us, in five tiers of a gallery that ran around our half
35 of the stadium, were the Balcony people.

Balcony people had season tickets. Balcony people had
small rooms, cupboard sized, about as large as the average
Salvadorean hut; I could see wine bottles, the glasses, the
plates of food. Balcony people had folding chairs and a good
40 view of the field. There were not many Balcony people –
two or three hundred – but at $2000 for a season ticket in
a country where the per capita income was $373 one could
understand why. The Balcony people faced the screaming
Suns and, beyond the stadium, a plateau. What I took to be
45 lumpish multi-coloured vegetation covering the plateau was,
I realised, a heap of Salvadoreans standing on top or clinging
to the sides. There were thousands of them in this mass, and
it was a sight more terrifying than the Suns. They were lighted
by the stadium glare; there was a just-perceptible crawling
50 movement among the bodies; it was an ant-hill.

From *The Old Patagonian Express* by Paul Theroux

Apply the skills

3 Look back at the task and the annotations. Now 'decode' the following task in the same way. Copy it out and add annotations, labelling the key elements.

> You are one of the 'Suns'. After the game, a reporter asks whether he can interview you about your experiences of attending the match. The reporter asks you three questions:
>
> - What did you see and feel both before and during the match?
>
> - What do you remember about other people watching the game and how their experiences differed to yours?
>
> - Would you go to another game if it was like this? Why/ why not?
>
> Write the words of the interview.
>
> Begin your interview with the first question.

Checklist for success

Remember to note down:

- ✔ your role
- ✔ the form and purpose
- ✔ the audience
- ✔ any other key details.

Check your progress:

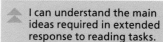 I can understand the main ideas required in extended response to reading tasks.

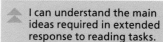 I can understand all the aspects required to respond to an extended response to reading task.

Extended response to reading: gathering information

The key elements in the question will guide you towards the information you need from the text. They will also help you decide on the tone and style of your response.

Explore the skills

One key element of the question is the list of bullet points. This is the content you *must* include in your response, so use it to find the key information you need from the text.

Look again at the bullet points from the task in Topic 8.1.

> You are Alfredo. You are hoping to organise guided tours including a visit to a football game like the one in Text A. You need to persuade your business partner that this is a good idea, explaining:
>
> * what it is like before the game
> * the different ways to experience the match
> * what tourists will learn or experience from going to one.
>
> Write a letter to your business partner.

Here is an example of some notes that have been started in response to the first bullet point.

Key part of question	Main points from text to use in the letter	Detail
what it is like before the game	the need to keep safe	watching out for 'thieves'
	how to get tickets	the 'conga-line' queue
	what it is like entering the stadium	

1. Copy and complete the table, adding details to the third column to support the overall points you might use in the letter. This could be specific factual information or particular descriptive details.

   At this point, you do not need to focus on how Alfredo might view things differently from Paul (the narrator). Stick to what actually happens or can be seen by anyone who is at the match.

Build the skills

Now consider the second bullet point: *the different ways to experience the match.*

2 What are these *different ways*? Scan the text for references to the following, and make brief notes on them:

- the 'Suns' and 'Shades' (what this means and who they are)
- the 'Balcony' people (how their experience is different to those of the 'Suns' and 'Shades')
- the people on the mound outside the ground (this may or may not be of use to you on the tour, so evaluate whether it is worth including).

Top tip

It is important to read the text carefully with the task in mind, to make sure that you include enough relevant details from the text in your writing. It can help to underline or highlight key details in the passage as you read it.

Develop the skills

Using inference is an important skill in tasks like this. For example, the writer states:

'The Balcony people faced the screaming Suns.'

they (the Balcony people) do not have the hot sun in their faces

the 'Suns' are making a huge amount of noise

3 Which of the following would be *reasonable* inferences from the given information?

a) The Balcony people hate the Suns.

b) The Suns hate the Balcony people.

c) The Balcony people are privileged.

d) The Balcony people are not as excited by the match as the Suns.

e) The Balcony people don't like football.

Apply the skills

The third bullet point in the question asks you to explain what tourists will gain from the experience. This requires a different sort of inference. For someone unused to the experience, it might not be particularly relaxing or comfortable.

4 Find textual evidence to support the following statements.

a) It is an exciting experience.

b) It is an important match that ordinary people do not usually get to see.

5 What else do you think tourists would gain from the experience? Look again at how Paul Theroux responds to what he sees: what does he learn about that he wouldn't have if he'd spent all his time at the beach?

Check your progress:

I can gather relevant information from a given passage.

I can select relevant information from a given passage and consider how it will be used.

Extended response to reading: developing a convincing role

For longer writing tasks, you will need to adopt a convincing role. In order to do this, you will need to understand the type of character and 'voice' you would have in this role and adapt your use of language to fit.

Explore the skills

A *role* is the part someone plays or the type they fit into – for example, a particular profession (bus driver), place in a group (eldest child) or even a state of mind (the hero in a story). *Character* refers to the person's personality or beliefs.

The role might have certain typical behaviours or traits. For example, a *tourist* might:

- want to see the sights
- use a map or phone app for directions
- be staying in a hotel or guesthouse.

Their character could be anything, but it might be suggested by the role. For example, they may:

- have an inquiring, curious mind
- be irritable about food or lack of comfort
- be worried about safety/security.

You can practise such creative thinking by taking some common roles in life and filling in the blanks. For example:

> *elderly professor, lives alone: thoughtful, bookish, dry sense of humour...*

1 Fill in the blanks for the following roles.

   a) taxi driver, father of five young children, in busy city: ...

   b) waitress, new to her job, very young: ...

Build the skills

It can help to build a mental image of the role you are 'playing'.

Ask yourself:

- Do I understand the role I have been given?
- What does this person feel about the situation or topic?

> **Top tip**
>
> Look back at Topic 2.10 for more information on voice and role in writing.

- How might this person spend their time? What are their interests or beliefs?

Imagine that your role is that of a ticket tout. You could use questions like the ones above to infer ideas about the character. Look at the table below.

Question	Detail from text	Explanation	Inference
Do I understand the role I have been given?	Touts are selling tickets for the 'Suns', before the game.	I'm selling unofficial tickets for the cheapest seats.	Touts like me rely on people being desperate to see the game at any cost, even for the worst seats.
What do I feel about the situation?	Alfredo says, 'Be very careful. Most of these people are thieves. They will rob you.'	Locals warn tourists about touts like me. They think I must also be a thief if I sell black-market tickets.	

2 Complete the inference for the second row of the table.

To flesh out characters and make them realistic, you could create a diagram.

3 Copy the diagram and complete it to build up an idea of the ticket tout and his life.

I'm hardworking and competitive – there are all the other ticket touts trying to out-sell me!

I'm crafty, but I'm not like the others. Yes, I'll sell dodgy tickets, but...

I'm worried, always checking around me. Police might turn up at any time and...

I have a family of... which means I...

I'm jealous of that man they call 'Alfredo' and his friends because...

4 Create a similar diagram for one of the 'Balcony' people.

- Use information from the text to build the mental picture.
- Consider any inferences about the 'Balcony' people suggested by the text.
- Use a range of different ideas.

Develop the skills

A key aspect of developing a convincing role is to get the voice of the person right. This means that the language you choose for that person must:

- fit their character (for example, if they are a positive, excitable person, you might use short exclamations and positive language)
- fit their role (a particular profession or type of person might use vocabulary linked to their job – for example, a football reporter might refer to 'waves of attack' or 'brilliant link-up play').

You also need to decide whether the language they use:

- is formal or informal
- contains **jargon** or other technical-sounding language
- contains **slang** and non-standard forms of English or is mostly in standard English.

Key terms

jargon: technical terms that people unfamiliar with the subject would not know

slang: very informal use of language (may include dialect words), often common to an area, city or group of people

5   Look at list of people who are attending the match and the different things they might say.

a) Match each role on the left to an appropriate phrase on the right.

b) What are the clues that tell you who is speaking?

child	'Can I have a drink? Please, Daddy! I'm so hot! Please!'
footballer	'After an uneventful first half, the match came to life on 52 minutes when Ribeiro saved the penalty.'
ticket seller	'Well, it was tough but we held out – great save by Marco – so we're still in with a chance of the Cup, which is great.'
reporter	'Four for the West Stand? Right, that will be forty dollars please.'

Look at these three extracts written in the role of the ticket tout.

> I have a highly sought-after position as a ticket facilitator who distributes tickets in return for monetary remuneration at public events.

> It's a right old laugh, innit, like? Know what I mean? Cos I just wanna make a packet before the fuzz catch me…

> I know people look down their noses at me, but they still want tickets, don't they? For the right price, I'll give them what they want.

6 Which extract seems most appropriate, bearing in mind both the role and character of the person concerned?

Now consider how to develop Alfredo's voice. Remember, the passage is not written by him so you will need to read the text and note down what you find out about him. Read the text on pages 179 to 180 again.

7 Match the inferences below to evidence from the text.

He warns Paul about his security.	He is worried for Paul's safety as a friend and a tourist.
He 'jumped the queue' and 'elbowed forward' to get the tickets.	He is very excited by the experience, which is special for him too.
His friends 'marvelled' at his ability to do so.	He could be seen as a leader or someone who takes responsibility.
He knows which tickets to get – not the Suns, but the more expensive Shades.	He might not have much money, but considers the event worth the extra cost.
He tells Paul 'such a match' would never be seen in his own town, Santa Ana.	He is determined, and perhaps slightly ruthless?

8 Now, consider his *voice*. What clues are there in the text about the way he speaks?

- Does he use long, rambling sentences or short, direct ones?
- Does he seem to be confident or timid in the way he speaks?
- What sorts of things is he likely to talk about (he is there as a fan of the team, and with his friends, so consider that)?

Apply the skills

9 Write a 100-word diary entry from Alfredo's point of view in which he describes arriving at the stadium and buying tickets.

Checklist for success

✔ Use language that matches what you know about Alfredo as a person and his likely character.

✔ Make sure that you draw from a range of different ideas in the text to create your role.

✔ Consider his perspective – remember that the text is *not* written from Alfredo's point of view so think how his perspective might differ from Paul's.

Check your progress:

> I can develop ideas from a text to create a role.

> I can select from a range of ideas in a text to create a convincing role.

Extended response to reading: structuring a response

To write an effective response, you need to organise your ideas so that they are clear and fit the form of text you have been asked to write.

Explore the skills

Look again at the task.

> You are Alfredo. You are hoping to organise guided tours including a visit to a football game like the one in Text A. You need to persuade your business partner that this is a good idea, explaining:
>
> - what it is like before the game
> - the different ways to experience the match
> - what tourists will learn or experience from going to one.
>
> Write a letter to your business partner.

There are two elements of structure in this task:

- the overall organisation of your text in letter format
- the structure of individual paragraphs to explain key ideas.

In terms of the overall organisation, you have the information you gathered for each bullet point from the task in Topic 8.2. You now need to consider how to organise this in letter format. For example:

- salutation: *Dear Raul*
- opening paragraph: explain your reason for writing
- middle paragraphs: use the information you have gathered for the bullet points in the task to persuade Raul
- concluding paragraph: what you want to happen next – any expected response from Raul.

1 Remember that this is a personal letter. What style of language would you use to address Raul? (He is your friend, but also your business partner.)

Build the skills

You now need to consider how to structure individual paragraphs so that you write 250–350 words in total. In Topic 8.2, you used a table to explore the text. This is a good starting point, but you need to think about how to adapt the information for *purpose*: to make it persuasive. For example:

- introducing your key idea/s to Raul
- anticipating any objections he might raise
- using persuasive language to get your point across.

2. How has this been achieved in the following paragraph? Copy the paragraph and annotate it.

> Tourists will love the whole build-up to the match. Yes, I know there are long queues for tickets, but, believe me, I know how to get them quickly. We can also make sure tourists are safe by giving them clear advice about valuables – this is something tourists have to do all over the world, so it's not a problem. Then, just imagine the thrill they will get entering the stadium and seeing the excited crowd and the pitch!

3 Complete the persuasive details for each of the points below about different ways of experiencing the match. Remember – stick to what is in the original text.

   a) Suns tickets – *don't worry, I'll ensure tourists don't have these because...*

   b) Shades tickets – *these are perfect because...*

   c) Balcony tickets – *these are good, but...*

4 Construct a paragraph using a similar model:

   - topic sentence introducing the idea
   - follow up sentence/s anticipating any objections that Raul might raise
   - finish with key positive points using persuasive language.

> **Top tip**
>
> You will not find much explicit information in the text that will help you address the second bullet point. You need to use your skills of inference here.

Develop the skills

Now think about the final bullet point: *what tourists will learn or experience from going to a match.*

5 Use a table or a spider diagram to come up with ideas – but remember, they must be specific details from the text.

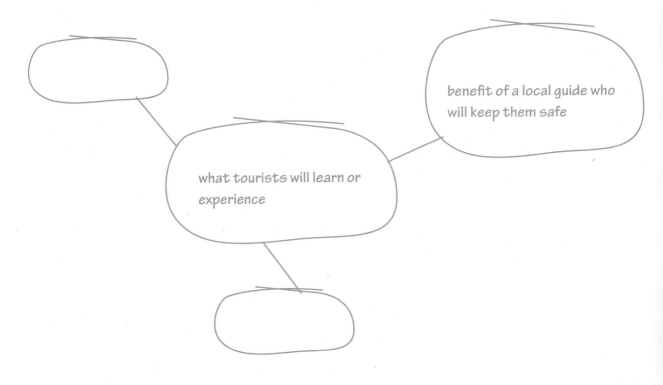

benefit of a local guide who will keep them safe

what tourists will learn or experience

Apply the skills

6 Write out a full plan for the task, with a number for each paragraph and letters for each point or detail you wish to include. Then, draft your response.

Checklist for success

✔ Use the bullet points to help you organise the order and content of your response.

✔ Remember the purpose of the letter – to persuade Raul.

✔ Make sure that you stick to the form – a letter.

✔ Use only the information from the text.

Check your progress:

 I can create an overall plan for a task and include relevant points.

 I can create an overall plan, and construct paragraphs that illustrate my points clearly.

Understanding directed writing questions

Directed writing questions may be based on one or two passages. They may ask you to:

- evaluate the material that you read, analysing the ideas that it contains

- express your own views on the issue or issues

- write in a form that allows you to express your own ideas.

Explore the skills

Read this task. It is based on Texts A and B below, but you do not need to read them yet.

Write a speech for a school assembly, giving your views on whether money raised through school fund-raising events should be given to a charity called Save Our Tigers, or used in some other way.

In your speech, you should:

- evaluate the views given in both texts about 'single species' conservation

- give your own views, based on what you have read.

Base your speech on what you have read in **both** texts, but be careful to use your own words. Address both of the bullet points.

Begin your speech, 'Thank you for attending my speech today...'

Write about 250 to 350 words.

Up to 15 marks are available for the content of your answer and up to 25 marks for the quality of your writing.

---

1. List the key elements of the question.

   Identify:

   a) the form of the text you are being asked to write

   b) its audience and purpose

   c) the core issue or focus

   d) the content you must include

   e) any other key information.

Top tip

If necessary, look back at Topic 8.1 to remind yourself how to identify the key points in a task.

Build the skills

You will need to analyse and evaluate the ideas from the passages in your own writing. In doing so, it may help to keep a running log or list of notes of the main points made by each writer.

For example, here is the opening paragraph of Text A:

> I don't want the panda to die out. I want species to stay alive – that's why I get up in the morning. I don't even kill mosquitoes or flies. So if pandas can survive, that would be great. But let's face it: conservation, both nationally and globally, has a limited amount of resources, and I think we're going to have to make some hard, pragmatic choices.

Look for *clear expressions* of viewpoint (that is, the first sentences make clear the writer wants species to survive).

Look for signals of *alternative points* (that is, the connective 'But' suggests that the writer has more to say).

Look for *evidence* that suggests a point of view (that is, lack of money for conservation, so choices have to be made).

So, the point you note down here could be:

> The writer believes in conserving all species, ('I want species to stay alive' but there's a lack of resources so it may not be possible).

2 Now read the two passages, making notes as you do so.

Text A

The following passage is an article in which a television presenter and naturalist, Chris Packham, asks a difficult question about conservation.

Should pandas be left to face extinction?

I don't want the panda to die out. I want species to stay alive – that's why I get up in the morning. I don't even kill mosquitoes or flies. So if pandas can survive, that would be great. But let's face it: conservation, both nationally and globally, has a limited amount of resources, and I think we're going to have to make some hard, pragmatic choices.

5 The truth is, pandas are extraordinarily expensive to keep going. We spend millions and millions of pounds on pretty much this one species, and a few others, when we know that the best thing we could do would be to look after the world's biodiversity hotspots with greater care. Without habitat, you've got nothing. So maybe if we took all the cash we spend on pandas and just bought rainforest with it, we might be doing a better job.

10 Of course, it's easier to raise money for something fluffy. Charismatic megafauna like the panda do appeal to people's emotional side, and attract a lot of public attention. They are emblematic of what I would call single-species conservation: i.e. a focus on one animal. This approach began in the 1970s with Save the Tiger, Save the Panda, Save the Whale, and so on, and it is now out of date. I think pandas have had a valuable role in raising the profile of conservation, but perhaps
15 'had' is the right word.

Panda conservationists may stand up and say, 'It's a flagship species. We're also conserving Chinese forest, where there is a whole plethora of other things.' And when that works, I'm not against it. But we have to accept that some species are stronger than others. The panda is a species of bear that has gone herbivorous and eats a type of food that isn't all that nutritious, and
20 that dies out sporadically. It is susceptible to various diseases, and, up until recently, it has been almost impossible to breed in captivity. They've also got a very restricted range, which is ever decreasing. [...] Perhaps the panda was already destined to run out of time.

Extinction is very much a part of life on earth. And we are going to have to get used to it in the next few years because climate change is going to result in all sorts of disappearances. The last
25 large mammal extinction was another animal in China – the Yangtze river dolphin, which looked like a worn-out piece of pink soap with piggy eyes and was never going to make it on to anyone's T-shirt. If that had appeared beautiful to us, then I doubt very much that it would be extinct. But it vanished, because it was pig-ugly and swam around in a river where no one saw it. And now, sadly, it has gone for ever.

30 [...] I'm saying we won't be able to save it all, so let's do the best we can. And at the moment I don't think our strategies are best placed to do that. We should be focusing our conservation endeavours on biodiversity hotspots, spreading our net more widely and looking at good-quality habitat maintenance to preserve as much of the life as we possibly can, using hard science to make educated decisions as to which species are essential to a community's maintenance. It may
35 well be that we can lose the cherries from the cake. But you don't want to lose the substance. Save the Rainforest, or Save the Kalahari: that would be better.

From www.guardian.co.uk

Text B

The following passage comes from a naturalist's autobiography.

A love affair with nature

I want you to picture a scene. It is a Sunday afternoon, twenty-five years ago. A child wanders around a zoo with his parents, until he is drawn to the panda enclosure. At first, there is nothing to see. Then, little by little, a bundle of fur emerges from behind a tree. Large eyes gaze out at the visitors. In that moment, the child is entranced by the gentle panda, as if he had been
5 offered the largest teddy in the world. But he also begins a love affair with nature itself.

That child was me. Little did I know that visit would change my life – but it did. For since then I have been a powerful advocate for 'save the panda' campaigns even in the face of mounting criticism of 'single species' conservation and its cost. After all, who can put a price on life? Yes, there are those who object to saving cuddly creatures like the panda and who claim that focusing
10 on individual species misses the bigger picture, the need to protect habitats for a diverse range of animals. They assert that piling effort into saving a creature, like the panda, who may have died out in any case through evolutionary forces, is a diversion, a waste of money … perhaps even a waste of time. But why should extinction be something we accept? Humanity has the power to change life for the better.

15 Yet I think this misses the point in another way. Not everyone can be a naturalist obsessed with the tiniest insect or ugliest mammal, or devoted to studying the life cycle of obscure plants. As I write this I remember what I was like as a child back then, and think of what I am like as an adult now: someone who reacts emotionally to animals, and if it is a cuddly panda that grabs my attention then what's wrong with that?

20 The money we give to campaigns to save such creatures does far more than just support that animal. It provides education and employment for local people; if people have jobs, they are less likely to de-forest, so it supports habitats too. Also, providing for the tiger inevitably means providing a better habitat for the prey it feeds off. But most importantly, it reminds us how close the creatures we most cherish are to extinction. There are only about 1800 giant pandas still in the
25 wild, and this is not yet enough to sustain the population. As I grew up I was forced to face the key question: was I happy to lose the giant panda, the white rhino, the Madagascan tree lemur, or the snow leopard? Would I be happy for such magnificent beasts to become relics of history? For me, the answer back then was 'no' – and it still is today.

Develop the skills

3 Check your points – are there any that could be directly compared or contrasted? Record your ideas in a table such as the one below.

Text A: Pandas – worth saving?	Text B: A love affair with nature
Conservation has 'limited resources'.	You can't put 'a price on life'.

Apply the skills

4 Based on your initial reading, what is your view on whether the school money should be spent on a Save Our Tigers campaign? Write one paragraph summarising your viewpoint. Check that you have enough evidence from the text in your notes to support this viewpoint.

Check your progress:

- I can select key points from a source text.
- I can select key points and compare them with ones from a contrasting text.

Directed writing: analysing and evaluating texts

You need to demonstrate that you have considered the key ideas in texts carefully, so that you can write an analytical response supported by evidence.

Explore the skills

There are two stages to this process. First, you need to look at an idea in detail to fully understand what the writer is saying. For example:

The truth is pandas are extraordinarily expensive to keep going.

the intensifier 'extraordinarily' suggests the cost is incredibly high

'keep going' – means help to survive, support

So, the point is: *it costs a huge amount to keep pandas alive (according to the writer).*

1. The table below contains two quotations from Texts A and B in Topic 8.5. Copy and complete it to identify the point being made and the inferences. If there is more than one inference, use the final column.

Quotation	Point being made	Do I agree/ disagree?	Why? Why not? (explain your reasons with new information or ideas)
Text A: 'Of course, it's easier to raise money for something fluffy.'	People are happy to donate to save appealing-looking animals.		
Text B: 'the child is entranced by the gentle panda'			

Build the skills

The next stage in the process is to **synthesise** two ideas from the texts, for example:

Text A: 'Extinction is very much part of life on earth. And we are going to have to get used to it in the next few years because [of] climate change...'

Text B: 'But why should extinction be something we accept? Man has the power to change life for the better.'

2 Start by making notes about:

- what each idea is saying and any inferences you can make
- what your own viewpoint is.

Key term

synthesise: bring two ideas together to make a new one

Develop the skills

Now evaluate. This means making your own judgement about the points. Bear in mind that you are not directly quoting from the given text or texts, but writing your own material – in this case, a speech for the school assembly. The sample response below synthesises the two points of view into one evaluative comment:

> I know that we are all captivated by the sight of the proud tiger with its unique coat, but I agree with Chris Packham: <u>surely</u> we should make honest judgements about conservation on more than just a creature's visual appeal?

uses a similar word to 'entranced' ('captivated') and phrases the point using the positive adjective 'proud' (like 'gentle' in Text A)

uses the phrase 'honest judgements' and links back to Packham's 'the truth is'

ends with a question and the phrase 'more than just' which suggests that the student *does not* think the money should be spent on the tiger campaign

There are a number of different ways of saying 'I agree' or 'I disagree'. For example:

I am in agreement with…	I am in disagreement with…
Likewise, I feel…	In contrast, I feel…
I share the same point of view	I don't share the view that…
I concur with…	I differ from…
I believe…	I don't believe…

3 Rewrite the evaluative paragraph above as if you disagreed with Chris Packham. Use at least two of the phrases in the right-hand column.

Apply the skills

4 Take the points from the 'running log' you completed in Topic 8.5. Turn these into evaluative sentences like the one above. Where there is not a 'parallel point' in the other text, try to evaluate that point on its own.

Check your progress:

⬆ I can synthesise points from two texts.

⬆⬆ I can synthesise points from two texts and evaluate what they are saying.

Directed writing: structuring your response

Once you have a good understanding of the points that each text makes, you need to write down your ideas in a clear and engaging way.

Explore the skills

Reread the task.

> **Write a speech** for a school assembly, giving your views on whether money raised through school fund-raising events should be given to a charity called Save Our Tigers or used in some other way.
>
> In your speech, you should:
>
> * evaluate the views given in both texts about 'single species' conservation
> * give your own views, based on what you have read.
>
> Base your speech on what you have read in **both** texts, but be careful to use your own words. Address both of the bullet points.
>
> Begin your speech, 'Thank you for attending my speech today...'.
>
> Write about 250 to 350 words.
>
> Up to 15 marks are available for the content of your answer and up to 25 marks for the quality of your writing.

You created a list of points that both texts comment on in Task 3 of Topic 8.5. You now need to decide how you will organise your work to deal with these points. There are different options available:

Option 1	Option 2	Option 3
Start with ideas you agree with from both passages.	Start with most important common area covered by both writers.	Start by going through Packham's ideas one by one, agreeing or disagreeing.
Continue with those ideas you don't agree with.	Continue with other common areas (but less important ones).	Continue by tackling the second writer's ideas one by one.
End with a conclusion summing up your views.	End with a conclusion summing up your views.	End with a conclusion summing up the ideas.

1 Look at the set of example notes below. Which of the three options do these notes follow?

- Paragraph 1: extinction – is it natural or can it/ should it be stopped?
- cost of conservation
- Paragraph 2: appeal of 'fluffy' animals: hard science versus emotion
- Paragraph 3: whether single species campaigns are 'out of date' given today's concerns (i.e. climate change)
- Paragraph 4: habitat campaigns better than single-species ones?
- Paragraph 5: naturalists' knowledge of the real facts versus the views of ordinary people
- Conclusion

Build the skills

Once you have decided on the order in which you will tackle the key points – whether synthesised from both passages, or each passage in turn – you need to think about the structure of your paragraphs.

Here is an example of a straightforward paragraph addressing one of the second writer's key points.

Some argue that most ordinary people are not able to focus their whole lives on the more detailed aspects of nature and conservation. Instead, they respond to the beauty or power of nature through their feelings, and that is why symbols such as the panda or tiger are important. I think this is very true and a good reason why we should support the 'Save the tiger' charity: it will keep us involved with conservation and in the future may lead us to support other less well-known species too.

— topic sentence sums up writer's point
— develops explanation
— expresses student's own view
— backs up/supports view with own evidence/ideas

2 Copy the paragraph below, reordering it so that it follows a similar structure to the example above. Then complete the final sentence, which explains the student's view more fully.

> Yet, I disagree because if that child is given a false view of nature then that is not healthy. It can turn people into strong supporters of conservation. It is also asserted that children first's experience with magnificent animals such as pandas can create a life-long interest in nature.
>
> They need to know the reality about...

Develop the skills

It is also important to consider the conventions of the form your writing should take. In this task, you are asked to write a speech, so you should think about the following conventions:

- Direct address: *I'm talking **to you**...*

- Personal and relevant perspective: *As **I** walk around **the school**...*

- Presentation of arguments through imagery, pattern of three, and so on: *Pandas may be **cuddly, cute** and **childlike in manner,** but...*

- Use of intensifiers or other powerful language: *It is **hugely significant** that...*

3 Decide which elements of the paragraph in Task 2 could be improved, using some or all of the points above.

Apply the skills

4 Choose a plan from Option 1, 2 or 3 on page 198 and write out how you will tackle the task. Then, choose any of the points that have not been covered in this topic and write a paragraph. Make sure that it:

- includes a topic sentence that makes clear what aspect of the passage or passages you are addressing

- includes explanatory sentence/s that explore the idea in more detail

- includes a sentence that shows clearly what your view is on the point you have selected

- is written in a style that suits a speech to the school.

Check your progress:

 I can create a basic plan for my chosen response and create informative paragraphs.

 I can select from a range of planning options and write clear paragraphs to convey my viewpoint.

Practice questions and sample responses: extended response to reading

Key skills

You will need to show the following skills in extended response to reading tasks:

- Identify the main ideas in a task in order to select relevant information.
- Consider how to use information form the passage effectively.
- Create a role with a convincing voice, based on ideas in a text.
- Plan and execute a suitable structure.
- Write paragraphs that clearly convey a point of view.

Your task

1 Read the following task, then write a response of 250–350 words.

> Imagine that you are Richard Branson and you have been asked to speak about extreme sports at a local college. Make sure that you include:
>
> - what happened that day
> - what Branson learned about himself
> - what he would say to students who are facing problems or in adversity.
>
> Base your report on what you have read in the text, but be careful to use your own words.
>
> **Begin:** 'I am delighted to have been invited here to share my experience with you…'.

Richard Branson is a very successful businessman. He founded the Virgin Records music stores when he was 22 years old. Since then, the Virgin brand has grown to encompass many different types of business, including a record label, an airline and a mobile-phone company. Branson has also made several attempts at breaking world records in sailing and hot-air ballooning.

In 1987, Branson attempted to cross the Atlantic by hot-air balloon with his partner, Per Lindstrand. In this extract, after a disastrous attempt to land, Per has leapt into the sea to save himself but Branson remains in the balloon.

Alone in the balloon

Whatever I did in the next ten minutes would lead to my death or survival. I was on my own.
5 We had broken the record but I was almost certainly going to die. Per, with no survival suit, was either dead or trying to swim on. I had to get somebody to find him. I had to survive. I cleared my mind and concentrated on the options in front of me. I hadn't slept for over 24 hours and my mind felt fuzzy. I decided to take the balloon up high enough so I could parachute off the capsule. I blasted the burners and then found my notebook and scrawled across the open page,
10 'Joan, Holly, Sam, I love you.' I waited until the altimeter showed 8000 feet and then climbed outside.

I was alone in the cloud. I crouched by the railings and looked down. I was still wheeling through the possibilities. If I jumped, I would be likely to have only two minutes to live. If I managed to open my parachute, I would still end up in the sea, where I would probably drown. I felt for the
15 parachute release tag, and wondered whether it was the right one. Perhaps due to my dyslexia, I have a mental block about which is right and which is left, especially with parachutes. The last time I had free-fallen I pulled the wrong release tag and jettisoned my parachute. At the time, I had several skydivers around me, so they activated my reserve parachute. But now I was by myself at 8000 feet. I slapped myself hard across the face to concentrate. There had to be a better way.

20 'Give yourself more time,' I said out loud. 'Come on.'

As I crouched on top of the capsule, I looked up at the vast balloon above me. The realisation dawned that I was standing beneath the world's largest parachute. If I could bring the balloon down, then perhaps I could jump off into the sea at the last moment before we crashed. I now knew I had enough fuel for another thirty minutes. It must be better to live for thirty minutes
25 than jump off with my parachute and perhaps live for only two minutes.

'While I am alive I can still do something,' I said. 'Something must turn up.'

I climbed back inside and took off my parachute. I made up my mind. I would do anything for those extra minutes. I grabbed some chocolate, zipped it into my jacket pocket, and checked that my torch was still there.

30 Peering out of the capsule into the fog below me, I tried to work out when I should stop burning, when I should open the vent, and when I should leave the controls and climb out on top of the capsule for my final jump. I knew I had to judge the last burn exactly so that the balloon would hit the sea as slowly as possible. Despite losing all our fuel tanks, the balloon was still carrying a weight of around three tonnes.

35 As I came out through the bottom of the clouds, I saw the grey sea below me. I also saw an RAF helicopter. I gave a last burn to slow my descent, and then left the balloon to come down of its own accord. I grabbed a red rag and climbed out through the hatch. I squatted on top of the capsule and waved the rag at the helicopter pilot. He waved back rather casually, seemingly oblivious to my panic.

40 I peered over the edge and saw the sea coming up. I shuffled round the capsule trying to work
out where the wind was coming from. It was difficult to be sure since it seemed to be gusting
from all directions. I finally chose the upwind side and looked down. I was fifty feet away, the
height of a house, and the sea was rushing up to hit me. I checked my life jacket and held on to
the railing. Without my weight, I hoped the balloon would rise up again rather than crashing on
45 top of me. I waited until I was just above the sea before pulling my life-jacket ripcord and hurling
myself away from the capsule.

The sea was icy. I spun deep into it and felt my scalp freeze with the water. Then the life jacket
bobbed me straight back up to the surface. It was heaven: I was alive. I turned and watched
the balloon. Without my weight, it quietly soared back up through the cloud like a magnificent
50 alien spaceship, vanishing from sight.

From *Losing my Virginity* by Richard Branson

Exploring responses

Now read this example response to the task.

Response 1

I am delighted to have been invited here today to share my experience with you. The experience I had was very exciting but very dangerous and I almost died.

— vocabulary is repetitive
— does not really say why the audience ought to listen

What happened was that I was attempting a record-breaking balloon flight but my balloon ran out of fuel. I was over the sea and it was foggy – I knew I was going to crash eventually. At first, I didn't know what to do as my mind felt all fuzzy. I wrote letters to my children and wife as I thought it was the end. Finally, I came up with a plan to survive. I let all the fuel out of the balloon and used it as a giant parachute, then just before it hit the sea I jumped out. I was wearing a life-jacket and the sea was icy but I was alive!

— uses Branson's exact words and doesn't even explain why he felt like this

I learned a lot about myself. One thing I learned was that my dyslexia made things difficult for me: I could not distinguish between right and left and this meant I didn't know how to open the parachute. But I was clever too because I realised there was another way to survive. I worked out I could use the balloon as a parachute to survive – and that is what I did. I also kept calm and realised that panicking doesn't solve anything.

So, if you are facing problems or things that frighten you, then I would say that you can definitely overcome them. There are lots of things you can do: for example, dyslexia didn't hold me back. You can use your intelligence and keep calm and work out answers to your problems. That is what I did and it saved my life. Thank you for listening to me.

Feedback

This response makes an attempt to take details from the text and integrate them into the speech. Unfortunately, the style is inconsistent and the content lacks structure and the sense of audience is missing. Vocabulary is mostly lifted from the original text, although there is some attempt at original ideas, if rather clumsily expressed.

2   Identify three further things in this response that could be
    improved. Use the 'Excellent progress points' on page 214
    to help you.

Now read this second sample response.

Response 2

concisely
paraphrases
information
from later in
text to sum up
predicament

I am delighted to have been invited here today to
share my experience with you. What happened had
a profound impact on me, and taught me incredibly
valuable lessons.

In essence, I was attempting a record-breaking balloon
flight but had got into terrible difficulty over a freezing
cold sea and was running out of fuel. Can you imagine
that? Faced with probable death, I wrote 'goodbye' notes
for my family; I couldn't think clearly and all the options
seemed to lead to my inevitable destruction, but finally I
cleared my mind and worked out a way to get through it.
Using the balloon as a parachute, I plunged into the sea
but without harming myself. I survived!

The experience taught me that I could work out solutions
to problems through cool thinking: that panicking doesn't
help. Equally important, it told me that I loved life and
that I would do anything to survive and see my family.
It showed me that even though I had problems such as
dyslexia I could overcome them through lateral thinking.

This, then, is my message to you. Whether the challenges
you face are big or small, don't fixate on your weaknesses.
You are more capable than you think! Keep a cool head
and consider all the options – somewhere inside you is
the answer you seek.

engages audience
by using powerful
adjectives
'profound' and
'valuable' and
adverb 'incredibly'

use of second
person creates
direct contact
with audience

Feedback

This is an excellent response. It instantly engages the audience
and keeps their interest by describing the incident in dramatic
detail. It used powerful language such as strong adjectives
and rhetorical questions. The speech develops logically, clearly
covering all three of the bullet points in the task.

3 Using the responses and feedback in this topic, and the progress points on page 214, evaluate your own response and improve it where you can.

Exam-style questions and sample responses: directed writing

Key skills

You will need to show the following skills in extended response to reading tasks:

- Select key points from a source text.
- Show that you understand explicit and implicit meanings in a text.
- Compare and contrast ideas from two texts.
- Synthesise and evaluate points.
- Choose an appropriate structure for your response.
- Write paragraphs to clearly convey your viewpoint.

Your task

1. Read the task and the passage that follows it. Then write your response to the task in 250–350 words.

> Write a speech to be given to students at your school about the effects of global tourism.
>
> In your speech, you should:
> - evaluate the views given in the text about the effects of tourism
> - give your own views, based on what you have read, about tourism to beautiful or historical places, and how it should be dealt with.
>
> Base your speech on what you have read in the text, but be careful to use your own words. Address both of the bullet points.
>
> Begin your speech: 'Thank you for giving me the opportunity to talk about this important issue…'.

Text A

Mass tourism is at a tipping point – but we're all part of the problem

By Martin Kettle

Nearly 30 years ago, […] I interviewed the zoologist, Desmond Morris. During that interview, Morris said something that was hard to forget. "We have to recognise," he said, "that human beings may be becoming
5 an infestation on the planet."

Those words came back to me as reports came in about the increasing reaction in many parts of Europe against the depredations of mass tourism. Last week I read a stress-inducing story in The Times about appalling passport-check
10 delays at Milan airport; three days later, I walked through those selfsame passport gates with only a brief and courteous check.

Nevertheless, when places from the Mediterranean to the Isle of Skye all start complaining more or less
15 simultaneously about the sheer pressure of tourist numbers in their streets and beauty spots, as has happened this August, it feels as if the always uneasy balance between the visited and the visitors has gone beyond a tipping point.

20 [….]

Predictably, Venice is one of the most agonisingly pressured of all. It embodies the increasingly irreconcilable forces of vernacular life, tourism and sustainability in historic parts of Europe. But that doesn't stop the millions arriving all the
25 time – 28 million this year, in a city with a population of 55 000, many disembarking from monstrous cruise ships that dwarf the ancient city as they approach the Grand Canal. Each day in summer is a humiliation of most of the things the world treasures about Venice. Not surprisingly,
30 many locals have had enough.

But these are only the hot spots. The tourism problem runs far wider. Human beings across the world make more than a billion foreign trips a year, twice as many as 20 years ago. In Britain, statistics this week show we took 45 million
35 foreign holidays last year, a 68% increase on 1996. And foreign trips cut both ways. Many of those who were

interviewed in the media when the narrow road to Glen Brittle on Skye became jammed with traffic this week were European visitors, attracted not just by the scenery but by
40 the advantageous exchange rate.

The problem shows itself in both supply and demand. There isn't enough room for the many to walk through the centre of Dubrovnik, or enough public [toilets] on Skye for the visitors. But the number of people wanting to visit such
45 places is rising all the time, fed by greater global prosperity, cheaper air travel and increased overall provision of hotels worldwide. Tourism is now the largest employer on the planet. One in every 11 people relies on the industry for work. Unsurprisingly, few governments want to put a
50 squeeze on such a source of wealth.

[…]

It would be wonderful if governments could find effective ways to at least mitigate the worst problems. Some, such as those of Thailand and Bhutan, have been bold, even
55 though most restrictions hit hardest at the less well-off and are most easily circumvented by the rich. The role of government action to ensure adequate and appropriate infrastructure in tourist areas is indisputable.

In the end, though, I think we have to take greater
60 individual responsibility too. […]

We have to re-examine the idea that we enjoy an unfettered liberty to travel at will or for pleasure. We have to rethink the impulse that says that a holiday from work – or retirement from work – is an open sesame to exploring
65 the world. We should learn […] that one can travel as much – and develop as much as a human being – in one's own locality as in the far-flung and exotic corners of the globe. Travel broadens the mind, they say. But is the person whose air-conditioned tour bus whisks them to a distant glacier
70 in Patagonia or to the Mona Lisa for a quick selfie before depositing them at a characterless international hotel richer in experience than the one who spends the same amount of time watching the birds or the butterflies in the back garden? I doubt it. We may not be an infestation yet. But we are a
75 problem. Travel can narrow the mind too.

From *The Guardian*

Exploring responses

Now read this example response to the task.

Response 1

Thank you for giving me the opportunity to talk about this important issue. I can see that tourism is on the increase and it needs to be looked at.

It is really clear that lots more people are now travelling around the world. So, this means lots of delays at airports, plus more people going to beauty spots and famous places. Like Venice where there are these monstrous cruise ships which must be very ugly to look at.

vocabulary is repetitive and limited

words taken directly from text

But it isn't just famous places but also places like Skye in Britain which are being spoiled by traffic jams. It is awful when a place like this is ruined because of visitors.

Also, there are places like Dubrovnik where you can't even walk in the centre because there are too many people.

personal view but no real sense of audience

But people want to travel, and I want to travel when I'm older. It's so much cheaper now and hotels are much better. Plus tourism makes a lot of money for cities and countries so that mustn't stop. Lots of people work in tourism, about 1 in 11 people.

So we all need to think hard before we take a holiday to some lovely place like Venice or Thailand. Because the traffic and the number of people will make it a bit unreal, not like it's supposed to be. Perhaps we won't enjoy it as much as staying at home, because we must not forget that there is a lot to do and see in our own country. Thank you.

Feedback

This response does deal with both sides of the issue at a basic level and sums up some of the key points made, but there is little attempt at synthesising them and drawing conclusions. There is also little sense that the speaker is trying to connect with the school audience.

2 Identify three further things in this response that could be improved. Use the 'Excellent progress points' on page 214 to help you.

Now read the second sample response.

Response 2

Thank you for giving me the opportunity to talk about this important issue. The gift of being able to travel the world is one I'm sure we all look forward to as we get older, but we need to question its effect.

The fact is that global tourism has seen a huge increase and this has had a profound effect on the world's most popular destinations. Venice, for example, sees 28 million visitors a year, many arriving on ugly cruise ships. I ask you – is this the best backdrop for such an ancient city? The sheer weight of traffic is also a major problem, with roads like the ones to the pretty Isle of Skye getting clogged up, and so too is the fact that people are unable to walk through the centre of popular cities due to the staggering number of visitors.

develops the point and responds to it from a personal perspective

What does this mean for us as young people? It is difficult because on the one hand I don't want to visit places that are so overwhelmed you cannot even see the sights, but I do want to expand my horizons. I also recognize that such tourism has benefits too: there is a good chance, for example, that one in every eleven of us in this room will end up with a job in tourism. And every government is pleased with the money tourism brings in.

synthesises points from both texts

Ultimately, I think the issue of what sort of travel we want is important. Will staying in a dull modern hotel and taking a few snaps on your phone as you battle the hordes really satisfy you? When we leave school, we have a choice – to blindly follow the crowd or do something different. As young people, we can blaze a trail for how we want travel to look in the coming years. For my part, I'm going to begin by getting to know my own country first – on foot or bicycle. I hope you do too.

clear expression of viewpoint and intentions

Feedback

This response covers the task in a logical way, addressing each of the bullet points and demonstrating a good understanding of audience and purpose. The writer successfully evaluates the points raised in the text and synthesises them to provide a clear, concise analysis in their own words.

3 Using the responses and feedback in this topic, and the progress points on page 214, evaluate your own response and improve it where you can.

Check your progress

Extended response to reading

Good progress

- I can understand the main ideas and points from a source extract.
- I can express ideas clearly and in a straightforward way, although they may not be well developed.
- I can use some details and examples to back up my ideas.
- I can focus on some of the bullets in the task.
- I can use some conventions of a speech.
- I can include a basic 'voice' in my writing that sometimes evokes a sense of personality.
- I can sequence my writing well and choose a broadly effective structure.
- I often get spelling, punctuation and grammar right.

Excellent progress

- I can look closely at a text and show my opinions about it.
- I can include well-developed and sustained ideas, using convincing and effective language to express these ideas.
- I can use examples and details to add power and purpose to my response.
- I can address all the bullet points listed in the task.
- I can use the conventions of a speech effectively.
- I can recreate a convincing voice that reflects someone's personality and sustain this throughout my writing.
- I can organise my ideas to have an effect on the audience.
- I almost always get spelling, punctuation and grammar right.

Directed writing

Good progress

- I can sometimes write using the conventions of a specified form.
- I can organise my response, sometimes choosing words that are powerful.
- I can sometimes use language appropriate to my audience.
- I can generally use accurate spelling, punctuation and grammar.

Excellent progress

- I can write in a variety of forms, using conventions appropriately.
- I can organise my ideas to influence the reader.
- I can choose words for their impact and effect.
- I can consistently use language to engage and influence my audience.
- I can use consistently accurate spelling, punctuation and grammar.

Composition

Composition tasks give you the opportunity to write at length. They allow you to show your understanding of the content and structure of either narrative writing or descriptive writing, and at the highest level to take risks or try out different approaches to produce an original piece of writing.

To write a composition, you will need to use your writing skills to:
- articulate experience and express what is thought, felt and imagined (W1)
- organise and structure ideas and opinions for deliberate effect (W2)
- use a range of vocabulary and sentence structures appropriate to context (W3)
- use register appropriate to context (W4)
- make accurate use of spelling, punctuation and grammar (W5).

Links to other chapters:

Chapter 3: Key writing forms

Chapter 4: Writing for purpose

Understanding composition tasks

You will have to make quite a few choices in your composition writing. It is important that you fully understand what those choices are and how they will affect your response. Composition tasks usually give you a choice of two types of writing – descriptive or narrative. A composition should be 350–450 words.

> **Top tip**
>
> Look back to Topics 4.9 and 4.10 to remind yourself of the key features of descriptive and narrative writing.

Explore the skills

1 Look at the two example tasks below. Which is a descriptive writing task and which is a narrative writing task? Make notes on why each task matches the type you have decided on.

a)

> Describe an occasion when two people meet for the first time.

b)

> 'Although it was almost midnight, I heard the sound of footsteps approaching our house. I opened the door…'. Use these two sentences to start a story.

Build the skills

Each type of writing has its own conventions. These might be *structural* (how ideas and information are sequenced or ordered) or *stylistic* (how language is used).

2 Copy and complete the chart below.

	Conventions of good narratives	Conventions of good descriptive writing
structure	structure adds interest by revealing or concealing information strong opening that hooks the reader use of flashbacks? surprising ending?	Individual elements are tackled in turn in detail.
style	vividly paints picture of setting and characters in reader's mind using imagery	

Develop the skills

You can develop your understanding of the conventions and practise using them. However, in exam conditions you will need to deal methodically with the tasks. It can help to follow a process such as the one below.

1 Read the four tasks (two descriptive writing and two narrative writing).

2 Select the one task from the four for which you:

- understand the conventions (the form/purpose and its style and structure)
- have a good range of ideas (it is no good choosing a topic or theme that you know nothing about or cannot picture in your mind)
- can write in a complex, sophisticated way (not just stating the obvious but providing detail and depth of language and ideas).

3 Quickly plan your answer.

3 Reread the two questions in Task 1. Which would you choose? Why?

Apply the skills

Once you have selected the task, make sure that you understand *what* it is asking you to do. You can do this by highlighting the key words in the question.

Narrative writing

'Although it was almost midnight, I heard the sound of footsteps approaching our house.

I opened the door...' Use these two sentences to start a story.

to be told in the first person ('I')

make sure I only write the beginning

a narrative is a story, so I must use what I know about good storytelling

the content: a person hears someone coming to the house and opens the door

4 Identify the key words in the following question.

Descriptive writing

Describe a scene in which a customer complains to a shop manager about an item he/she has bought.

Check your progress:

I understand what each task is asking and can select a form that I can write competently.

I understand the range of tasks on offer and can draw creatively on what I know of them.

Planning ideas for a descriptive task

Highlighting the key words and phrases in the task is important, but how does it help you to develop a response?

Explore the skills

Look again at the following task. The key words have been highlighted.

> **Descriptive writing**
>
> Describe a scene in which a customer complains to a shop manager about an item he/she has bought.

1 Quickly generate ideas about the *content*, based on the key words. Jot down:

- what the *customer* and *manager* are like
- what the customer is *complaining about*.

2 Create two spider diagrams to help you focus on the *descriptive elements*. Copy and complete these spider diagrams, or come up with your own.

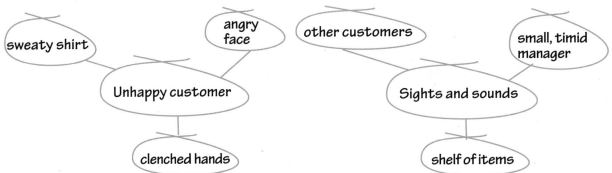

The grid below collects some possible notes on the initial ideas you might have.

Paragraph	Overall focus	Descriptive elements	Up close
1	customer entering the shop	his/her speed of walking carrying object clothing – coat	wooden crate with pet's eyes just visible
2			

3 What would you put in your second paragraph? Jot down some ideas.

Build the skills

4 Follow the same process for the task below. Pick out the key words and then jot down:

a) the main content of the task (and what you should/ should not include)

b) the descriptive elements (the things you plan to describe – for example, swings, flowerbeds, benches).

> **Descriptive writing**
> Describe a summer afternoon in a park.

Develop the skills

Another way of generating ideas is to use word associations or links to add related ideas and build each descriptive element. For example:

child chasing pigeon – *pigeon pecking in the grass – flies up in old man's face – green grass – scared face*

> **Top tip**
> Look back to Topics 4.9 and 9.1 for help if you need to.

5 Note down linked words or phrases for each of the following.

a) children with football – *shouts...*

b) water fountain – *stone basin...*

c) old men playing chess – *square table...*

6 Now consider how you can look at your descriptive task in an original or unusual way. For example, think about the shop task: how would the description change if:

- the shop was one from 100 years ago
- the shop sold very unusual, out of the ordinary objects
- the customer complaining was a small child
- the shopkeeper was someone you (or your narrator) knew?

7 Choose one of these options. Write a list of key nouns or noun phrases related to the shop, the customer or the shopkeeper or manager.

Apply the skills

8 Read the descriptive task below. Note down the key words and then generate ideas using one of the methods above.

> **Descriptive writing**
> Describe someone exploring an underground cave.

Check your progress:

▲ I can generate basic ideas for a descriptive task.

▲▲ I can generate a range of ideas and choose one that is original or striking.

Structuring description creatively

Descriptive writing is about creating a vivid picture through your choice of words. It is also about how, and in what order, you reveal that picture.

Explore the skills

Look at the following task:

> Describe someone's impressions of a new town or city.

There are several ways you could approach structuring a response. You could look at it through *time*:

- Has the person just arrived or are they *arriving?* (For example, you could describe their impressions as they come into the city on a train.)
- Are they just waking up in a new place, ready to see it in the light? If so, is it dawn – or when?
- Could the impressions be at different times – for example, as they wake up, then later in the day?

Alternatively, you might decide to structure your description according to *place*.

- Are you describing the whole of the city – the cityscape?
- Could you describe different locations (a café, a busy crossroads, then a peaceful park)?
- Could you contrast this new place with the one your narrator has just come from?

Here is a plan for structuring a description.

Paragraph 1: Late night: arriving by train – city lights

Paragraph 2: My first view of the city up close as I leave the station

Paragraph 3: Dawn. Sunlight. The view from the hotel window.

Paragraph 4: Lunchtime: more to be seen from my balcony....

Paragraph 5:

1. What structural device does the plan mostly use to divide up the description?

2. Add a further change for paragraph 5.

Build the skills

Structure also relates to how you reveal details within and between paragraphs. Will you describe a whole scene? Will you focus on small, individual details?

Note how in this example below, the paragraph begins by setting the whole scene, then 'zooms in' on more precise detail.

topic sentence gives the general view

> Through the window, a row of office buildings opposite slowly come to life. A modern glass tower reflects the rising sun as the blinds are slowly lifted. One window reveals a businesswoman in a smart blue suit who sits at her desk sipping a cup of coffee, reflecting on the day ahead.

compound sentence gives a specific example of one of the buildings

complex sentence provides even more detail of what is happening in the 'glass tower'

3 Write a paragraph following a similar structure.

- In the first sentence, describe a new scene from your window.
- In the second, add more detail – what can you 'paint in' to make the place more vivid?
- In the third, describe a specific person or object connected to the scene you are describing (use a longer sentence to provide more detailed information).

Read an example of how this idea could be developed.

Top tip

Think of this technique as the 'camera' method: you zoom in from a general wide-angle view to a close-up of a particular person or object. It can give your writing a strong sense of **perspective**.

> From my hotel window, I watch as the long street lined with shops, shuttered and shut, slowly awakes [1]. At one end [2], a café's lights flicker before they illuminate fully, while at the other [2] blinds lift up on a fashion display. Here, a young girl stands outside and stares at the mannequins [3], then retreats inside and steps into the glass box. [4] Like a ballerina, on tiptoes, she reaches and adjusts an amber scarf on a pale and static neck. [5] On the pavement, a sparrow picks at crumbs in the gutter.

4 How does this response apply 'camera techniques? Link the types of camera shot below to the numbered sentences in the text.

a) wide angle

b) panning from side to side

c) long shot framing a person

d) tracking shot

e) zoom-in to close up

Key term

perspective: the particular angle or direction from which something is seen or experienced; it can also refer to someone's attitude towards something

5 Here are some ideas for a further paragraph. Match each one to the type of camera shot.

crumpled can of fizzy drink on pavement	long shot framing one thing
school student on bike cycling past	zooming in
sun coming up over distant hills	panning from one side to another

6 Put these ideas together to create your own 'zooming-in' paragraph. Begin with the wide-angle view before narrowing to a close-up.

Develop the skills

It is important to be clear in the way you link or sequence words, phrases or sentences. Prepositions can help you.

Prepositions can indicate the time or sequence of events, or the place or position of people or objects. The table below shows some common prepositions.

Prepositions of time	Prepositions of place/position
on, in, at, since, for, before, to, past, from, til/until, by	in, at, on, by, next to, beside, near, between, behind, in front of, under, below, over, above, through, across, towards, onto

7 Identify the prepositions of time or place in the examples below. Note down what each preposition tells us.

a) Through my window I see the row of office buildings opposite come to life.

b) … a businesswoman in a smart blue suit sits at her desk…

c) … a cafe's lights flicker before they illuminate fully…

8 Here is a further paragraph from the city scene. Copy and complete it, adding appropriate prepositions.

The sun has risen and… the dawn the quiet hush of the morning has been replaced by the bustle of life… the lamppost a little mouse sniffs and scurries past… the yellow light splutters and goes out. A jogger runs… it, and screams in fright… running off… the street to her waiting car.

Conjunctions are also useful in descriptive writing. Conjunctions that indicate events happening concurrently (at the same time) can stop you from slipping into telling a story. For example:

> A modern, glass tower reflects the rising sun **as** the blinds are slowly lifted.
>
> At one end, a café's lights flicker before they illuminate fully, **while** at the other blinds lift up on a fashion display.

9 Rewrite each pair of sentences below, using a conjunction to make them a single sentence.

  a) The fisherman hauls in the nets. The small fish slither free.

  b) The businesswoman stands up. Her first visitor enters the room.

Apply the skills

10 Write two or three paragraphs in response to the task below.

> Describe a street market as it opens up for customers.

Checklist for success

✔ Decide how you will structure the text as a whole.
✔ Use camera-style techniques to control the perspective.
✔ Use linking words and phrases to sequence your ideas.

Check your progress:

I understand how different structures can help me organise my work.

I can use a range of structural devices at whole text and paragraph level to enable the reader to follow my perspective clearly.

Using the senses and imagery in descriptive writing

Explore the skills

Imagery is the creative use of words to create sensory pictures in the mind. **Similes** and **metaphors** are both types of imagery. Images play a key role in bringing your descriptive writing to life. The senses are also very important to descriptive writing. Good descriptions often evoke sounds, smells, textures, sights and tastes.

Here are two good examples of imagery in description:

- The man's hoarse voice was like a **broken brick on sandpaper**. (simile)
- The child's fingers on mine as I opened the door were **tiny splinters of ice**. (metaphor)

1 Make notes on the following questions.

a) What different senses does each description appeal to?

b) What is particularly effective about each description?

Key terms

simile: using *like* or *as* to compare things

metaphor: which describe one thing in terms of another

Build the skills

The best imagery is about choosing your ideas carefully.

- The man's hoarse voice **was like flowing honey**.

2 Read the beginning of each description below, then decide which of the similes fits best with what is being described.

a) The customer's angry words hit the manager like a *soggy towel / sharp whip / bowl of warm rice*.

b) His powerful serve crossed the net like a *speeding missile / gentle butterfly / hovering helicopter*.

3 Now have a go yourself.

a) *The light burst through the wide gap onto the floor like...* (add your simile; think of a liquid)

b) *A narrow... of light shone onto the floor.* (add your metaphor; think of something thin, nasty and sharp)

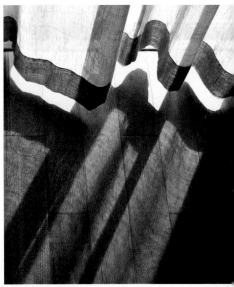

Develop the skills

The best descriptive writing combines images to create an *overall effect*.

> The midnight lake shone like a huge, silver brooch, and around it, in the swaying grasses, glow-worms glittered like miniature diamonds. A cool mist frosted my skin. The moon, which hung from the sky's dark neck, was an enormous locket which I felt I could reach out and touch. I was poor in terms of money but living in such a beautiful place, I was like the richest prince on earth.

4 a) Identify the three similes and two metaphors in the text.

   b) What *main* sense do these images appeal to? What other senses you can identify?

   c) What links all these images together? (Is there one overall comparison or **analogy** being made?)

Here is another paragraph on a different topic.

> There was a wild rush to get to the front to see the band. Like bees racing towards their favourite lily, we sped towards the stage. From the sides of the arena, other people swarmed over the barriers like soldier ants or a tide of beetles swallowing up the space.

5 Look at the three possible final sentences below. Which fits best with the paragraph above? Why?

   • I was a tiny leaf swept up in a huge, unstoppable storm.
   • I felt like a leader of an army.
   • I was a shark speeding through the water.

Apply the skills

6 Write your own description (100–125 words) about a journey into an unknown town or city. Create a mood that suggests the experience is like enjoying a delicious feast.

Key terms

analogy: a developed comparison between two ideas

Check your progress:

 I can use the senses and imagery in my descriptive writing.

 I can select from a range of sensory ideas and imagery to create the greatest impact.

Narrative writing: structure and detail

Narrative writing needs:

- a strong opening to hook the reader
- a complex, interesting narrative (the events are told in an original way)
- a carefully managed ending (that fits with the story as a whole)
- detailed description and ambitious vocabulary used when appropriate.

Explore the skills

Look at the following task, which you came across in Topic 9.1.

> 'Although it was almost midnight, I heard the sound of footsteps approaching our house. I opened the door...'. Use these two sentences to start a story.

How can you respond to this task, fulfilling the requirements of narrative writing listed above?

1. Think about creating an interesting narrative. This means writing the start of a story that will engage the reader. Copy the table below, then add more ideas to the right-hand column.

Who is approaching?	A stranger in the house?
	Another member or members of the family?
Who are 'you'?	Are you a teenager in a house like your own?
	Or are you someone else, older, an adult?
Why has the person come to the house?	To meet someone?
	To reveal a secret?
	To steal something?
What will happen next?	An argument?
	A chase?
	A mysterious event?
What might have happened earlier?	Other visitors?
	Someone watching the house for weeks?

You may have come up with lots of ideas, but now make your key decisions (for example, who the person is and why they are there). Bear in mind that the more original the idea is (without it being ridiculous), the better the story will be.

2 Make your key decisions based on the table you created in Task 1.

Build the skills

A good narrative often:

- uses flashback (the writer recalls or goes back to an earlier time)
- includes a surprise and/or suspense (things are not as they first appear)
- withholds information (does not tell the reader everything at once).

The beginning of the narrative is a vital element. It will shape and form what follows, including the use of these techniques.

3 Here are two potential openings to the story. Decide which one uses the techniques above.

> Although it was almost midnight, I heard the sound of footsteps approaching our house. I opened the door. In front of me stood my brother, Paulo. He had gone missing ten years earlier and although he had changed, I knew it was him.

> Although it was almost midnight, I heard the sound of footsteps approaching our house. I opened the door. For a moment, I peered into the darkness. Was there someone there or not? I took a step forward and a hand grabbed my shirt.
>
> 'You?' I gasped.
>
> Suddenly, I was five years old again, playing in the yard, making a mess, making our mother yell at me.

4 Using the second example, note down your own ideas for what happened to the brother. Consider the following questions.

- Did he run off and get lost?
- Did he go off to find work and not return?
- Did he get into trouble?
- How old was he?
- What sort of person was he?

5 Continue the flashback from this point (writing about 100 words). For example:

> *We were always close, even though he was much older than me, but that day in the yard was the last day I saw him – Paulo. My brother…*

6 If possible, compare your flashback with a partner's.

   a) Did you come up with similar ideas?

   b) Whose works best? Why?

7 Flashbacks only really work when they have some impact later in the story. Imagine that the person at the door is the brother who has disappeared. Note down some reasons for his return – for example, he is in trouble and needs help.

Develop the skills

Good stories work towards a **climax**, when everything comes together in a dramatic moment, followed by an ending that resolves or completes what has occurred, for good or bad. For example:

Stage 1: grab reader's attention	Mysterious stranger at the door turns out to be brother, Paulo.
Stage 2: development or complication	Flashback – why he left, has returned because he is penniless, living rough. Wants me to steal food for him from the cupboard. Makes me promise not to tell parents.
Stage 3: climax	Parents catch me and brother in the kitchen.
Stage 4: ending	They forgive him for running away – all is well.

8 This plan ends 'all is well', but the best stories often contain twists – something surprising – in their conclusions. What could be the twist or unexpected ending here?

9 Read these two endings and complete one of them with a final twist, or come up with a completely new ending of your own.

> My parents hugged my brother, and we all sat down around our small wooden kitchen table. My father poured us all some water with lime juice. Then my brother sighed, 'I have something else to tell you.' He got up, went to the door and opened it…

Key term

climax: the most interesting or exciting point in a story

Top tip

Look back to Topic 4.10 to remind yourself about the basic five-part story structure.

As we sat there drinking lime water, I looked at my brother again as he raised the glass to his lips. There was something wrong – something not right…

Another way in which you can organise and structure a story is through your use of sentences – and in particular, your use of tenses. For example:

I am waiting here, hoping to be rescued. I remember how it all began – the moment when I decided to explore the caves.

present progressive

present simple

past simple

The use of the two present tenses plunges us straight into the action. The past tense sends the reader 'back in time' to how the narrator got into this position.

10 Which of the sentences below would fit both grammatically and in terms of making sense? Think about where the writer is taking us – forward, back or keeping us in the present.

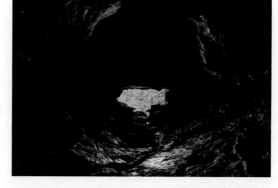

a) It had been a glorious day – perfect for exploring.

b) It is a glorious day – perfect for exploring.

c) It will be a glorious day – perfect for exploring.

11 Now, imagine that the trapped narrator begins to think of the future – he dreams of escape. Use future tense forms *(I am/he is going to or I/he/they will/might/may*, and so on) to write the next paragraph. Begin:

I try to think about the future. How someone…

Apply the skills

12 Now return to the original task ('Although it was almost midnight…') or think of an entirely new story of your own. Plan and then write the first draft of your narrative piece. It should be 350–450 words long.

Check your progress:

- I can plan and write a story which has an effective plot.

- I can plan and write a story using a range of techniques to engage the reader's interest and sequence my ideas in an interesting way.

Narrative writing: characterisation

You will not have much space in which to tell your story, so you need to balance dialogue and description, and use language cleverly to reveal characters.

Explore the skills

It is important that you *show*, rather than *tell*, the reader about a character or situation. For example, your story may hinge on the actions of a bored child that lead to a dramatic event.

Which of the following examples is more interesting to read?

> Mina was bored. She spent all day in her room thinking about what to do.

> Mina lay on her tiny bed staring at the ceiling. She had already counted the rows of dull, fading flowers on her wallpaper and had read her tatty school book three times. She sighed heavily and listened as her bedside clock ticked slowly.

Top tip

When implying character and context, small details can reveal a lot: for example, tatty school book implies that Mina is perhaps untidy and disorganised as well as bored!

1   The second example not only implies something about Mina's character – that she is bored – but cleverly shows her being bored. How is this done? Note down answers to the following questions.

   a) What is Mina doing?

   b) How is she acting? What details add to the overall tone?

Build the skills

Try not to spend too much time on just one part of your story. You must create a *balance* between the different elements. For example, if you spend too much time on Mina bored in her room, you might not have enough space to write what this makes her do. A good plan might look like this.

Introduction:	Mina is bored in her room.	75 words
Development and complication:	Flashback: she's been sent there for not doing her homework. She climbs out of window, tries to find her friend's house but it is dark and she gets lost.	150–175 words
Climax:	She is chased by someone or something and cornered; it turns out to be her father, desperate to find her.	100–125 words
Resolution:	Back at home, she now finds her room a comfort.	75 words

2　Complete the section about Mina in her room using 35–40 words.

Develop the skills

Dialogue can help bring your story and characters to life.

3　Read these two dialogue extracts, then complete the improved version.

First version

'Well, Mina, I have to say that I'm very disappointed in you because you haven't done your homework so I'm really, really cross,' said Mina's mother angrily.

'It's not my fault I haven't done it, you know. It's because I've been helping with Granddad. So, I don't think that's fair,' replied Mina stubbornly.

Improved version

Mina knew she should have done her homework, but she sat down with a thump and...

'I'm very disappointed, Mina,' said her mother, angrily turning her back and starting to wash the plates.

Apply the skills

4　Write your own narrative in response to this task or complete the story about Mina:

'The Escape' – write a narrative with this as a title.

Checklist for success

✔ Keep the conversation simple; make it reveal something about the characters.

✔ Make sure that the speech is broken up with action or description.

Check your progress:

I can create main characters in a well-organised plot.

I can create interesting characters through a range of effective techniques.

Practice questions and sample responses: composition tasks

Key skills

You will need to show the following skills when answering composition questions.

Descriptive writing:

- Generate a range of interesting ideas, including ones from an unusual or original perspective.
- Include vivid details, using the senses to express what is felt or experienced.
- Use imagery or other techniques to create a strong impact.
- Organise your description in interesting ways, through time, place or a combination of both.
- Use a variety of 'focusing' techniques to move from wider overviews to close detail.
- Link ideas structurally through prepositions, conjunctions, and so on.

Narrative writing:

- Generate a range of interesting plots, including ones with unusual forms of narration.
- Use structural or organisational devices such as flashbacks or changes of tense to engage the reader.
- Create compelling and engaging characters.
- Use dialogue accurately and to add meaning and impact to your stories.

Your task: descriptive writing

1. Read the following descriptive writing composition task. Then write a response of 350–450 words.

> Describe a hidden or secret place.

Exploring responses: descriptive writing

Now read this example response to the task.

Response 1

The secret place I enter is through a tall hedge. There is a door with a large handle and when I pull it, the door opens slowly. Through the door, the garden opens up and I can see, feel, hear and smell so many things.

> clear opening sets the scene but with no sense of where the garden is or how the writer got there

The first thing to attack my senses is the smelliness of the flowers. It is almost overpowering and hits me in a great wave. I am not sure I like it all that much, but the discovery of the garden is so amazing that I control myself and continue walking. It's just so amazing.

> use of the senses to convey feeling

Now I see old trees bending down over me with curved branches like old men's arms which seek to grab me. I push them to one side and find I am standing on a stone bridge over a sparkling stream. There are lots of fishes to see.

> use of imagery, if a little unoriginal

All around the garden is the tall hedge, like a box, and inside there are lots more hedges creating a maze-like effect. I feel like I am inside a game and don't know where to turn. Now I am not sure of the way out so I go back the way I came over the little bridge and past the old man trees. But I cannot find the door.

I look up above and the sky is a brilliant blue. Birds from the garden, ones I don't recognise – they don't look very nice or friendly – well, they swoop down and peck close to me. I think they are some sort of seabird, which seems strange because we are not near the sea. The grass by the path is like a green blanket, soft and inviting, so I sit down while I consider what to do next.

Now the smell of the flowers is really getting to me. They are so sickly and suffocating. It is surely time for me to leave so I go to have another look for the door, which will let me escape. This time, miraculously, it is there.

> intriguing idea that could have linked to the game concept, but not really fully explored

I feel like Alice in Wonderland waking up but I haven't been asleep so this is not a dream. I will come back to this garden again if it is still here.

Feedback

While the response presents a clear and vivid picture, there is something lacking here. There is little sentence variety and the descriptions, though easy to visualise, are sometimes a little dull and repetitive given the possibilities. Ideas are suggested but not fully developed. There is evidence of original thought, but it never quite gets going. Having said that, this is a more than competent response that does have imagery, control and a fluent structure.

2 Identify three further things in this response that could be improved. Use the 'Excellent progress points' on page 240 to help you.

Now read this second sample response.

Response 2

At the top of my parents' dull, grey apartment block is a set of iron stairs that lead onto the roof – or so I thought. The metal sign warns, 'No entry – danger,' so I can't tell you what gets into me that afternoon when I decided to climb them. — change of tense correct?

Forcing open the heavy trap door, I stepped into another world. For there, facing me was the most lush, luxuriant — good variety of sensory adjective
garden I have ever seen. An arch, twisted round with the delicate fingers of fragrant pink roses confronted me, and — zooms in, using imaginative metaphor
beyond was a matted walkway, sprinkled with sand, like golden paper. — effective simile, if not the best comparison

As I took my first tentative steps, the tinkling sound of tiny fountains at either side rose up, like a thousand mini- — excellent, original simile
orchestras tuning up. They glimmered as water spouted from sculptures. Below, the sound of the brutal city streets continued. Cars snarling like wild cats. People chattering like monkeys. I am at peace. Away from it all. — short sentences provide effective contrast

Yet there was more. Off the main pathway were further — new topic sentence and connective links to new description
routes. I explored each in turn, each revealing a new delight. Down one, a hammock swung between bamboo trees, as if its owner had just disappeared. Down another, were rows of tiny flowers I didn't recognise, which seemed newly planted. I had no idea what was watering them but despite the intense tropical heat they were thriving.

How could I have missed this place? Who created it? Whoever it was must have realised that we all need an escape from the speed of everyday life. This was a real oasis, not a mirage. It felt like mine, as if I was the first explorer.

My dreams were broken by a melody interfering near my side. I glanced down at the pathway railing. On it, a row of tiny bluebirds, six or seven, I can't recall exactly, sat like a little choir, chirping out their song – just for me! I reached down and one hopped onto my hand and tilted its head as if checking me out. Then, in a flash of blue it was gone and so were the others. Perhaps they'd heard something.

focused attention on physical movement adds to atmosphere

I suddenly felt like an intruder. Time to leave. Will I tell my parents? I felt like I wanted to keep the place to myself, like a dream which you think you will ruin if you reveal it.

feelings of the writer

I closed the door behind me. Immediately it was as if the garden had never existed. Below I could hear the sounds of couples arguing in their apartments, pots bubbling in kitchens, televisions blaring out.

excellent list of details provides contrast at distance

I was back in the real world.

effective single sentence paragraph to conclude

Feedback

This is an excellent piece that really conveys the setting and atmosphere of the garden. The description is built up very well, with each paragraph developing what has gone before or taking the reader down new pathways (literally). There is a real variety of vocabulary and imagery, although for the answer to be improved it would need to be inventive and perfectly matched to the desired atmosphere. We also get a real sense of the 'interior voice' of the writer and his or her feelings. Occasionally it feels as if the description is going to spill over into storytelling but fortunately that does not occur. Very occasionally, too, tenses are a little insecure, although overall the account is consistent in this respect. The use of sentences is excellent, with shorter sentences used for effect. All in all, a very impressive piece.

3 Identify three further specific features of this response that are an improvement on Response 1.

4 Using the responses and feedback in this topic, and the 'Excellent progress points' on page 240, evaluate your own response and improve it where you can.

Your task: narrative writing

 5 Read the following narrative writing composition task. Then write your own response of 350–450 words.

> Write a story that begins with you overhearing a phone call which is meant to be secret.

Exploring responses: narrative writing

Read the example response to the task below.

Response 1

I was on the stairs in the middle of the night when I heard the phone call. It was a very hot night and I couldn't sleep and needed a drink. I was coming down the stairs, rubbing my eyes, when I saw my father by the phone. He was speaking quietly and he had his back to me so he couldn't see me. The hall is long and narrow so there was no way he could spot me.

'He mustn't find out. Have you got that?' my father whispered.

I could not tell if he was worried or angry, but I began to ask all sorts of questions to myself. Who was 'he'? I was the only boy in the house, so it must be me. My father and mother had been acting quite secretively, it was true. They seemed to be whispering to each other all the time.

'I realise this is the best time to phone, but be careful. Don't call again. I'll call you,' my father said.

Be careful about what? Was my dad involved in something bad? Had he got into debt? But why hide it from me?

The next day, I watched my parents carefully. But they didn't give anything away. I even followed my dad to the train station one morning before going to school, but nothing strange happened.

In any case, my mind began to think about other things. It was my birthday at the weekend. That was when it all made sense! Of course, my dad had been talking to someone about my present! He wanted to keep it secret from me. But why speak to someone in the middle of the night? That was still weird.

good use of questions, but we need to find out more about the narrator

The day came. I opened my presents which were what I'd asked for – like a new bike but no real surprises. Then my dad said he needed to pop out to get something – and could I help him? I said yes of course.

Suddenly, we seemed to be going to the airport. What was going on?

Our car pulled up at the short stay parking. I saw someone walking towards us. No. It couldn't be! It was! It was my older sister who had emigrated to America five years ago. She had come back just for my birthday. So that was why my dad was talking in the middle of the night.

'Hello, little brother!' she said, hugging me.

needs detail or imagery to create pictures in the mind

good, concise ending that shows us how close they are

Feedback

The structure of this response is clear, achieving a balance between dialogue and events, although it ends very suddenly. The characters are clearly drawn but they are not described in any detail. There is a lack of imagery and sense of location or setting, and rather too much 'telling' of information to the reader rather than 'showing'.

6 Identify three further things in this response that could be improved. Use the 'Excellent progress points' on page 240 to help you.

Now read the second sample response on the next page.

Response 2

I heard my older brother Fabrice's hushed tones as I walked past his room. The door was slightly open, a shard of light slicing the air, and I could see him, in his tracksuit, sitting on the edge of his bed, speaking on his mobile

good opening tells us how brother is speaking

'No way, man. I can't do it! You got me?'

realistic speech and good characterisation

Fabrice sounded anxious, upset. What was going on?

Suddenly it went quiet. The call was over. I heard footsteps padding over the floorboards coming towards me. I froze. My brother opened the door wide.

'What you doing? Listening, huh?' he said, angrily. He pushed me up against the wall, his eyes sparks of fire.

'No – well – I heard something, but I didn't understand,' I replied worriedly. 'I mean…', I didn't have time to finish.

a bit repetitive and not really a proper word

'Keep it that way!' He slammed the door.

That weekend we were at a big athletics meeting at Wood Park. My brother was a brilliant runner and he was the favourite for the 100-metre race. It was mid-afternoon, the sun baking the sandy track. He was prowling about beside it, like a caged cheetah, his muscles rippling in his back. In his own world. But then, just before the race began, the cheetah seemed to melt away. I saw him talking to a gang of older boys. One of them – a thin, pale boy with a ring in his nose – grabbed him by his white vest. The boy poked a finger into Fabrice's chest. What about those muscles, Fabrice, I asked in my head? You don't have to take this!

good 'showing' rather than 'telling'

But next I knew, Fabrice was coming towards me. He had tears running down his face, but walked straight past.

Something got into me. Maybe a little bit of that cheetah spirit. I needed to know what was going on. So, I followed them. Hid out of view while they gathered behind the old pavilion, smothered in graffiti, smears of white and red. Tears, they looked like. I heard it all.

Soon I was back in the grassy arena, and tracked my brother down. He was tying up his running shoes – left shoe first, always the same routine.

'I know what is happening,' I told him. 'You mustn't lose the race. It's not right!' I added, as forcefully as I dared. He didn't look up, just paused and then moved on to the other shoe, meticulously folding the perfect white laces over each other.

He stood up, stared for a moment into the distance, at nothing it seemed…

Before I knew it, the race had begun. At first my brother was a long way behind. But that was his usual style. His strength would batter through in the last 30 metres. But he'd left it late. Too late, surely? He was going to lose because of that gang, because someone wanted to fix the race for a bit of cash. But no… I was wrong. Suddenly he was surging through! It was like he was in his own corridor of air, swift as the cheetah, swifter maybe. He dipped on the line. He'd won! He'd won!

Soon a man in a business suit was giving him a long red sash with a shiny medal on it. When the man had shaken Fabrice's hand, I went over.

As I approached I saw the gang of boys walking over too. They did not look happy at all.

'What are you going to do?' I asked.

Fabrice put his arm around my shoulders.

'Guess we'll just have to face the music together, won't we?' he said, gripping me tightly.

this is the climax but it is over too quickly

good ending – resolves situation between brothers but leaves us wondering too

Feedback

This response demonstrates good characterisation by showing characters' individual actions and contrasting ways of speaking. There are also some nice pieces of descriptive detail, but more is needed. Elements of the plot are a bit unbalanced: there could be more suspense at the climax (for example, would Fabrice lose the race deliberately or not?).

7 Using the responses and feedback in this topic, and the 'Excellent progress points' on page 240, evaluate your own response and improve it where you can.

Check your progress

Sound progress

- I understand what a task is asking and can select a form I can write competently.
- My understanding and planning of the task shows that I know what the form is and have some ideas for my response.
- I am able to use basic sentence structures in descriptive texts.
- I can use some imagery to make my writing memorable.
- My stories contain the main structure of introduction, development, climax and ending.
- I can sequence stories clearly and use simple sentence structures and vocabulary.
- I can include easily understood characters and a recognisable setting.
- I can include all the main elements of a story with equal balance.

Excellent progress

- I can think creatively of detailed and original ideas for my chosen task before I start.
- I can use a range of structural devices to enable the reader to follow my perspective.
- I can select from a range of imagery and sensory ideas to make my writing memorable.
- My stories contain the main structure of introduction, development, climax and ending, and include features such as flashback, twists and holding back information.
- I can manage elements such as the climax and ending well, fitting them to the story in a way that satisfies the reader.
- I can use complex, but appropriate and varied sentence structures and ambitious vocabulary for effect.
- My characters are clearly drawn, detailed and believable with the right balance of dialogue and action.
- My settings and descriptions are vivid and interesting.

Approaching written coursework 10

Your coursework assignments will give you the opportunity to explore ideas at length, and to select unusual or original ways of responding, giving your own views on your experience of the world about you. One assignment will be written in response to a non-fiction text.

Coursework assignments are a real chance to impress! You will have time to experiment with different viewpoints, structures and time sequences, to try out unusual forms and to develop characters in detail.

This chapter takes you through the different assignment possibilities, allowing you to develop your skills.

You will write *three* assignments:

Assignment 1: writing to discuss, argue and/or persuade in response to a text or texts
Assignment 2: writing to describe
Assignment 3: writing to narrate.

You will need to focus on these writing skills:
- articulate experience and express what is thought, felt and imagined (W1)
- organise and structure ideas for deliberate effect (W2)
- use a range of vocabulary and sentence structures appropriate to context (W3)
- use register appropriate to context (W4)
- make accurate use of spelling, punctuation and grammar (W5).

For Assignment 1, you will also need to use your reading skills:
- demonstrate understanding of explicit meanings (R1)
- demonstrate understanding of implicit meanings and attitudes (R2)
- analyse, evaluate and develop facts, ideas and opinions, using appropriate support from the text (R3)
- select and use information for specific purposes (R5).

Links to other chapters:

Chapter 3: Key writing forms

Chapter 4: Writing for purpose

Chapter 8: Extended response to reading and directed writing (directed writing sections)

Chapter 9: Composition

Developing personal writing

Your coursework assignments give you a wonderful opportunity to reflect at length on ideas and issues, as well as to find your own personal 'voice' and to write about your own interests and experiences.

Explore the skills

Writing personally can mean writing honestly about your own thoughts and viewpoints, developing a style of writing that is your own, or choosing titles or tasks that interest you. Read the two examples below – both of them are descriptive accounts of childhood memories.

A

The Thought Tree

There, under the huge, curving branches of the willow, I would lie with my back against the knotty trunk, staring up at the clouds that flickered through the leaves, forming and reforming themselves in greys and whites.

This is the place my dreams and hopes began.

B

The Worst School Bus Ever

Let's be honest – the ride was <u>not</u> pleasant. I'm talking thirty smelly eleven-year-olds; I'm talking a rickety old bus hitting every pot-hole in the road; I'm talking being squashed at the back with my nose pressed like a squashed tomato against the greasy windows. What fun!

1 What differences do you notice in:

   a) the subject matter chosen by each writer?

   b) the style and mood each creates?

Build the skills

Writing does not need to be entirely truthful to be personal – for example, the bus might not have 'hit every pot-hole', but when you draw on something detailed and concrete from your own life, you can embellish it to create an impact.

2 What impression do you get of each writer in the two extracts?

3 The style of each example is quite distinctive. Which style do you think is closest to your own? What 'childhood memory' would you choose to write about?

Develop the skills

To express ideas that sound convincing and have impact, you need to be able to sustain and develop them. Exploring ideas in detail shows your reader that you have fully engaged with the subject.

Here is part of a plan for example A above.

> ✓ The old willow – me sitting under it – the clouds.
>
> ✓ The tree in more detail – its setting at the end of the garden.
>
> ✓ My life at that time – why I used to go there.
>
> ✓ How I stopped sitting there as I grew older and made friends.
>
> ✓ The tree now – or how I imagine it now we no longer live there.

4 The writer uses 'change' as a means of developing and extending their ideas.

   a) What personal changes do they include?

   b) What change in time do they refer to?

This structure of beginning with a core idea then developing it works equally well for persuasive writing. Below is the start of some notes about the influence of social media.

> My memories of my first mobile phone and how I felt.

5 How could this account be developed? Think about:

   • the same idea of change due to getting older

   • adding linking ideas related to other aspects of social media in the writer's life.

Apply the skills

6 Think again about a childhood memory you would choose to write about. Make brief notes about:

   • what your title and focus would be

   • what details you would include

   • how you could develop or sustain the account (for example, through changes in time)

   • what impression you would like to give the reader.

Check your progress:

⬆ I understand how personal ideas can help my writing.

⬆⬆ I can consider some personal ideas and apply them to writing tasks.

Approaching Assignment 1: Writing to discuss, argue and/or persuade

For Assignment 1, you will write in response to a text or texts you have read.

Explore the skills

You will:

- explore the ideas in the text/s
- express your own views on the information and ideas you have read about
- write in a particular form, such as a news article, a speech or a letter, and for a particular purpose.

What topics or issues interest you? You could consider:

- personal or local issues (for example pocket money, traffic issues in your neighbourhood)
- wider issues or ideas (for example, your thoughts about nature, wildlife, the older generation, gender issues, cultural ideas).

1 Note down ideas about all the different things that interest or concern you. Then draw up a short-list of key areas.

2 Choose one or two of the topics from your list and think about how you would:

- find articles or other forms of writing about them
- research information (facts, statistics and other ideas).

Which of the following would be particularly useful for you?

- looking in the local newspaper or local news website
- looking in national newspapers or magazines
- using general online search engines
- talking to, or interviewing, people
- finding data or statistics online or from printed reference books or records.

Build the skills

In this type of writing, you need to show your ability to *evaluate* ideas or arguments in a text.

3 What does 'evaluate' mean? Think about each of the definitions below. Which one best matches what you will need to do?

- Give your clear viewpoint on the topic you have chosen and give supporting evidence.

- Explain the different arguments on the topic as a whole without giving your personal view.

- Reflect on the different ideas given and make a judgement about whether they are convincing or not, before giving your personal view.

Develop the skills

Once you have evaluated the key ideas in a text, you need to respond to them in a specific form. Imagine that you have chosen as your issue the subject of ebooks versus printed books. You have found an interesting article about the revival of printed books.

Here are three possible forms that your own writing could take:

- a letter to a bookshop owner about the issue of ebooks
- a speech to 11–12 year olds about the topic
- a newspaper article in response to the article you read.

4 For each of the three forms above, note what conventions you might include. For example:

> **Top tip**
>
> Look back at Topics 3.1, 3.5 and 3.6 to remind yourself of the conventions of speeches, articles and letters.

Letter to bookshop owner	Speech to children	Newspaper article
opening salutation – formal: *Dear Mr...* first paragraph – explaining reason for writing	welcome introduction using 'we' to draw students in	

Apply the skills

5 Think again about a topic that interests you. Create your own task – like the ones above – that allows you to evaluate the ideas and express your own viewpoint.

Topic: …

Article that I will respond to: …

Form of text I will write in response: …

Conventions required: …

Check your progress:

↑ I understand the main requirements of Assignment 1.

↑↑ I can apply what I have learned about Assignment 1 to make my work more effective.

Assignment 1: Responding to a text

When writing to discuss, argue or persuade, you will need to select information, evaluate it and adapt it for your own purposes.

Explore the skills

Imagine that you have decided to explore the issue of ebooks and printed books, and have found the following article. How will you respond to it?

Vocabulary

Mintel: a company that carries out market research

pc: per cent (%)

How printed books entered a new chapter of fortune

by Sam Dean, *Daily Telegraph*
15 JULY 2017 • 1:26PM

It will not come as a surprise to anyone with even a brief understanding of the British high street that the number of independent bookshops has almost halved in the past 11 years, according to the Booksellers Association.

But there is hope – the book revival is gathering pace. Once seen as doomed to an ebook-inflicted death, the physical version has been creeping back into the mainstream after years of decline. Fresh research has found that sales of ebooks are expected to fall for the first time. **Mintel** predicts that ebook sales in 2017 will decline by 1**pc**. At the same time, print sales are forecast to grow 6pc this year and 25pc over the next five years.

Those gains in print sales are driving the book market in the UK, which is estimated to surpass £2bn this year, an annual rise of 4pc. In short, the tide has turned. And all of a sudden, the book business does not seem like such a daunting place to be.

[...]

"The print book revival continues as consumers, young and old, appear to have established a new appreciation for this traditional format," said Rebecca McGrath, Mintel's senior media analyst.

As ever, there are multiple theories for the return of the old fashioned book. A widely held belief is that it is a manifestation of our digital-heavy lives, where days and nights are spent staring at screens, and all we want is a moment of respite.

"Consumers are placing growing value on physical goods in a digital world," adds McGrath. "In such a connected world, many people increasingly value time when they can get away from screens. When it comes to print readers, many value the chance to enjoy some digital-free time at home."

Mindy Gibbins-Klein, the founder of publisher Panoma Press, agrees. "People spend so much time on their screens," she says. "We need a break."

For Simon Key at the Big Green Bookshop, it is more to do with the tangible nature of books, their designs and their feel.

"It is the physical book that evokes a memory," he says. "It is about seeing that book, rather than just being about the story itself. That is a big selling point. It is not just the content, it is the memories they bring back to you when you have finished reading them. You do not get that with an e-reader."

This, Key says, is one of the main reasons that consumers appear willing to spend more money on a printed book, rather than buying a cheaper electronic version. It is also why he believes more focus is now going into their design.

"We are based in one of the poorest boroughs in London and we can sell, and do sell, hardback books for £25, which is not what you would expect in an independent shop in Wood Green," he says. "It is partly because they look so wonderful that people want to touch and feel them."

Alan Staton of the Booksellers Association adds that "publishers are publishing more beautiful books and booksellers are creating more beautiful places to discover them".

The "shelfie" interior design craze, where people show off their intellect through their book collections, also adds value to the physical book. "There is prestige about people coming to see your office and books," says Gibbins-Klein, whose publishing company focuses mainly on business and personal development books.

As the leader of a firm that tries to publish their books in as many formats as possible, Gibbins-Klein sees first-hand that consumers are happy to fork out the cash for a hard copy even when other options are available. "It does not seem to be price-sensitive," she says. "People are willing to pay more."

This is backed up by the Mintel research, which says that nearly 70pc of UK consumers are happy to invest more than £6 on a hardback book, but just 17pc are willing to spend that much on an ebook.

[....]

For Key there are still "wobbles". He says: "We go through patches where we are looking at the bank statement every day to see if we can pay the bills."

The signs are undoubtedly encouraging. On a simplistic level, more people are willing to pay more money for more books. The question, then, is whether that will be enough.

From www.telegraph.co.uk

1 Begin by getting an overview of the argument. To do this, look at each paragraph in turn and jot down six or seven key points. For example:

Title: 'How books entered a new chapter of fortune' – why books are having a more 'fortunate' existence!

Point 1: Fact: number of independent bookshops down almost 50% in ten years.

Point 2: 'there is hope – the book revival is gathering pace' – Opinion: things are getting better; ebook sales are falling; print book sales rising.

Point 3: …

Top tip

Read Topics 8.5 and 8.6, which give more information about analysing and evaluating texts.

Build the skills

Next, you need to evaluate the points: to decide whether you agree or disagree with what the writer says, and add a comment of your own.

Here is an example, based on the information above. You can use the idea:

> E + E + E (*explain, evaluate, express*)

The writer of the article comments on the number of independent bookshops as being down almost 50%. This may be true, but the assumption that this is down to ebooks may be mistaken. For example, research shows that viewers of e-sports has 'exploded from 204 to 292 between 2014 and 2016' (source: bigfishgames.com). I would argue that people are just choosing other ways to spend their leisure time – not just on ebooks.

explains the key idea (from paragraph 1) from the article *in own words*

draws on *personal research/ evidence* to *evaluate* how accurate or important the information given is

expresses own view based on the evaluation

The table below contains one of the points from the article and a suggested response from a student (you do not have to share their view!).

Point/quotation from text	Meaning or implication	Agree	Disagree
'there is hope – the book revival is gathering pace'	Ebook sales are falling and people are buying more print books – this is a good thing!		

2. Copy and complete the table, adding the points from the list you made in Task 1. You do not have to agree *and* disagree but, as in the model paragraph on page 248, you must evaluate the points.

Develop the skills

The text you have to write about may be chosen by your teacher, or you may be given a choice of related texts to choose from. Whatever the text is, you should:

- draw on any conventions related to that text type
- use language that matches your purpose (this relates to **register** – which will show that you are able to express your ideas appropriately)
- write in the role you have chosen or that has been assigned to you
- draw on any additional information or research you have done. (For example, how many bookshops are there left in your local town or city? How many of your friends use e-readers like Kindle or smartphones to read books? Do they buy books from online retailers?)

Top tip

Additional research can really help in this type of writing task. Use the internet, books, magazines and newspapers to find out more about the topic. If appropriate, go out in your local area and find out more. This can help you to personalise the task.

Top tip

To remind yourself about voice and formality/informality, look back at Topics 2.9 and 2.10.

Key term

register: the level of formality in a piece of writing

Look at the two example assignments below.

> You are an avid reader and feel very strongly about what you have read in the article. Write a response to the editor of the newspaper in which you argue for or against the changes described.
>
> You can respond in any form you wish – for example, through an article or a letter.

> Give a speech to younger students at your school in which you discuss a topical issue that might affect them.
>
> In this case, the issue will be the importance – or otherwise – of printed books.

3 Decide which of these two pieces you would prefer to write. Start by thinking about your own opinion on the topic or your own experiences of printed books or ebooks.

4 Now, plan your response. (Look at Topics 8.5, 8.6 and 8.7 for more information on planning and writing this type of task.) Take into account the points you have selected and commented on. Remember, you will need to:

- begin with an appropriate introduction that fits the type of text and audience (for example, *Thank you for letting me talk to you today about…*)
- use clear paragraphs to explore each point and comment on it
- end with a conclusion that expresses your view – and, if relevant, calls for action.

For persuasive writing, you need to use:

- rhetorical questions or statements (*Surely it is not the case that…?*)
- powerful, emotive language (*incredibly sleek machine*)
- repetition or lists (*no cover, no paper, no turning of pages*).

Top tip

Remember, the three 'e's:

- *Explain* the points in your own words.
- *Evaluate* the points or information either as they stand, or in relation to other evidence or research you have.
- *Express* your viewpoint.

Apply the skills

5 Write your article, letter or speech. Remember that it must be 500–800 words, so make sure you comment on each point fully.

Check your progress

⬆ I can develop a clear and effective response to a given passage.

⬆ I can express my ideas on a given passage thoughtfully, and for deliberate effect.

Approaching Assignment 2: Writing to describe

For Assignment 2, you need to produce a piece of descriptive writing that creates a convincing atmosphere.

Explore the skills

It is likely that whatever type of description you choose to write, it will involve some of the following elements:

- a particular setting or building (for example, a wintry beach, a magical tower)
- weather or natural event (for example, mountain storm, heatwave in the city)
- an event or experience (for example, a birthday party)
- a person or group of people.

1 Which of these ideas would you choose to describe? Why?

Build the skills

Whatever the task, your descriptive writing should:

- create a convincing picture offering depth and detail
- provide a variety of focuses, for example using 'camera-style' techniques – zooming in on detail or widening out
- create a vivid or powerful atmosphere, mood or setting
- use well-chosen imagery, sensory language and sentence variety to bring the description to life
- have a clear structure: this could be chronological, or include a change of mood, setting or perspective
- include details that 'show' rather than 'tell' the reader about the scene or a character's feelings

2 Review your understanding of each of these key features – are you clear what each one refers to? If not, read Topics 9.3 and 9.4, which show you how to structure description effectively.

Develop the skills

Successful descriptive writing often shows individuality. Here are three extracts, which all demonstrate distinctive styles of description.

For bleak, unadulterated misery that **dâk**-bungalow was the worst of the many that I had ever set foot in. There was no fireplace, and the windows would not open; so a brazier of charcoal would have been useless. The rain and the wind splashed and gurgled and moaned round the house, and the **toddy palms** rattled and roared.

From *My Own True Ghost Story* by Rudyard Kipling

We wandered along intersecting avenues, until we came to one broader than the rest, at the end of which stood a little house. Tiny streams flowed round and about it, flowed under its walls and into its rooms; fountains splashed ceaselessly in front of it, a soft light wind swayed the heavy folds of the patterned curtains hanging half-way down across its deep balconies.

From *'In Praise of Gardens'* by Gertrude Bell

My mother was the archetypal Cockney sparrow and was much loved by all the family. She was small, but moved quickly, possessed a sharp wit and considerable intelligence. Her school reports were excellent: the family Bible was just one of several prizes she had won. No tradesmen ever managed to cheat her, although some tried – she could always add up faster than they could!

From *From Stepney to St Tropez* by Peter Gould

Vocabulary

dâk: a traveller's rest-house

toddy palm: a type of tree which produces a sort of wine

3 Which of the features in the list on the previous page can you identify in each text?

4 What is distinctive about each of the texts? Think about:

- the narrative viewpoint (who, if anyone, seems to be speaking)
- the use of tenses or time
- the mood or atmosphere created.

Apply the skills

5 Think of one memorable person, one memorable place and one memorable event. Which would you choose to write about? Make notes about your choice, trying to visualise as much detail as you can.

Check your progress

 I understand what the requirements of Assignment 2 are.

 I can apply what I have learned about Assignment 2 to my work.

Assignment 2: Writing a descriptive text

Your descriptive text does not have to be based on your own personal experiences, but it may help to draw on places or people you know. You can then adapt or develop the setting or character to make it even more memorable.

Explore the skills

Look at the table below, which shows some notes in preparation for a piece of descriptive writing about 'a memorable event or experience'.

Event – the opening match of the season between my team and another	
Ideas	Developed
• went with my family – big football fans!	• perhaps just go with my mother
• lovely sunny day	• holding her hand
• sat halfway up the stands	• wintry, cold day?
• next to a boy like me	• imagine we are at ground level by the side of the pitch – can bring in all the action from the game
	• next to… an old man in a wheelchair

1. How has the original idea been developed?

2. Why might the writer have suggested these changes? Think about some of the key ideas in description, such as:

   • having a focus or different focuses

   • creating convincing, vivid pictures

   • use of change or contrast.

3   Now, think of your own memorable experience. Remember that this is a descriptive piece – you should not create a *story*, you should focus on what you or your narrator sees and hears.

a) Jot down your original idea (like the one on page 254, based on personal experience if possible).

b) Develop it to make it more interesting or allow for a tighter focus (it is often better to focus on a specific individual or individuals in a description rather than just describe broad groups).

Build the skills

Take the same idea of an exciting event or experience. The notes below begin to build the ideas from the table on page 254.

sight: huge, cubed, silver floodlights

touch: my child hand holding my mum's hand

sound: roar of fans, songs and chants

Football match with my mother

smell: wafting scent of hot coffee and tea from flasks

> **Top tip**
>
> Chapter 4 and Topic 9.2 show you how to generate ideas for your descriptive writing. This might involve using the senses to build ideas.

4   Create a similar sense diagram for your choice of exciting event or experience (you could consider a music gig, a ride at a funfair, getting caught in a tropical storm – or whatever you can think of, real or imagined).

Remember that whatever description you write, you need to sustain it over 500–800 words. To achieve this, you will probably need seven or eight key ideas – and each one of those needs to be well developed.

> The huge, cubed floodlights, flashing silver in the early evening, captured the lines of rain that fell across their glare. The rain slanted down, turning the white lines by the pitch in front of me from straight, neat stripes to a blurry mess. Players slid or crashed into the hoardings or slipped over, like clowns – except it was not deliberate.

5 How has the description of the floodlights been developed? Think about the highlighted sections:

- what aspect of the weather the floodlights lead to
- what feature of the pitch is then described
- what people/characters are then brought into the picture.

6 Take one aspect of your chosen exciting experience and develop it in the same way.

- Begin with one focus.
- Lead into a second.
- Add a third.

Develop the skills

Because this is coursework writing, there are many styles and approaches you can take (see Topic 10.1).

7 Look at the descriptive pieces below and on page 257. What do you notice about the different forms, structures and uses of language they adopt? Make notes on each, perhaps jotting down what you like, or would like to use in your own writing.

A

> Dusk: mothers with children dragged behind, raced by, their feet pitter-pattering through the thin, grey puddles. The neon lights at the crossing blinked and winked like naughty schoolboys and red buses screeched to a halt to let passengers tumble off.
>
> Dawn: empty streets. A single starling sat on a lamp-post high above the pavement, opened its little beak and sang out. But no one except me heard.

B

> Slowly now
>
> The sea's tide creeps by
>
> Along the valley of the sandy dunes,
>
> Eats up the level land, the grassy marshes,
>
> Swallows, spreads and covers all with water.

C

Supper is a riot. Ma stands at the top of the long table, dispensing chicken and cous-cous from a huge pot, while six pairs of hands shout 'Me first! Me first!'. Hot, fruity sauce dribbles down the ladle while plates clatter and battle for attention.

D

The old man in the corner shop has a face like a wrinkled map; it creases when he smiles, and unfolds when he sits back on his wobbly stool to have a nap. When he opens his palm to take my money, his fingers are like bent twigs as they grasp the coins. He wears a tatty red beret and a scratched medal hangs from his jacket: a war hero I wonder? Or something he has acquired?

8 Now, imagine that you have been given the following task:

> You have just spent your first night in a new town or city. Describe your surroundings and feelings as you awake.

  a) Do any of the structures and styles you have just looked at appeal to you?

  b) Would any of them *not* be suitable?

  c) Can you think of any texts you have read that could provide inspiration for your own work?

  d) What other original or interesting ways could you structure or present your ideas?

9 Using the skills you have learned here, and through your reading of Topics 9.2 and 9.3, plan a response to the task, considering how you will apply descriptive writing features effectively.

Apply the skills

10 Complete the first draft of your descriptive response. Remember that in your coursework, your draft will be handed in with your final piece, so make sure that you use it thoughtfully to improve your work.

Check your progress:

⬆ I can create an effective response to my chosen descriptive task.

⬆⬆ I can create an original and distinctive descriptive piece.

Approaching Assignment 3: Narrative writing

Assignment 3 is a great opportunity to tell a compelling and original story of your own. You will be able to draw on your own reading, as well as on new ideas that you develop as part of the coursework process.

Explore the skills

It is important that your chosen narrative has a well-defined, engaging plot with interesting characterisation. How can you achieve this?

Look back at the five-part story structure described in Topic 4.10. Then look at this palette of characters, locations and general plot ideas.

a one-armed shop-keeper

a brilliant young pianist

a father whose children have all left home

a highly successful businesswoman

a small hut by a lake

a border crossing-point

a luxury penthouse flat

a huge hall in a castle

a peaceful forest glade

a palace made of ice

a tale of revenge

a journey of discovery

a secret revealed

a terrifying experience

an unexpected relationship

a sad memory

1. Create three stories based on or inspired by these ideas. Share your ideas with others, then amend or add to your original plots to improve them.

Build the skills

As well as the core content (the main plot ideas and characters), you will also need to consider how to make your work original and interesting. Spend some time exploring original ways of telling or structuring your work.

Read this example narrative task:

> Write a fictional or autobiographical account of a secret that is revealed with an effect on others.

As well as the core content, there are several narrative choices you can make. For example:

Form	Narrative voice(s)	Style or mood
short story	first person narrator	formal and/or informal
diary or diary entries	third person narrator	reflective
letter(s)	multiple narrators	dramatic, and so on

2 Copy the table, then add any other forms, voices or styles you can think of.

Top tip

You could even mix the styles according to character – for example, an elderly 'posh' character might speak in a more formal way than a teenage tearaway!

Top tip

If you are not sure what each of these narrative choices refers to, look at Topics 4.10, 9.5 and 9.6 for more information about narrative writing.

Develop the skills

Here is a set of choices based on the idea of a secret revealed.

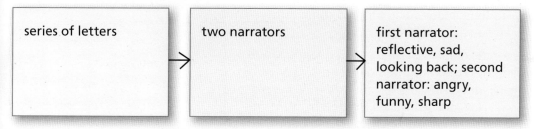

series of letters → two narrators → first narrator: reflective, sad, looking back; second narrator: angry, funny, sharp

3 Using the task above, or one of the storylines you developed earlier, make your own choice of narrator(s).

Apply the skills

Assignment 3 rewards boldness and originality.

Complete the plan using the following steps:

- Write out your chosen storyline clearly (from the opening to this lesson).
- Underneath it, write out clearly your choice of narrator(s).
- Add any further details that come to mind (name of character, more detail on place...).
- Evaluate the idea – is there anything you could change or improve to make it more original or striking (change character, add a twist or surprise to the storyline)?

Redraft your plan as needed.

Check your progress:

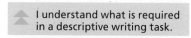

I understand what is required in a descriptive writing task.

I can apply what I have learned about descriptive writing to consider a range of options for success.

Assignment 3: Developing narrative writing

In Topic 10.6, you explored some of the broader choices available to make your story engaging and effective. Now remind yourself of some of the skills that narrative writers employ to achieve such an impact.

Explore the skills

What makes an interesting account and interesting characters? In this extract, the novelist John Braine explores the process that should go on in your head when you *imagine*.

Let us consider another example of how not to write. I made it up, but it's an absolutely typical passage from any unpublished novel and I have seen passages like it in more than one published novel.

'Tom walked over to the window. The sun had come out. He went upstairs and awakened Hilda.'

This is remarkable for the number of questions it doesn't answer. How did Tom walk over to the window? Slowly? Briskly? What did he see through the window? How did he go upstairs? What did he notice on the way? How did he awaken Hilda? If he went into the bedroom, what did she look like when she was asleep?

You don't just walk over to the window in a novel. Walking is a physical action and every physical action is revealing. And the sun doesn't simply come out in novels. *Had come out* is three dead words. Nothing is seen. But what happens in real life is that the sun, in shades from pale yellow to bright orange, is reflected from water, from windows, from car reflectors; it brings out the colour of the grass and the trees and the flowers; it makes new things look newer and old things older. What has happened isn't a general unremarkable fact, but a physical happening in the specific place you're writing about, seen by a specific person.

[….] And how does Hilda sleep? If it doesn't matter, then Hilda doesn't matter. Does she smile or frown when she's awakened? Or grunt? Is she easy or difficult to awaken? And what does she look like when she's asleep? What does Tom feel when he looks at her?

From *Writing a Novel* by John Braine

1 What advice do you think is most important from this passage? Why? What will you pay attention to in *your* story?

Build the skills

One piece of key guidance from John Braine is that you must 'show' not 'tell'. You cannot completely avoid giving information, but generally it is better to show a character's personality rather than tell the reader what sort of person they are. For example, *She was a lonely old woman* is better expressed as: *The old lady sat in the rocking chair staring sadly out of the rain-swept window.*

 2 How is this achieved in the following extract?

The snake and Ántonia

I was walking backward, in a crouching position, when I heard Ántonia scream. She was standing opposite me, pointing behind me and shouting something in **Bohemian**. I whirled round, and there, on one of those dry gravel beds, was the biggest snake I had ever seen. He was sunning himself, after the cold night, and he must have been asleep when Ántonia screamed. When I turned, he was lying in long loose waves, like a letter 'W.' He twitched and began to coil slowly. He was not merely a big snake, I thought – he was a circus monstrosity. His abominable muscularity, his loathsome, fluid motion, somehow made me sick. He was as thick as my leg, and looked as if millstones couldn't crush the disgusting vitality out of him. He lifted his hideous little head, and rattled. I didn't run because I didn't think of it – if my back had been against a stone wall I couldn't have felt more cornered. I saw his coils tighten – now he would spring, spring his length, I remembered. I ran up and drove at his head with my spade, struck him fairly across the neck, and in a minute he was all about my feet in wavy loops. I struck now from hate. Ántonia, barefooted as she was, ran up behind me. Even after I had pounded his ugly head flat, his body kept on coiling and winding, doubling and falling back on itself. I walked away and turned my back. I felt seasick.

Ántonia came after me, crying, 'O Jimmy, he not bite you? You sure? Why you not run when I say?'

From *My Ántonia* by Willa Cather

Vocabulary

Bohemian: a native or inhabitant of Bohemia – in the present-day Czech Republic

3 Make brief notes about:

    a) what we are told about Jim, his feelings and behaviour

    b) the impression we get of Ántonia, through what Jim says and how she speaks and behaves

    c) the way in which the excitement of the event is conveyed to the reader.

4 Does the extract pass the John Braine test? In what ways? Note down effective aspects of the text. For example: How did Jim move? (*in a crouched position* and *whirled round* show his care, and fear – he wants to protect Ántonia)

Develop the skills

Look at the task below.

> Write a narrative piece in which the following words appear: 'I knew we didn't have long…'

5 Using what you have learned about generating ideas and planning for narrative writing, make notes about how you might approach the task.

- Start by coming up with ideas suggested by the title – for example, who is 'I'? Why don't they 'have long'? You could use a spider diagram, a list of ideas or any other method.

- Construct a 'well-defined' plot, using the five-part story sequence outlined in Topic 4.10.

- Consider settings you might use, but do not have too many.

- Decide on your main character or characters.

- Think about where the given sentence will come in the story.

6 Next consider the variety of ways you could *tell* the story. Think about:

- the form or text type

- narrative voice(s)

- style and/or mood.

7 Finally, create a story table like the one below that captures all your decisions. Leave the third column blank for now.

Features	Details	Change or improve?
Who is the story about?		
What is the basic (five-stage) plot?		
What will be the main setting or locations?		
What form will it be told in?		
Who will tell it?		
In what style/mood?		

8 Review your decisions and the story you have planned. Is there anything you could change or improve to make your story or characters more distinctive? Complete the last column of the table.

Apply the skills

9 Write your first draft.

As you do so, go back to John Braine's guidance and look again at what makes Willa Cather's account successful. You should not copy what she has done, but use it as a template for good writing – memorable characters, situation and action.

10 Now consider what might need improving or changing. Remember that your draft will be handed in with your final piece, so make sure that you use it thoughtfully to improve your work.

Check your progress:

I can create an effective response to my chosen narrative task.

I can create an original and distinctive narrative piece.

Drafting and improving your work

Coursework assignments give you the opportunity to hone and improve your ideas – and perhaps most importantly, the way you express them.

Explore the skills

What do you think will be the biggest challenges you face when writing your coursework assignments? Think about what you have done well previously, and what you have found more challenging.

1 Copy and complete this self-evaluation checklist.

Skill	Not a problem	Could be better	Needs a lot of work
Using or adapting the basic conventions of particular text types (for example, speech, letters, news articles)			
Using an appropriate range and variety of vocabulary			
Getting basic grammar right			
Organising or sequencing work so it is clear to follow – using paragraphs effectively, using linking words			
Punctuating work for clarity and meaning			
Spelling correctly			

Explore the skills

2 Use your completed table to identify areas that you might struggle with in your coursework.

Build the skills

You will have the opportunity to redraft your work and improve it.

First – check the *overall structure* of your text:

- Is it logical? Does it create impact in the right places?
- Are you able to follow the argument, story or description without getting confused? Look again at your plan and try shifting ideas around.

Second – check for *technical accuracy*: do not get 'caught up' in the flow of the text but instead look at each word individually.

Third – identify *individual problem sentences or paragraphs,* and start to redraft them. For example:

First draft

> There, under the branches of the tree I would lie with my back against the notty trunk. I stared up at the clouds. They flickered past through the leaves. They changed themselves in greys and whites. This is the place my dreams and hopes began.

Final version

> There, under the huge, curving branches of the willow, I would lie with my back against the knotty trunk, staring up at the clouds which flickered through the leaves, forming and reforming themselves in greys and whites.
>
> This is the place my dreams and hopes began.

3   What changes has the student made between the two versions? Think about:

- any change in vocabulary (see the reference to the clouds)
- the end of the paragraph (what effect is created by separating information like this?)

4   In what ways does the final version work better than the first draft?

Apply the skills

5   Review the three-stage proofreading process outlined in Topic 2.8, and make notes to ensure that you are clear about what you need to do.

Check your progress:

I understand what the drafting and proofreading process requires.

I can apply my drafting and proofreading skills to my own work.

Coursework-style tasks and responses

Assignment 1

Key skills

In Assignment 1, you will need to show the following skills:

- demonstrate understanding of explicit meanings
- demonstrate understanding of implicit meanings and attitudes
- analyse, evaluate and develop facts, ideas and opinions, using appropriate support from the text
- articulate experience and express what is thought, felt and imagined
- organise and structure ideas and opinions for deliberate effect
- use a range of vocabulary and sentence structures appropriate to context
- use register appropriate to context
- make accurate use of spelling, punctuation and grammar.

Your task

Read the task. It is based on the article in Topic 10.3: 'How printed books entered a new chapter of fortune'.

> You have read an article about a topical issue. Write a response to the article giving your views on the issue and arguing your case. (In this case, the article explores the revival in the sales of printed books.)

1 Identify the key requirements of the question.

Exploring responses

Read the following extract from a response to the task.

Response 1

This response is a letter to the editor of the newspaper that published the article. Read the opening to the response, and consider in what ways it meets the criteria for a letter arguing a case to the reader.

Dear Sir,

I read the article about print and ebooks in your paper. The writer states how 'the book revival is gathering pace' and how sales of ebooks are going down. This makes it sound like this is a good thing as 'revival' means coming back to life. But I think this makes it sound like ebooks are really bad, and I don't agree.

The writer also mentions someone who says, 'consumers, young and old, appear to have established a new appreciation for this traditional format.' But I am not one of them. I do not wish to go back in time to old books as they do not fit in with my lifestyle. Who wants to lug a great big old mass of paper with them? Not me.

Another point that the writer makes is that people are sick of looking at screens all the time. They need a 'respite' which makes reading ebooks sound like an illness! However, I do not feel ill when I read an ebook. Lots of ebook electronic devices have screens that do not affect your eyes as much as the usual ones, so I don't agree there.

The writer says it is 'to do with the tangible nature of books, their designs and their feel. It is the physical book that evokes a memory'. This is rubbish – I don't agree.

Annotations:

- clear opening, but a little blunt – could give more of an overview
- comment on use of words and what this implies
- clear viewpoint on issue but not developed
- short sentence creates persuasive impact
- effective rhetorical question
- paragraphs used for each new point of discussion
- some development from the student's own personal views
- viewpoint clear but no argument – and no detailed comment on the point made

Feedback

This response provides a clear view of the writer's opinions. However, points from the article have not been evaluated in any depth and no additional research is referred to.

2 Identify three things that could be improved in this response. Use the 'Excellent progress points' on page 275 to help you.

3 Rewrite the final paragraph of the response so that it works more persuasively.

Now read an extract from a second sample response.

Response 2

This response to the task is in the form of a speech to children aged 11–12 about print books versus ebooks. This is the opening of the speech.

I am delighted to be able to talk to you all about one of my favourite things – books! Now, you might not think this is a big issue – everyone loves a good book! – but you'd be wrong. You see, for the last few years people like you have been choosing to read ebooks rather than the paper ones. There was a real danger that printed books would die out – but, thankfully, it seems this is not the case.

a suitable opening that refers to the audience

slightly informal register is suitable here

explains point in own words

The reason I am talking to you is that I read an article recently which said that for the first time for many years, ebook sales were going down. Print books were having a 'revival'. This sounds like they are coming back to life, and that's wonderful news. Can you imagine a world without brightly coloured covers and paper you can flick through? Boring, dull and deadly.

comment and viewpoint clearly expressed in same sentence

rhetorical question skilfully uses visual detail

pattern of three hammers home the point

paragraph for new point

The article also stated that we all spend too long staring at screens, 'day and night' and we need a break. I agree – I get fed up of staring at my phone or my tablet; the light from the screen really hurts my eyes. Research has shown that people who have work roles involving substantial screen time are more likely to suffer sleep problems, headaches and similar issues. It seems clear that staring at that rectangular white space can't be good for you.

effective personal reference

Another important point from the article which I want to share with you is that experts believe people like the 'traditional format' of books. I think this is a good point. Tradition is very important, isn't it?

viewpoint clear but this is an assertion – no evidence or support provided

Feedback

This is an excellent response, well-suited to its target audience and offering a clear point of view on the topic. It makes use of language devices effectively, including rhetorical questions, patterns of three and personal experience. It could be slightly improved by adding evidence for the final assertion, but overall this is an effective, engaging opening to a speech.

4   Look again at your response to this task from Topic 10.3. Using the responses and feedback in this lesson, and the 'Excellent progress points' on page 275, evaluate your own response and make improvements where you can.

Assignment 2

Key skills

You will need to show the following skills:

- articulate experience and express what is thought, felt and imagined
- organise and structure ideas and opinions for deliberate effect
- use a range of vocabulary and sentence structures appropriate to context
- use register appropriate to context
- make accurate use of spelling, punctuation and grammar.

Your task

Read the task, which you began to explore in Topic 10.5.

> You have just spent your first night in a new town or city. Describe your surroundings and feelings as you awake.

Exploring responses

Read the extract from the response below.

Response 1

From the top floor of the hotel I saw a tangled network of dusty streets and sand-coloured buildings topped with red or brown roofs. I heard a symphony of sounds, like the clatter of cattle and the distant horns of cars and trucks which weaved between the crowded inhabitants. There were cyclists and motorbikes too, dodging in and out of the crowds, stopping, then going again. No one waited for the traffic lights, although all took notice of the police officer in white gloves waving people past. From the dawn onwards it seemed this place is a hub of noise and activity.

Later I went back to my apartment as the evening faded and the baking sun slowly slid down over the edge of the city. But nothing stopped and the city never slept. Just new people appeared. New cars and workers going to night-time work. Everything seemed jumbled up like whoever built the city just threw all the buildings up in the air and let them fall on the ground as if playing a game.

I was really nervous about my new job but decided I needed to welcome my new life.

- good 'long shot' of the city
- opens up the possibilities of description
- vivid sensory details and vocabulary
- close up detail provides focus
- new paragraph good for switching time
- repetitive vocabulary

Feedback

There are some details picked out and some precise use of vocabulary, but this response begins to slip into a narrative towards the end.

1. Identify three specific things that could be improved in this response. Use the 'Excellent progress' points on page 276 to help you.

Now read this extract from a second sample response.

Response 2

The City is an Ocean

I wake to the sight of a huge, silver eel. It is the highway which curls around the coral buildings, suffocating the little roads and paths, like tiny minnows. It growls and snarls and swallows onrushing vehicles and throws them out again, forever hungry and never satisfied.

- very expressive and original opening metaphor/image
- present tense suits description

In offices, I can see sharks patrol the corridors in business suits, their jagged words cutting down their enemies. Smaller fish – little frightened crabs – scuttle into rooms to avoid their bosses and cower behind doors or under desks, afraid they'll be netted. The shark's narrow eyes settle on a useless bloater, a slow-moving salesman who failed to hide. He's not been selling much so the shark snaps him up and sends him home, never to return.

> inappropriate word choice – sharks can't 'patrol'?

> clever link

> metaphor cleverly extended and developed

> perhaps too literal – him being sacked?

Above the city, I look up and see the sky is another ocean. It is serene, still and deep blue. It reminds all fish of other peaceful worlds, where no nets come and food is free.

> change of focus

Back on the streets below, my eyes pick out married couples and friends who cling to each other like sea-urchins, wrapping their fronds and spines around each other's bodies. They sway along the pavement in the breeze, fearful of being swept up by the tide of time. It's only six hours till work begins again.

> excellent simile and vocabulary choices

Slowly as I settle to my new surroundings, the waves sleep and the eel settles too. It eats but now more slowly. Half-watching, waiting, ready for the rush of the new day.

> structurally links end to the beginning

Feedback

This is an outstanding response, which is both original, engaging and effective. The structural decisions, splitting the description into different views and times, help the reader visualise the scene.

2. Using the responses and feedback in this topic, and the 'Excellent progress' points on page 276, revisit the plan and the draft you made for this task in Topic 10.5. Make any changes to the plan that you need, then write a final version.

Assignment 3

Key skills

You will need to show the following skills:

- articulate experience and express what is thought, felt and imagined
- organise and structure ideas and opinions for deliberate effect
- use a range of vocabulary and sentence structures appropriate to context
- use register appropriate to context
- make accurate use of spelling, punctuation and grammar.

Your task

Read the task, which you began to explore in Topics 10.6 and 10.7.

> Write a narrative piece in which the following words appear: 'I knew we didn't have long'.

Exploring repsonses

Now read this extract from a sample response, which comes from the end of the narrative.

Response 1

Stranded by the sea

So we were stuck and it was all Carla's fault.

'I didn't want to come to this stupid cave in the first place,' I said.

Carla didn't say anything. We both felt so cold and I could see the water levels creeping up. We huddled on a ledge but it was very narrow and we weren't sure if it would be high enough. — good detail but more description would help

Then something stirred in the surface of the water. — good use of suspense

'What's that?' Carla screamed.

'I don't know.' I replied. — speech punctuation error

There was another movement, and then a sort of hand reached up for our ledge. It looked like a young woman's hand as it has slim long fingers. Then slowly the rest of the person emerged from the grey-looking water. It was a beautiful lady with long, flowing hair, like a doll.

I had no idea how she got there, because the water was so cold no one would survive for long. The huge waves were now crashing into the cave's entrance and I knew we didn't have long. — sensory detail

'Come,' the woman said, holding out her hand.

'I'm not jumping into that!' Carla stated.

'If you do not follow me, you will die, it is your choice.' Said the woman. —— punctuation needs correcting
Then she added. 'I know a tunnel under water, but you must trust me, you
need to hold your breath for a few seconds.'

I took one look at Carla and jumped. Then the water hit me like a slap —— good attempt at imagery
in the face from an ice-block. Then I was underwater and to my shock
I saw what the woman looked like. She had a tail of a fish which was
shimmering green and blue. —— narrative twist, but perhaps more could be made of writer's shock
Perhaps the cold water was blinding me and I couldn't see properly that
would explain it.

Next I heard Carla splosh into the water too.

Feedback

The structure for the story seems clear and easy to follow.
However, there are several errors of punctuation, tense and
grammar. In places, there is some effective description, but the
ideas are only partially developed.

1 Identify three specific things that could be improved in this
response. Use the 'Excellent progress' points on page 276 to
help you.

Now read this extract from a second sample response. This time it
is the opening to the story.

Response 2

The shrinking land

I knew we didn't have long. Now the sand had shrunk to a tiny —— excellent first line plunges the reader right into the action
area of about two metres square around me. The cold easterly
wind howled and in the dark I could no longer see my fellow —— good use of sensory details
fishermen.

They say that when your life is under threat your past flashes
before your eyes. In my case, all I could remember was my wife's
face that morning when I left. —— use of flashback to set scene

'You don't have to go out on the sands. Everyone says it's
dangerous,' she told me.

We were standing in our one-room hut; the baby was crying,
and the electricity meter had run out. The radiator was cold as
stone, and I could feel the icy winter draught sliding through the
gap under the door.

'I do,' I told her. 'We have no money.'

She was right of course and perhaps now I wouldn't see
her again. I thought of my fellow fishermen and women —————— rather repetitive
and wondered if they knew the sands and tides better than me. vocabulary
Perhaps they were safe at home now with their families.

I looked for a light or any sign of life. Where was the beach?
There was no moon or stars to guide me, but I had to
move or I'd be dead. I plunged waist up into the swirling ————— excellent use of
water, hooked around me like some ghastly grey snake, imagery
and headed in a straight line.

But the water rose even further. Now it was at my chest!
There was nothing for it: I just dropped my baskets of fish –
the fish that paid my paltry wages – so that I could swim. I
felt utterly miserable. Even if I survived I would lose my job.
I didn't like the gang boss, the smug man in the expensive ————— concisely expressed charac-
coat who'd picked me out of the line of men looking for work, terisation
but I needed this. Yet if I came back with no catch they would
get rid of me. Discard me like an unwanted bit of useless
seaweed.

I imagined my wife and baby. My son with his sharp, blue eyes – like ————— use of short sentence for
the little pebbles on the beach. I had to make it for them. impact

Suddenly I saw a light! A hazy oval shimmering and dipping up
and down. It pulled me like a magnet towards and it, and finally I
felt hope – surely I could survive now? We would see in the next
few horrible minutes.

Feedback

A very effective response, with well-developed ideas and a
highly effective characterisation and content.

② Using the responses and feedback in this topic, and the
'Excellent progress' points on page 276, evaluate the
response to this task that you drafted in Topic 10.7. Then
write the final version of your response.

Check your progress

Assignment 1

Reading

Sound progress

- I can include relevant ideas from the text.
- I can begin to explore simpler and more explicit ideas and say whether or not I agree with them.
- I can write a response that is appropriate to the task, using some of the correct conventions and voice required.

Excellent progress

- I can fluently pick out ideas from the text and explain them.
- I can explore and offer my views about implicit and explicit ideas from the text.
- I can write a response that uses my own research and experience, and which shows a high level of understanding of the issues discussed.

Writing

Sound progress

- I can write in a way that gets my views across and engages my reader.
- I can usually organise my ideas into a clear sequence.
- I can sometimes use powerful words.
- I can sometimes choose the words and tone that match the purpose and audience of my text.
- I can use generally accurate spelling, punctuation and grammar.

Excellent progress

- I can write in a way that gets my meaning across very precisely and powerfully.
- I can organise my writing carefully so that it helps my reader to understand my ideas.
- I can select words carefully to create precise meanings and effects.
- My choice of register is effective and suits the purpose and audience.
- My spelling, punctuation and grammar is almost always accurate.

Assignment 2 & 3

Writing

Sound progress

- I can choose ideas and details relevant for the task.
- My organisation is straightforward and my writing feels purposeful and complete.
- I use some precise vocabulary and a range of sentences sometimes chosen for their effect.
- My register is sometimes appropriate for the context.
- My spelling, punctuation and grammar is generally accurate.
- I can describe objects, people and scenes by using helpful details (descriptive writing).
- My plot is suitable and ideas link together (narrative writing).
- I can create characters and settings that are interesting (narrative writing).

Excellent progress

- I can write in a way that is interesting for my reader.
- I organise my writing so that it has an effect on the reader.
- I use well-chosen vocabulary precisely, and vary my sentences for effect.
- My writing makes it easy for the reader to imagine people, objects or scenes (descriptive writing).
- I can write stories with a clear sense of development and characters and places that are convincing (narrative writing).
- My spelling, punctuation and grammar is almost always accurate.

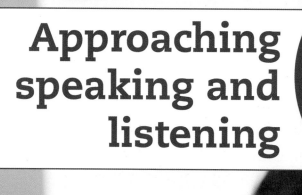

Approaching speaking and listening

11

You use your speaking and listening skills all the time and to succeed in employment and further study you will need to be a clear, confident communicator. As part of your Cambridge IGCSE course, your speaking and listening skills are assessed in a formal situation. This chapter will help you to build your skills both for this task and to help you communicate effectively at school and in your everyday life.

You will use your speaking and listening skills to:
- articulate experience and express what is thought, felt and imagined (SL1)
- present facts, ideas and opinions in a cohesive order which sustains the audience's interest (SL2)
- communicate clearly and purposefully using fluent language (SL3)
- use register appropriate to context (SL4)
- listen and respond appropriately in conversation (SL5).

Using the right language

Your audience is a vital consideration in any speaking and listening situation. A talk or presentation to a teacher should be in a fairly formal register. If you choose to deliver a **monologue** in the role of a character, you can speak less formally as long as that suits the character. However, in the conversation part of the assessment, you should always speak formally. Answer questions using **standard English**, rather than the casual language you might use with friends.

Explore the skills

You are going to deliver a presentation on how your school's rules should be changed. Remember the following points when working through the tasks below.

- Focus on using formal standard English.
- Use a suitable style and include content that will engage your audience.

1 With a partner, decide how you would vary your content and style for:

    a) the head teacher

    b) your classmates

    c) a meeting of interested parents.

In each case, ask yourself:

- What will they already know?
- What do I need to tell them?
- How can I put across my views most persuasively?

2 The example on the next page is part of an unsuccessful presentation. Read it, then decide what needs to be improved.

Key terms

monologue: a speech, in role, by one character without interruption

standard English: the most widely used form of English that is not specific to a particular location or region (for example, in standard English, you would say: *we **were** going* not *we **was** going* and you would use the word *argument* rather than *tiff* or *barney*)

> Thing is, nobody likes rules. They're rubbish. And the ones we have in this school are brainless. You've gotta be here to know we suffer. Man, do we suffer! Parents? They don't know nothing about stuff happening to us every day. We was told off for eating our lunch outside on the field yesterday. Maybe they thought the grass was, like, going to get worn out. Mental!

To do well in speaking and listening, you will need to be able to use standard English in your tasks. That means:

- avoiding slang or language that is too informal
- speaking in full sentences, using correct grammar
- using vocabulary that will be widely understood.

3 Deliver the speech in Task 2 to a partner, changing it to standard English that would be more suitable for an audience of parents. Alter words and sentence structures where necessary.

Build the skills

The tone you use is always important. Here is a good example of a conversation about healthy diets.

Sara: ... So, really, healthy eating is something we should all be aware of.

Teacher: I'm sure we would all agree with that.

Sara: We would, sir, but agreeing is not necessarily the same as acting, is it? After all, it is easy to say, 'Yes, let's eat more vegetables and consume less sugar', but it's much harder to apply that philosophy when we arrive at the supermarket.

Teacher: Well... aren't we all very aware that our diet is crucial if we are going to live a long and healthy life?

Sara: I guess... So... are you suggesting that fundamentally affects the products we choose?

Teacher:	Maybe... Does it?
Sara:	Perhaps... But probably not often enough. You need to consider clear examples... Like my family... or even your family... I mean... How often do you weigh yourself? Do you think your diet is healthy enough, sir...? Do you get to the shop and think... 'Mm, I'd better buy less chocolate and more oranges'. Or is it easy for all of us to accept being a few kilos heavier...

Written English can be reconsidered and reworked; spoken English is formulated moment by moment and demands an instant response. In the example above, Sara works out her ideas as she speaks ('I guess... So...') and uses part-sentences. However, she still uses appropriate English and her tone is perfect for her audience. She is thoughtful and makes points without becoming too casual or offending her teacher.

4 How does Sara make her conversation effective and engaging? Consider her use of the following features:

a) rhetorical questions

b) quotations

c) sensitive challenges to her teacher

d) vocabulary.

Develop the skills

The example below is an imaginary conversation between a student, Majid, and his teacher about transport problems. Notice how Majid sometimes struggles to use effective English, which would clarify his ideas.

Majid:	I get sick of traffic jams. Boring traffic jams.
Teacher:	It's a problem we all face, isn't it? Have you had particular problems?
Majid:	I've been stuck for hours sometimes. Ages. Take last week. Hardly moving at all. We need better roads made.
Teacher:	Was there something actually wrong with the road?
Majid:	Too true! And it's not enough to say 'ride bikes'. We need to get to places quickly. You can't cycle across the country, can you? And the trains are rubbish.
Teacher:	In what way?

Majid: They're rubbish. We need someone new in charge, if you ask me... Someone who knows what's wrong. And puts it right...

5 Rewrite Majid's words, trying to improve:
- the variety of sentence lengths and types
- the style, making it less chatty but still natural
- the details, so that the ideas are developed.

Now read this sample opening to a presentation in which the speaker talks about her favourite country.

> Greece is a place that attracts people from all over the world nowadays: in fact, some resorts are just too popular. However, if you don't want that kind of holiday, there are still secluded spots, hidden from the main tourist traffic, which remind you of what the whole of Greece was once like and even today offer an experience that will prove unforgettable. There are wonderful attractions: for example, in the tumbling town of Hora, on the island of Serifos, you can stand by the church, thirty metres above the port, look out across the sea and dream, just the way the philosophers must have done all those years ago...

6 Answer these questions, considering the speaker's vocabulary, sentences and tone.

   a) What makes this opening engaging?

   b) How does she show she has thought about her audience?

Apply the skills

7 Prepare the opening of a presentation describing your favourite place and explaining why you like it. Use an appropriate style to engage your audience, and varied vocabulary and sentences. You might include:
- a precise description of what it is like
- why it is special for you, or your earliest memories of it.

8 Now rewrite it as a monologue, recounting your first visit to this place.

Choosing and researching a presentation topic

When making a presentation, it is important to choose a good topic and research it well.

Explore the skills

Always think carefully about how to make a presentation interesting for your audience. Check that you know your topic in detail, so you will feel confident when talking and answering questions about it. If necessary, carry out research.

1 Which of these topics could you talk about most successfully? Why?

- Argue that problems caused by teenagers are sensationalised in the press.
- Advise the parents of primary school students to send them to your school.
- Explain why teenagers prefer technology to real life.

Build the skills

Once you have chosen your topic, think about what angle you could take on it. For example, it is more difficult to persuade someone that your football team is the best than it is to describe what happened during a match. You should not necessarily choose the easiest approach – a more complex one is likely to be more engaging and successful.

2 Choose one of the topics below and use notes, a mind map or a spider diagram, to explore the angles you could take on it. Remember, at the simplest level you might be arguing for or against a point.

- Some television presenters being very highly paid
- Pressure on teenagers to do well in exams
- Zoos

Read the following sample extracts from presentations, showing different responses to the same topic.

Top tip

When asked to give a presentation, try to choose a topic that will allow for a good discussion, to show your skills at analysis and debate.

Response 1

> The trip was a huge success. We met at 6:45, which was really early for most of us, then the bus arrived at about seven. I rushed straight to the back, to sit with Jenny and Asma, and a whole gang of us were on the back seat. Mind you, we didn't feel like singing that early in the morning. I swear Lucy was still chewing her breakfast when she got on …

a clear topic sentence

sets the scene

adds humour

Response 2

> I know what the reaction from most of you will be when I ask this, but… how can anybody justify a trip to a theme park in school time? And before you start, yes, I know everyone enjoys it – but what in the world does it have to do with education? Wouldn't it be better to sit in lessons during the week and go to an amusement park at the weekend? It's lovely to see the teachers having fun and running around, of course, but weekdays should be for learning…

direct address to audience/rhetorical question

an engaging approach

challenging

light humour

3 With a partner, identify what is good about Response 1. Then identify the more advanced skills shown in Response 2.

Develop the skills

If your content is not relevant, you will lose the attention of your audience. Researching your topic carefully to find the most interesting material is vital. This means being selective and finding information from different sources that suits your purpose. Avoid copying material from any source.

4 List facts about the city, town or area where you live. Make them as different as possible, to cover a range of interests. Then select facts from your list that you could use in a talk presenting the place as:

- a tourist destination
- a good place for a major company to relocate to
- somewhere deserving special government funding.

> **Top tip**
>
> Each point you make needs to be clear and precise. If the audience misses a point, they have no second chance to hear it.

Read the extract from a presentation below. The speaker chose her topic, then her approach to explain what made Muhammad Ali 'the greatest'. Note how the topic has been well researched. It is *full and well organised* and uses a *range of language devices*.

> Most boxing experts agree that Muhammad Ali should be considered the greatest boxer of all time. As Cassius Clay, he won the gold medal at the Rome Olympics in 1960, then turned professional and became world heavyweight champion in 1964, defeating Sonny Liston, the boxer everyone else feared. Clay was handsome, 'floated like a butterfly and stung like a bee', and the world loved him. However, he courted controversy. Ali refused to fight for the USA in the Vietnam War. He had his title taken from him...

5 With a partner, discuss the following questions.

a) How many facts does the response above include?

b) How does the speaker use the facts?

c) What is the main point?

d) How does the speaker try to make her audience interested in Muhammad Ali?

The presentation on Muhammad Ali:

- offers facts that give a clear picture of what was happening
- indicates what was special about him
- gives an impression of why he was such a great boxer
- only includes facts relevant to the main topic – Ali and why he was outstanding.

Even a fairly everyday topic, such as school rules, can be made more interesting by including:

- statistics (for example, how many rules are broken)
- survey results (for example, how students feel about particular rules)
- comparisons (for example, with other schools).

Top tip

When planning a presentation, remember that each detail needs to support your overall purpose. Finding the facts is just the start. What counts is how you use and develop your ideas around them.

Apply the skills

6 Prepare a talk for your class on your favourite hobby. Complete a table like the one below, which is about running.

Points you would select	Why you would choose the points	How you would develop the points to show their effects or go into more detail
Running is healthy.	health issues important at any age	how much weight I lost/how my life changed as I became healthier
15 million British people run.	pleasure/competition/feeling of well-being	age no barrier: Constantina Dita became world marathon champion at 38; Buster Martin ran in the London marathon aged 101

7 Now make notes on possible angles for the presentation about your hobby. For example, is it unusual? Does it help you in other areas of your life? Could you ever make a career of it?

Structuring your presentation

In a well-structured presentation, the speaker knows what they are going to say and in what order. In particular, you will need to think about the different ways to begin, develop and end your presentation.

Explore the skills

1 Imagine that you are going to give a presentation about your favourite school subject. First, list the points you might make, then put them into a logical order. For example, you might group points as follows:

- how it is taught
- why it particularly appeals to you
- how it could help you in the future.

Think particularly about how you would begin your presentation and how it might end.

You should plan your ideas in detail, then summarise them so they fit on a cue card that you can refer to when giving your presentation. Remember that you will only be talking for about four minutes.

2 Complete a table like the one below to develop your ideas. Add more detailed information to the right-hand column. Then, using your plan, run through what you would say.

Main idea	Points to be included
teachers	Miss Spivey (brings cakes to school)
	Mr Jenkins (simply adores volcanoes)
lessons	lots of videos
	drama improvisations about other countries
trips	include field trips, camping

> **Top tip**
>
> Planning a presentation is similar to planning an essay. However, when you are talking, you can develop ideas on the spot and interact with your audience, using different tones of voice and gestures.

Build the skills

Your *opening* sets the tone for what follows. It should make it clear what you intend to talk about. It should also immediately engage your audience.

Some possible techniques to use in an opening include:

- rhetorical questions: *Have you ever wondered why the sea is salty?*
- relevant humour: *We recently learned about the Leaning Tower of Pisa – not to be confused with pizza...*
- powerful facts: *The 1933 California earthquake killed at least 115 people.*

3 Use the techniques above to write three interesting openings for the presentation about your favourite school subject.

Develop the skills

Your choice of ending will depend on your topic and purpose. Try to make a powerful impression using one of these techniques:

- a summary of your argument
- a joke
- one final, convincing point
- a rhetorical question.

4 Use one of these techniques to write a conclusion to a talk on why it is important for schools to have history lessons.

5 Write an alternative ending to the history-lesson talk using one of the other techniques listed above.

Read this example conclusion to a presentation about a favourite subject.

> Anyone coming to our school should look forward to doing Maths. We really do have the best teachers. The equipment and books are all new. What is more, the way they present the subject makes it fun from the start to the finish. And they manage to find things to do outside the school, so we get away from our desks for a while. The Maths department really could not be any better. It's my favourite subject, and I bet it will be yours.

6 Rewrite the conclusion above to improve it.

- Organise the material more effectively so that the ideas develop more logically.
- Add more detail and comment appropriately.
- Rephrase or rewrite where necessary to leave the audience with a memorable idea.

Apply the skills

7 Plan a presentation to persuade your local community to donate to a charity supported by your school.

- Make a plan in bullet points and add details.
- Prepare what you are going to say to open and close the presentation.

Engaging your audience

Including imagery and repeating key words or phrases will help you to emphasise important points. Careful use of humour, rhetorical questions and exaggeration will appeal to listeners.

Explore the skills

Read the following sample extract from a presentation. The speaker has chosen to do a monologue, in role. The response is in standard English, but it has been enriched by imagery and repetition.

> I curse that man – Prospero! – and everything about him. He demands and he demands. Always craving more. He holds himself like a god and wields his power as if he even ruled the world. As if he would be worthy to bow and crawl at my mother's feet; as if he would be worthy to sit at her table; as if, were it not for the sprite who does his bidding, he could look down on me today. He is mendacious. He is truly the serpent on this island...

1 Identify the imagery and repetition in the extract.

a) Comment on each example and its effect.

b) 'Always craving more' is not a conventional sentence. Why is it used? What effect does it have?

2 With a partner, discuss why each example you have found is appropriate for the purpose.

Build the skills

Read the following extract from a sample presentation spoken in role as Miranda from *The Tempest*.

> My father is a wonderful man. He does everything in his power to keep everything under control and he has led a very difficult life. He has so much trouble with Caliban, because he behaves so badly, and my father simply has to discipline him. It seems that punishment is all Caliban understands...

3 Rewrite this extract to improve it, adding imagery and repetition.

Develop the skills

Rhetorical questions can be used to challenge the audience to think more actively about an issue. For example:

- 'Can this ever be acceptable?' (The desired reaction is: *Probably not!*)

4 Add two rhetorical questions to this extract to add interest.

> When we look across the world, there is no reason why we should not all work together, towards a common future. Someone from Asia is really no different from someone in Canada. We have lives that may vary and we may have different beliefs, but we are all human beings, who love, laugh and cry.

Adding humour and witty touches can encourage the audience to warm to you. Try:

- a funny anecdote (short story) to support your point, for example: 'I caught measles on holiday. Well, actually, measles caught me. What happened was…'

5 Add a funny follow-on to each of these sentences.

a) Anyone can dress well if they know where to shop.

b) I try to help my cousin.

Top tip

Exaggeration can also make a considerable impact, for example: 'Her make-up was so thick her nose was only just poking out of it'. But use exaggeration sparingly.

Apply the skills

6 Produce a presentation opening about the job you would like when you are older. Use the following techniques, underlining each example: imagery, repetition for effect, rhetorical questions, humour and exaggeration.

Checklist for success

- ✔ Use imagery and repetition in your presentation to create more of an impact.
- ✔ Use rhetorical questions, humour and exaggeration sparingly and only when suited to a topic or an audience.
- ✔ Plan in advance which of these techniques you will use.

Developing a role

You may choose to make your individual presentation in character – for example, as a fictional character or someone from history.

Explore the skills

You need to prepare in advance to create and develop a convincing character. If you have chosen a fictional character, such as the examples of Caliban and Miranda from *The Tempest* in Topic 11.4, you must be prepared to discuss their role in the novel, play or film they come from. If you have chosen a historical figure, you may be asked questions about what they hoped to achieve, or their importance in history.

In order to portray someone convincingly, you need to consider the following:

- their history: what has happened to them
- their attitudes: what they think about different issues and people
- their behaviour: how they speak to and treat others
- their relationships: with people around them
- their motivations: why they behave as they do.

1 Choose one of the following roles. Make notes about the character for each of the areas in the list above:

- an older relative
- a famous painter
- a prison guard
- a film star.

2 In groups of three, choose a character each from the list above. Introduce your character, describing your life and what has happened to you.

Build the skills

When performing in role, you need to use language that is appropriate for your character. For example, a politician will speak differently from someone who works in a burger bar.

3 Work with a partner. You are talking about whether space exploration is a waste of time and money. Take it in turns to deliver a monologue while the other listens.

- One of you is Neil Armstrong, the first astronaut to walk on the moon, in 1969.
- The other is a volunteer worker for a charity fighting against homelessness.

Before you begin, note down some appropriate words or phrases for your character.

Develop the skills

When you are in role, you need to speak clearly, but you also need to speak in the way your character would.

Read the example improvisation below. The speaker is in role as a television reporter. Notice how she speaks, giving the audience a vivid feeling of what happened at the end of a marathon, how people reacted and an impression of the sort of person she is.

> Only rarely in my life have I felt so many people united in joy: when Alexandro crossed the finish line, there was an outpouring of emotion the like of which many here today will never have witnessed. He had run the entire race in absolute agony, but was not prepared to give in, and 42 kilometres is a long, long way to suffer. As he finished, the whole crowd was cheering and many were crying. I cried too…

4 With a partner, discuss what features of her speech make it successful.

5 Continue the report, making up any details, but maintaining the tone of the reporter's speech.

Apply the skills

Choose a character from the media or real life. It could be the character you chose in Task 2. Other possibilities include:

- a leading politician
- a singer
- someone in your favourite television show
- a sports star.

6 Demonstrating clearly how they speak, deliver a three-minute speech as your character about a significant event: perhaps you have lost your job, won a medal or fallen in love.

Preparing for conversation

How you need to prepare for a conversation will depend on your topic. For example, for a conversation about teenage crime, you could research facts, figures and opinions. If you are asked for ideas to improve your local community, you might assess a range of options and then adopt a point of view.

During your conversation, you might be asked to:

- expand on what you have already said, adding details or considering other angles
- clarify facts or opinions.

Explore the skills

When preparing for the conversation about your presentation topic, think about what questions your teacher might ask, and note down any information and ideas.

1 What would you need to decide and research to give a presentation and answer questions on the topic below?

> The greatest individual the world has ever known.

Top tip

Brief notes are fine, but never read directly from them. Make sure that you do not develop them into any form of script.

Build the skills

Try to anticipate questions that you might be asked, and have the information ready. For example, if you were talking about 'My life outside school and what makes it interesting', you might have prepared information on:

- your hobbies or interests
- a job you have
- how you spend the rest of your time.

2 With a partner, decide what other details you would need to know in case a range of questions were asked on this topic.

3 List ten facts or points you would have to research about someone you admire. In pairs, take it in turns to read out your lists. Your partner should try to think of three questions seeking further information on your chosen person and why you admire them.

Look at these sample responses to the presentation topic:
What more can we do to help old people?

Response 1

I have a friend who suggests we should all think about what it will be like when we get older. If we all thought about that, I am sure we would treat old people much more kindly. It is not just about raising money for charities; it's important to be nice to old people every day.

Response 2

Obviously, it's never easy. Charities like Age Concern give out leaflets like this one, with advice, but we can't just wave a magic wand to transform the lives of old people. Nevertheless, to just give up on them isn't an option. And even little things matter. Last week, for instance, the paper boy knew my grandma was unwell and asked if she would like an extra magazine the next day…

4 With a partner, discuss why Response 2 is better.

Develop the skills

You need to be ready to answer questions following your presentation.

5 With a partner, imagine that you have given a presentation supporting the view that teachers are a school's most valuable resource. Your partner asks you questions about why you hold that view and challenges your opinions. Try to make use of some of their points and reach a compromise. Follow the example below.

> **Teacher:** But couldn't you learn just as well from an online resource?

> **Student:** Well, it's true that computers are good for revising something you've forgotten, but you need a good teacher to assess what you need in the first place.

Apply the skills

6 Working in pairs, prepare a talk responding to the following statement:

> Poor people don't want charity; they want jobs and a decent wage.

Then take it in turns to act out a conversation between teacher and student in which the student acknowledges the teacher's points and either reaches a compromise or sticks to his or her own conclusion.

Responding to talk, seeing implications and paraphrasing

During a conversation, it is important to show that you can both talk *and* listen.

Explore the skills

Effective listening allows you to absorb other people's ideas and develop new ones of your own.

Read this example extract from a group discussion about people we respect.

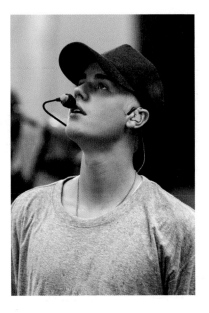

Kamal:	OK. So, you think that Justin Bieber is as important a world figure as Mahatma Gandhi?
Lucy:	He was only my age when he released his first full-length album. How cool is that?
Kamal:	That's quite impressive, but Gandhi's non-violent protest helped to secure Indian independence.
Lucy:	Well, I think celebrities can do a lot of good.
Kamal:	Can you give an example?
Shabnam:	Like footballers. There's that Suarez for one.
Kamal:	Didn't he bite another player?
Lucy:	Well, it might have been a misunderstanding.

1 With a partner, discuss:

a) how Lucy's listening skills are limiting the conversation

b) how she fails to respond to prompts and implications.

> **Top tip**
>
> In a conversation, always respond directly to what someone says, counter their ideas, ask them for more detail or develop what they have said.

Build the skills

Responding sensitively means not only engaging with what people *say directly* but with what they *imply*. People regularly say things that imply something else, for example: 'I love your new dress. It's so... different'. A good listener picks out what is implied and comments on it.

2 Look at the sample conversation extract below, then answer these questions.

    a) Which teacher responses could be challenged by a perceptive listener?

    b) What is implied in each response you have identified?

Top tip

Look out for what your teacher is implying and for any inconsistency. Challenge them if necessary.

Dan:	Geography's like RE – a total waste of time.
Teacher:	Have you ever been on holiday abroad?
Dan:	Yeah, we went to – where was it – some place in Italy, or Spain.
Teacher:	So, you're not sure what country you went to.
Dan:	Oh... yeah, it was Mallorca. Is that a country? It was a lot hotter than we expected and everything was shut on a Sunday.
Teacher:	Might a bit of research have made the experience more rewarding?

Develop the skills

Paraphrasing what is said during a discussion proves that you listen and understand well. For example:

Teacher:	I think that for many people, travel is an education as well as fun. It broadens our horizons.
Sonia:	You think that seeing other parts of the world expands our thinking and perception.
Teacher:	Absolutely.

3 In groups of four, prepare a conversation entitled: 'Space exploration is a waste of time. The money could be spent on more worthwhile things'. Two of you should take up each viewpoint.

- Note down the points made by each speaker taking the opposite view.
- Summarise what each speaker thinks.

Apply the skills

4 In a group of three, discuss this topic:

> Out of school, most teenagers waste most of their time.

- Look out for implications and challenge them.
- Use paraphrase to acknowledge what people say, and to check your understanding.

Checklist for success

✔ Focus on listening carefully because what you hear affects how well you respond.

✔ Offer a clear paraphrase of any comments or questions to show that you have listened well and understood any implications made.

Developing and supporting ideas with confidence

You will feel more confident if you are well prepared and can develop your ideas in detail, using evidence and examples.

Explore the skills

Imagine that you are going to talk about the following topic:

> There should be a ban on competitive sport.

1 List the points you make in favour and those that might be made against you. How would you counter each one?

2 Look at this example of a conversation about this topic. How does Abi show that she has prepared well, and can confidently support her ideas?

Teacher:	What kind of money do top players earn?
Abi:	They earn obscene amounts of money. Arsenal's Alexis Sanchez earns $186 000 a week, and has just been offered $530 000 a week to move to China.
Teacher:	That's certainly a bit more than most of us earn, but aren't these players an inspiration to others?
Abi:	Up to a point, but their earnings might just encourage young people to have unrealistic expectations. Many young people won't be able to see a live Premier League football match – not when the cheapest tickets can cost up to $69. That's for Chelsea. Even a ticket for Leicester costs at least $29!
Teacher:	Excellent point. But what's wrong with just watching on TV?
Abi:	And becoming even more of a couch potato? Teenagers would be better off going out and actually playing in an amateur game themselves.

Questions may be used to test you and to encourage you to do your best. They may:

* request extra information: 'So, if you think Pythagoras was the greatest mathematician ever – what did he do that has improved my life?'

* encourage you to extend an idea: 'Excellent, James – can you develop that point?'

* challenge you: 'Surely not! What about Van Gogh?'.

3 In pairs, identify how the teacher uses questions in the conversation above.

4 Think of another three questions that the teacher might ask on this topic, and suggest how they could be answered.

Top tip

Confidence is not just about talking at length. Careful listening, followed by a pertinent comment or question, can show your confidence just as well.

Build the skills

5 If someone raised the points and questions below in a conversation, how could you develop them or argue against them?

Statement	Development	Counter argument
Surely football doesn't actually make the world a better place.		
The whole world seems to be obsessed with America.		

Develop the skills

6 Write down what you would say in response to these challenges. Remember: you can, if you wish, acknowledge that someone has a point, but then disagree.

a) But isn't education all about getting a good job one day?

b) Shouldn't we ban cars completely if we value human life?

c) Don't you think everyone should learn at least two languages?

Apply the skills

7 In pairs, prepare a presentation on the following topic:

> You don't need to travel to enjoy life.

Practise giving your presentations, following them up with the kind of conversation you might have.

Checklist for success

✔ Extend your own ideas by adding supporting evidence.

✔ Get your partner to clarify questions if necessary, by using phrases such as *By that, do you mean… or … ?*.

✔ Develop an idea yourself, by using phrases like *Yes. And that reminds me of…*; *Not only that, but…*

Practice tasks and sample responses

You will have to give an individual presentation. You will then discuss the topic with your teacher.

Part 1: Individual task

You will give a presentation, a talk, a speech or a monologue. For example, you might talk about your reaction to meeting a famous person or about a recent film you have seen, suggesting why others might also like it. You can use a dictionary to prepare for the task, but you cannot take one into the assessment.

Key skills

For the individual talk, you will need to:

- articulate experience and express what is thought, felt and imagined (SL1)
- present facts, ideas and opinions in a cohesive order which sustains the audience's interest (SL2)
- communicate clearly and purposefully using fluent language (SL3)
- use register appropriate to context (SL4).

Part 2: Conversation

The individual talk leads into a conversation about your chosen topic. So, for example, you could develop an account of meeting a famous person into a discussion of wider issues such as the nature and role of 'celebrity' and media intrusion into celebrities' lives. You could develop a talk about a film into discussion of wider issues such as censorship, popular culture and the film industry.

Key skills

For the conversation, you will need to:

- articulate experience and express what is thought, felt and imagined (SL1)
- present facts, ideas and opinions in a cohesive order which sustains the audience's interest (SL2)
- communicate clearly and purposefully using fluent language (SL3)
- use register appropriate to context (SL4)
- listen and respond appropriately in conversation (SL5).

Exploring sample responses: Individual task

Read this sample extract from an individual presentation entitled 'My week in Italy', along with the annotations showing its good and bad points.

My holiday was with my brother, my mother and father. —————— appropriate but unoriginal opening
We decided to do something different this year, so we flew to Rome. Then we rented a car and drove down to the bay of Naples. That was quite an experience, because some of ————— offers some relevant detail
the drivers were crazy. When my mother was driving, my father kept covering up his eyes but in fact she was much safer than him. ————————— journey is touched upon but lacks development

When we arrived at the accommodation, it was great. It was miles from anywhere on a hillside in a converted farm. The people who ran it had a family of cats who seemed to fight with each other all the time but never bit us. They lay next to ————— engaging details about cats
us when we were next to the pool and they were waiting outside the door every morning. My favourite was Nero. He followed me everywhere. They said that he adopted someone every week, from the people renting the property. I wonder if he liked me because I get up much earlier than my brother so there was more time to play. Also, I don't grunt as much as my brother does!

We went off to see things some days, like Pompeii and ————— sensible organisation of material into sections
Herculaneum. Both of those towns were buried when
Vesuvius exploded back in Roman times and you can see just ————— including place names adds interest
what life was like back then. They had central heating and
wall paintings and you can walk in the buildings themselves.
It's very hot though, so you have to take water with you, to ————— emotive vocabulary although 'erupted' would be more precise
stop dehydration... ————— appropriate use of details

offers quality of 'being there' but ideas put together without firm sense of structure

Feedback

The speaker uses some varied vocabulary (including names) and has organised the presentation logically. There are some engaging touches. The language is suitably formal most of the time and there is some sentence variety. The presentation lacks more imaginative touches, such as the use of anecdote or extension of ideas, and sentences and vocabulary are accurate but do not exhibit flair or great variety. However, it is clear (without ever being exciting).

1 In addition to the annotated points in this response, find:

- an overly casual expression
- repetition of a word very soon after it has been used once
- two short, simple sentences that would be better turned into a single complex one
- a good use of humour to engage the listener.

Now read the following sample extract from a presentation, in which the speaker talks about looking after a grandmother with Alzheimer's disease.

I imagine most of you will have some idea of what Alzheimer's disease is: it progressively takes away the memory, so that sufferers lose touch with reality more and more, until they eventually can't even recognise their wife, their husband, or their children. They jumble the past and present. Until there is no past or present for them. They can't even recognise night or day. And my grandmother has Alzheimer's.

— precise vocabulary

— complex sentence introduces the subject

— broken sentences, making it seem disturbing and emphasising 'Until'

We noticed it starting when her memory suddenly got worse. She struggled to cook our special meal on Friday night, which had always been her treat for us at the end of the week. Then she wasn't sure what day it was. She didn't know what she had done earlier in the day. People's names were forgotten even more easily than they had been before. She needed – help.

— examples to shock and emphasise the seriousness

— possible pause before this word for effect

We actually thought that we needed help too, but as time goes on, you discover that the early stages were nothing. It is a degenerative disease, which can only get worse. She takes tablets and somehow manages to still live alone, but now it is as if she is in a different kind of world altogether. Conversations are always the same:

— personalised – showing effect on family

'What day is it?'

'Wednesday.'

'Do I have meals on wheels tomorrow?'

'Yes, they'll be here.'

'Do I have to pay for them?'

'No, they're all paid for.'

'What day is it?'

'Wednesday.'

'Do I have meals on wheels tomorrow...'

— reality of the conversation makes situation clear and tragic

---

Feedback

This speaker engages the audience and offers a variety of information, presented in interesting ways. Sentences are varied, there is some excellent vocabulary and the grandmother's situation is brought to life with the examples and conversation. Standard English is used with great confidence.

2 In addition to the annotated points in this response, find:

- a short sentence used as the dramatic climax to a paragraph
- simple sentences used as dramatic examples of the condition worsening
- sophisticated vocabulary showing that the speaker has researched the subject
- dialogue used to show the tragic reality of the situation.

Exploring sample responses: Conversation

Noor has already delivered a presentation on the fundraising she carried out for victims of Hurricane Matthew in Haiti. She talked about her sponsored silence, baking cakes for sale and a 20 km sponsored walk she undertook with her friends. Read this sample extract from her conversation with her teacher, along with the annotations.

Teacher:	That was all very impressive, Noor. Tell me: did you reach your target for the funds you hoped to raise?
Noor:	Yes, I did. In fact, I collected more than I was expecting, because people were so generous. And they were worried about the people who were suffering, obviously.
Teacher:	Yes, we all were. So, do you think it's right that we should have to try to raise money like this?
Noor:	We try to give money to the people who need it so badly.
Teacher:	Of course – but might it not be better if all the money needed came straight from governments? After all, you raised a good deal, but they could give so much more, because they have so much more, haven't they?

clear and appropriate answer, offering a reason

possibly doesn't quite understand the intention of the question

Noor:	I suppose so. The governments do send money to help, don't they?

— responds to new idea

Teacher:	Yes, indeed. But do you think it's enough?
Noor:	I haven't really ever thought about that – but I suppose they give as much as they can, just like everybody else, because they have other things they need to spend money on too. I know what you mean, though. It would be good if they gave some more.

— honest answer, recognising a good new idea

— shows she has taken idea on board

Teacher:	Do you think rich countries give enough in foreign aid generally?
Noor:	It would always be better if they gave some more, especially when there has been a volcano or an earthquake or floods. People living in villages can't help themselves if they have no homes and no jobs and they've lost everything. I think governments should give more.

— makes significant, relevant points

Feedback

The student makes significant points throughout, listens carefully and responds to what is obviously an idea she had not thought of before. She mostly responds to what is asked, but does also challenge the teacher in an appropriate way. She speaks in formal English and presents her ideas in sentences.

3 Find examples in this response of the student doing the following:

- challenging and encouraging a response
- developing an idea and, in doing so, showing she is listening well.

Now read this extract from another sample conversation. In this case, Shane is talking with his teacher about the football World Cup, following his individual presentation about recent tournaments.

Teacher:	World Cups make a lot of money. Isn't it true, though, that the host countries make relatively little? Doesn't the organisation, FIFA, make an absolute fortune?
Shane:	I'm afraid you're right. They even demand that they are not taxed on the profits they make,

— sensitive response

so they can just walk away with the proceeds. Countries like Brazil, who hosted the competition in 2014, got publicity and built new stadiums, but that was all: it's so bad that the people who had to build the grounds were only paid a fraction of what they deserved every day. It's shocking.

adding vital and relevant details, using well-chosen vocabulary

Teacher: Yet you still think the World Cup is wonderful?

Shane: Yes. You have to split the football and the excitement away from the corruption behind it...

intelligent response, expressed with balance

Teacher: Can you do that? Should we do that?

Shane: I see what you're saying – but if you love football, what's the alternative?

mature interchange with teacher

takes initiative with a challenge

Teacher: Watch tennis?

Shane: Well... you could only watch your favourites on television most of the time, not live; and, frankly, tennis doesn't have the passion. At football, you can sing and shout and even be tribal again if you want. It's a release from the problems of the world, just for 90 minutes each week. Unfortunately, tennis doesn't offer you that. Have you ever been to a live football match?

new idea, expressed with conviction

pattern of three used for effect

sense of conversation, rather than just responding to teacher

Teacher: No, though we all see it on television...

Shane: People can say what they like about players being over-paid and behaving like huge babies – which we all know they do – but the excitement generated is amazing. I took my mother to a match and she goes regularly now. I still cannot believe it, but she is swept away by the drama of it all. There are many things wrong with football finance and there is corruption too but that cannot really detract from all that it represents to hundreds of millions of people around the world...

Feedback

The student interacts with the teacher in a mature fashion, listens sensitively, uses formal standard English and offers a range of ideas that move the conversation on as he presents and expresses his ideas and arguments clearly. He has knowledge of the subject and sustains the conversation intelligently.

4 Find four examples of effective speaking in Shane's final speech. Look especially for his use of language, how he really engages in a conversation with the teacher – quickly responding to what the teacher says, and how he concludes.

Check your progress

Sound progress

- I can use varied vocabulary.
- I can communicate clearly and engage the listener.
- I can organise my presentation to engage the interest of the listener.
- I can choose a topic that I can talk about adequately, and do some research on it.
- I can work out a basic order in which to make my points.
- I can engage the interest of the audience with some language devices.
- I can anticipate questions on my subject.
- I can prepare to answer questions and respond appropriately.
- I can show a readiness to listen to my teacher and to respond appropriately.
- I can respond to prompts.

Excellent progress

- I can use an appropriate style consistently, with varied sentences, vocabulary and expression.
- I can speak confidently for a given purpose.
- I can use standard English confidently in an appropriate register.
- I can choose a topic that allows me to respond with authority and enthusiasm, and research it effectively.
- I can organise my content well for the given purpose.
- I can select and use a wide range of language devices.
- I can prepare to discuss issues that might arise.
- I can acknowledge points in a conversation and develop them.
- I can show that I understand implied meanings.
- I can listen carefully and take the initiative.

Practice papers and guidance

This section of the book will take you through the type of tasks that you will be asked to complete for formal assessment, to offer you a realistic rehearsal under examination conditions of the skills you have learned throughout your course.

When using these practice assessments, it is important that you complete them with an eye to the timings required to complete a whole examination. For example, the most sensible way to approach a set of comprehension or short-answer questions is to use the marks allocated for each one to work out what proportion of the total marks available this represents. You can divide the time available by these proportions to work out how much time to spend on each one.

Sample assessments provide a valuable opportunity to assess your own strengths and weaknesses. You can then adjust your revision plans accordingly. For example, if you realise that you need further clarification of how to write a summary, you might revisit Chapter 6 to brush up your skills. You might also add another five minutes to your time allocation for the summary when doing your next practice assessment.

Approaching examinations is demanding because examination questions require certain techniques – you need to apply the appropriate skills and knowledge to answer each question, remembering to look out for command words and precise instructions. Use these practice assessments and the marking process to see which areas you are weaker on and focus on those key areas the next time. This should help to improve your exam technique.

Links to other chapters:

Chapter 1: Key reading skills

Chapter 5: Comprehension

Chapter 6: Summary writing

Chapter 7: Analysing language

Chapter 8: Extended response to reading and directed writing

An introduction to Practice Paper 1

The exam-style questions that follow on pages 307–313 are based on the model of the 2020 Cambridge IGCSE examination. They have been written by teachers, not by the examination board.

Which skills should I be using?

Question 1 (a) to (e) asks you to show only reading skills.

- You will need to use the key skills of *skimming*, *scanning* and *selecting* (Topics 1.1–1.3 and Chapter 5). In addition, you will need to use your understanding of *explicit* and *implicit meanings* (Topics 1.5–1.7 and Chapter 5).

- Question 1(f) asks you to show both reading and writing skills.

- You will need to use the *summary* writing skills (Topic 1.4 and Chapter 6).

Question 2 asks you to show only reading skills.

- You will need to use the key skills of *skimming*, *scanning* and *selecting*, and your ability to understand *explicit* and *implicit meanings* (Topics 1.1–1.7 and Chapter 7).

- You will need to show the skills of identifying language choices and understanding how writers achieve effects (Topics 1.8–1.9 and Chapter 7).

Question 3 asks you to show reading and writing skills.

- You will need to use the key skills of *skimming*, *scanning* and *selecting*, and your ability to understand *explicit* and *implicit meanings* (Topics 1.6–1.7).

- You will need to write clearly and accurately using your extended response to writing skills (Topics 8.1–8.4).

Tips for success

- Manage your time well. Spend slightly longer on higher-marking questions.

- Make sure that you *use your own words* if you are told to *explain*.

- For Question 1 (f) you must write in continuous prose and *use your own words* wherever possible, basing your summary on your notes.

- For Question 2 (d) it is important that you use quotations in your answer and explain effects by referring to the meaning and associations of words.

- It is important that you show detailed knowledge of the text in your answer to Question 3. This means that you must base your own ideas on *ideas and details from the text*, although it is usually best to use your own words to present these.

Practice Paper 1: Reading

Reading   **2 hours**

Answer **all** questions.

The number of marks is given in brackets [ ] at the end of each question or part question.

Read Text A and then answer Questions 1 (a) to (e).

Text A

Brady Barr has a TV series on the Geographic Channel. Here is an extract from an article that he wrote for the channel's website about filming a particularly dangerous episode.

The cave was literally a chamber of horrors, probably the worst place I have worked in the ten years I have been at Geographic. The cave was filled with the usual customers (scorpions,
5 roaches, maggots, spiders, millions of bats, lizards, and snakes), but it was the unbelievable amount of bat guano that made it unbearable. There were places where you had to wade through chest-deep liquefied bat guano. The stuff was like quicksand, almost sucking you down and making progress very slow and cautious. This bat guano soup along with low oxygen levels eventually prevented our expedition from going deeper into the cave.

10 On day three, about 200 feet (60 meters) into the cave, walking along the right-side wall where the fecal soup was the shallowest, I spied a large python partially exposed in a crack in the left wall, on the opposite side of the cave across the deepest part of the fecal river.

[With cameras rolling] I frantically waded across the middle deepest portion of the fecal river (waist deep on me) and to the other side of the cave, where I was successful in grabbing the
15 last few feet of the snake's tail before it escaped into the wall.

By this time Dr Mark Auliya, a python expert working with me on this project, arrived to assist me in pulling this large snake out of the wall. I handed over the tail to Mark while I attempted to free more of the large snake's body from the crevice as Mark pulled.

After a brief power struggle, the python popped out of the crack in a blur of coils and quickly
20 started to wrap us up. In the waist-deep fecal soup, the darkness of the cave and myriad of coils, it was difficult to locate the head, which was our major concern. With Mark still holding the tail, the big snake wrapped its powerful coils around Mark's body once and around both of my legs down low at least once, and maybe two coils. The snake's head was horrifyingly all over the place, popping in and out of the fecal soup and making securing it almost
25 impossible. Before we could formulate a plan to get out of the quicksand-like fecal soup, where drowning was a serious issue while trying to subdue a giant snake, it bit me.

I felt the snake attach to my leg right below my left buttock, which sent me literally through the roof with pain. These guys are armed with dozens of strongly recurved razor-sharp teeth. After securing its hold, it threw the weight and power of its muscular body into the bite and
30 started ripping downward. The power of these snakes is beyond comprehension... remember, they are constrictors, and power is the name of their game.

Question 1

(a) Give **two** reasons why the cave was an unpleasant place to be, according to the text.

....

....

.... [2]

(b) Why was it so important to get out of the quicksand in paragraph 2?

.... [1]

(c) Why do you think Brady described himself as 'frantically' wading after the snake when he sees it in paragraph 4?

....

....

.... [2]

(d) Reread paragraph 6 ('After a brief... bit me').

  (i) Explain, using your own words, what the writer means by the words in italics in the following phrases:

  • the python popped out of the crack in *a blur of coils* (line 19)

....

....

.... [2]

  • the snake's head was *horrifyingly all over the place* (line 23)

....

....

.... [2]

  • *popping in and out* of the fecal soup (line 24)

....

....

.... [2]

  (ii) Give two reasons why catching the python was a dangerous activity.

....

....

.... [2]

(e) Explain why the snake wound was particularly painful for Brady.

....

....

.... [2]

[Total: 15]

Read Text B, a transcript of a blog posted on a forum for viewers of The Nature Channel, and then answer Question 1 (f).

Text B

Just flick on the television on any given night of the week and you will be faced with a mind-boggling array of documentaries focusing on all manner of exotic beasts from every corner of the globe – and they're just the presenters! No, seriously, I now have access to virtually any creature, in any location from Pole to Pole.

5 Progress indeed, you may say. In my childhood we were lucky if we saw the occasional lemur peeling a grape or a rogue elephant knocking down the set on a kid's TV show. They were glamorous strangers imported for our viewing pleasure and usually accompanied by a zoo keeper in a smart uniform. How we laughed at their strange features and 'aahed' at their cute habits when they were let out of their boxes for a few minutes of air-time...

10 After our bed-time our parents watched their once-a-week dose of some exceedingly dull programme with close-up film of insects constructing elaborate dens and birds jumping off cliffs. The voice over was factual, often very knowledgeable, but awfully sensible... frankly I didn't mind that I wasn't allowed to stay up.

Nowadays young and old can see anything, anywhere, doing everything – including quite a
15 few things that frankly put me off my dinner! We see animals in their natural environments, living, dying, just as nature intended. It can be tough to watch but it is reality. Modern nature programmes often tell a story. We get involved with a family or a character. Recently we had to delay dinner just to check whether a little meerkat lived or died!

Of course, the presenters are a bit more high profile than I'm used to. They seem to be as
20 much on show as the animals but they really know what they're talking about and they certainly have a gift when it comes to making things interesting. I do wish they wouldn't do stupid things though: putting your hand in something's mouth doesn't strike me as setting a great example! I think I preferred it when the presenter just kept a polite distance and whispered to the camera.

25 You know we ought to think ourselves lucky. From the comfort of our sofa we can share the lives of all sorts of amazing creatures in a way that generations past could not even imagine. Perhaps soon we won't even need zoos at all – now that would be progress!

(f) According to Text B, what changes in wildlife-themed TV shows has the writer experienced since their childhood?

You must use **continuous writing** (not note form) and **use your own words** as far as possible.

Your summary should not be more than 150 words.

Up to 10 marks are available for the content of your answer and up to 5 marks for the quality of your writing.

[Total: 15]

Read Text C, an extract from *My Family and Other Animals*, then answer Questions 2 (a)–(d).

Text C

This text is taken from a longer narrative. It describes the experiences of a young boy, Gerald, and his family on the island of Corfu. In this extract Gerald describes one of his regular visits to a local naturalist.

Theodore would welcome me in his study, a room that met with my full approval. It was, in
5   my opinion, just what a room should be. The walls were lined with tall bookshelves filled
with volumes on freshwater biology, botany, astronomy, medicine, folk-lore, and similar
fascinating and sensible subjects. Interspersed with these were selections of ghost and crime
stories. Thus Sherlock Holmes rubbed shoulders with Darwin, and Le Fanu with Fabre, in what
I considered to be a thoroughly well-balanced library. At one window of the room stood
10 Theodore's telescope, its nose to the sky like a howling dog, while the sills of every window
bore a parade of jars and bottles containing minute freshwater fauna, whirling and twitching
among the delicate fronds of green weed. On one side of the room was a massive desk, piled
high with scrapbooks, micro-photographs, X-ray plates, diaries, and note-books. On the
opposite side of the room was the microscope table, with its powerful lamp on the jointed
15 stem leaning like a lily over the flat boxes that housed Theodore's collection of slides. The
microscopes themselves, gleaming like magpies, were housed under a series of beehive-like
domes of glass.

'How are you?' Theodore would inquire, as if I were a complete stranger, and give me his
characteristic handshake – a sharp downward tug, like a man testing a knot in a rope. The
20 formalities being over, we could then turn our minds to more important topics.

'I was... er... you know... looking through my slides just before your arrival, and I came across
one which may interest you. It is a slide of the mouth-parts of the rat flea... ceratophyllus
fasciatus, you know. Now, I'll just adjust the microscope.... There I... you see? Very curious.
I mean to say, you could almost imagine it was a human face, couldn't you? Now I had
25 another... er... slide here... That's funny. Ah I got it. Now this one is of the spinnerets of the
garden or cross spider... er... epeira fasciata...'

So, absorbed and happy, we would pore over the microscope. Filled with enthusiasm, we
would tack from subject to subject, and if Theodore could not answer my ceaseless flow of
questions himself, he had books that could. Gaps would appear in the bookcase as volume
30 after volume was extracted to be consulted, and by our side would be an ever-growing pile
of volumes.

'Now this one is a cyclops... cyclops viridis... which I caught out near Govino the other day. It
is a female with egg-sacs... Now, I'll just adjust... you'll be able to see the eggs quite clearly.
... I'll just put her in the live box... er... hum... there are several species of cyclops found here
35 in Corfu.'

Into the brilliant circle of white light a weird creature would appear, a pear-shaped body,
long antennae that twitched indignantly, a tail like sprigs of heather, and on each side of it
(slung like sacks of onions on a donkey) the two large sacs bulging with pink beads.

'... called cyclops because, as you can see, it has a single eye situated in the centre of its
40 forehead. That's to say, in the centre of what would be its forehead if a cyclops had one. In Ancient Greek mythology, as you know, a cyclops was one of a group of giants... er... each of whom had one eye. Their task was to forge iron for Hephaestus.'

Outside, the warm wind would shoulder the shutters, making them creak, and the rain-drops would chase each other down the window-pane like transparent tadpoles.

45 'Ah ha! It is curious that you should mention that. The peasants in Salonika have a very similar... er... superstition.... No, no, merely a superstition. I have a book here that gives a most interesting account of vampires in... um... Bosnia. It seems that the local people there...'

Tea would arrive, the cakes squatting on cushions of cream, toast in a melting shawl of butter, cups agleam, and a faint wisp of steam rising from the teapot spout.

50 '... but, on the other hand, it is impossible to say that there is no life on Mars. It is, in my opinion, quite possible that some form of life will be found... er... discovered there, should we ever succeed in getting there. But there is no reason to suppose that any form of life found there would be identical...'

Sitting there, neat and correct in his tweed suit, Theodore would chew his toast slowly and
55 methodically, his beard bristling, his eyes kindling with enthusiasm at each new subject that swam into our conversation. To me his knowledge seemed inexhaustible. He was a rich vein of information, and I mined him assiduously. No matter what the subject, Theodore could contribute something interesting to it. At last I would hear Spiro honking his horn in the street below, and I would rise reluctantly to go.

Question 2

(a) **Identify a word or phrase from the text** which suggests the same idea as the words underlined:

   (i)   Gerald <u>liked</u> the appearance and contents of Theodore's study. [1]

   (ii) Gerald believed that the collection of books contained a <u>good range</u> of fiction, non-fiction, fact and fantasy. [1]

   (iii) Theodore was quite <u>formal and distant</u> towards Gerald, despite knowing him well. [1]

   (iv) Gerald was <u>fascinated</u> and wanted to know about everything. [1]

(b) **Using your own words,** explain what the writer means by each of the <u>words underlined</u>:

> Sitting there, neat and correct in his tweed suit, Theodore would chew his toast slowly and <u>methodically</u>, his beard bristling, his eyes kindling with <u>enthusiasm</u> at each new subject that swam into our conversation. To me his knowledge seemed <u>inexhaustible</u>. He was a rich vein of information and I mined him assiduously.

   (i)   methodically [1]

   (ii) enthusiasm [1]

   (iii) inexhaustible [1]

(c) **Using your own words**, explain how the <u>phrases underlined</u> are used by the writer to suggest what Theodore is like.

> Sitting there, neat and correct in his tweed suit, Theodore would <u>chew his toast slowly and methodically,</u> his beard bristling, his <u>eyes kindling with enthusiasm</u> at each new subject that swam into our conversation. To me his <u>knowledge seemed inexhaustible</u>. He was a rich vein of information and I mined him assiduously.

[3]

(d) Reread the descriptions of:

- Theodore's laboratory in paragraph 1, beginning 'Theodore would welcome me…'
- Gerald's feelings about Theodore in paragraph 12, beginning 'Sitting there, neat and correct…'

Select **four** powerful words or phrases from **each** paragraph. Your choices should include imagery. Explain how each word or phrase selected is used effectively in the context.

Write about 200 to 300 words.

Up to 15 marks are available for the content of your answer.

[15]

[Total: 25]

Reread Text C, an extract from *My Family and Other Animals*, then answer Question 3.

Question 3

You are Gerald Durrell. Many years after the events described in this extract, you are asked to give a speech to a group of interested parents about the importance of introducing children to the natural world. The interviewer asks you three questions:

- What do you remember seeing and feeling on your visits with Theodore?
- What do you remember about Theodore, his behaviour and the way he treated you?
- Why do you think that this kind of experience is valuable?

Write the words of the interview.

Base your interview on what you have read in Text C, but be careful to use your own words. Address each of the three bullet points.

Begin your interview with the first question.

Write about 250 to 350 words.

Up to 15 marks are available for the content of your answer, and up to 10 marks for the quality of your writing.

[25]

[Total: 25]

An introduction to Practice Paper 2

The practice questions that follow on pages 314–316 are based on the model of the 2020 Cambridge IGCSE examination. These questions have been written by teachers, not by the examination board.

Which skills should I be using?

Section A requires you to show both reading and writing skills.

- You will need to use the key skills of *skimming*, *scanning*, *selecting* and *synthesising* (Topics 1.1–1.4). In addition, you will need to use your ability to understand *explicit* and *implicit meanings* (Topics 1.5–1.7). You will also use the ability to analyse and evaluate (Topic 1.11).

- You will need to use the skills contained in Chapter 8, which takes you through the process of responding to a directed writing task (Topics 8.5–8.7).

- You will also need to understand the conventions of three different writing forms outlined in Chapter 3: a speech, article or letter.

- Finally, you must be able to understand and incorporate the techniques of writing for different purposes, either to persuade, argue or explore an idea, as explored in Chapter 4.

Section B requires you to show only writing skills.

- You will need to be able to use all the key writing guidance contained in Chapter 2 and the guidance on descriptive and narrative writing contained in Chapters 3 and 4. Remember that some of the guidance about the way that writers write in Chapter 1 will also be helpful to you in your own writing.

- You should draw on the detailed guidance given in Chapter 9 for the type of composition that you choose.

Tips for success

- It is vital that you manage your time effectively and do not spend too long on one section at the expense of the other.

- It is important to show show *evaluation* of the text in your answer in Section A. This means that you must consider the *ideas and details from the text*, as well as giving your own views. *Planning is vital* for both tasks, but especially so for the composition task.

- Remember to *select language* and *make structural choices consciously* to fit each task, considering your form, viewpoint and audience.

Practice Paper 2: Directed writing and composition

Directed writing and composition   **2 hours**

Answer **two** questions in total:

Section A: answer **Question 1**.

Section B: answer **one** question.

Section A: Directed writing

Read Text A, then answer Section A, Question 1.

Text A

The following is taken from a blog by a mother (who is also a dietician) after she learned that local schools were checking the food that students had brought in from home, and removing items that they considered to be unhealthy.

My child's lunchbag is a crime-scene!

5 As a parent you might expect the odd school pick-up to end in tears. Friendship issues, forgotten homework, lost sports clothes – I've mopped up the misery of them all, but holding your sobbing child because they have a 'naughty lunch bag' sticker on their polo shirt was a first for me.

Apparently, this horrifying idea is all the rage nowadays. As the government starts to panic
10 over child nutrition, the food-hall has become a battleground. Now don't get me wrong – I'm all for healthy eating and I take my responsibilities as a parent seriously but making a child feel judged and embarrassed about what they have been given to eat is just wrong!

Firstly, can we remember that most food given to students is provided by parents. If there is a problem then how about sending a discreet note home rather than humiliating the innocent
15 recipient? Kids are incredibly sensitive. They hate being singled out at the best of times – but for something that they are not in control of? No!

Now let's look a bit closer at the whole 'name and shame' process. Apparently our government has decided that they will check what every school-age student eats whilst on the school site. Well-qualified as the staff are in our local school I doubt that every school has
20 an on-site nutritionist. Can Mrs Murray from K4 tell the difference between a nice bit of local cheese and a well-dressed piece of plastic mixed with preservatives masquerading as a cheese finger? Does she know how much sugar there is in the average 'health bar'? For that matter, is she aware that fruit juice is a sure-fire way to raise our little ones' blood sugar to a nice frenzied playground peak and then drop it again in time for a post-lunch sleep.

But okay. Let's say the food police manage to identify a rogue bit of food. Then what? If they
25   remove it then that is one less item for that offender (sorry, child) to eat that day. Are they
going to offer replacements or does the criminal (sorry, child) just go hungry? Good-luck
eliciting high-level analysis from my son when he's hungry!

I am not defending the type of meal or snack that bursts with e numbers and sports 12
brightly wrapped items each with a cartoon character and 300 calories minimum. I am not
30   the kind of parent who passes fast food through the school fence or thinks that a family-size
bar of chocolate is a suitable snack for a six-year-old child. However, I have been known to
pop the odd can of fizzy drink into the long line of lunch boxes I fill every morning. (It's hard
thinking of different ideas every day – there are 195 school days a year you know!) I'm going to
confess right here that we *do* get through 15 'snack-sized' chocolate biscuits per week on the
35   'production line'. But that's alongside 30 pieces of fresh fruit, endless home-grown tomatoes,
cucumbers and other veggies and wholemeal bread in abundance. It's all about balance – and
actually those lunchboxes are only about 20% of what my kids eat in a day. Where will it end?
Will my children soon have to complete a food diary when they arrive at school, confessing to
the food crimes committed at home and running laps until they've shed the excess calories?
40   What will we do with the students who have not had enough to eat? What about the schools
which provide unhealthy food or host vending machines packed with it?

I do understand that as educators the schools want to send out the right messages about
healthy eating. But how about doing something more positive than lunch-box policing?
Healthy cooking 'parent and child' sessions… menu cards for parents… one of our local
45   schools had an 'eating for exams' cook book on sale recently. Those are approaches that
tackle the problem at its grass roots – parental responsibility – and if needed, even provide
healthy food for students who cannot access it at home, rather than encouraging young,
malleable minds to associate certain foods with misery and embarrassment.

Question 1

Imagine that your school is considering introducing similar checks on the food that children bring to school.

Write a letter to your school in which you give your views about whether or not teachers should check the food that students eat at school.

In your letter, you should:

- evaluate the views given about the checking of lunches
- give your own views, based on what you have read, about whether the checking of food would benefit students.

Base your letter on the blog, but be careful to use your own words. Address both of the bullet points.

Begin your letter: 'Dear School Governors…'

You should write about 250 to 350 words.

Up to 15 marks are available for the content of your answer, and up to 25 marks for the quality of your writing.

[40]

[Total: 40]

Section B: Composition

Answer one question from Section B.

Questions 2 and 3

Write about 350 to 450 words on **one** of the following questions.

Up to 16 marks are available for the content and structure of your answer, and up to 24 marks for the style and accuracy of your writing.

EITHER

Descriptive writing

2   Describe a scene when a group of people meet to celebrate a happy occasion.

OR

Descriptive writing

3   Describe a quiet garden or park.

OR

Narrative writing

4   Write a story that includes the words, 'she stood in shock as the scene unfolded before her...'

OR

5   Write a story that involves a character who is determined to win.

[40]

[Total: 40]

Glossary

adjective: a word that describes a noun ('the *red* car', 'the *closed* shop')

adverb: describes a verb (usually an action)

adverbial of time: a word or phrase expressing when something happened

analogy: a developed comparison between two ideas

anecdote: a short story to exemplify or back up a writer or speaker's point

bias: a strong favouring of one side of an argument or debate, often without representing the other side of it

characterisation: how an author presents a particular character

climax: the most interesting or exciting point in a story

cohesion: how a paragraph is knitted together and linked to other paragraphs around it. Topic sentences, connectives and linking phrases all help to make a text cohesive.

conjugated: when verbs change form, usually taking on a different ending

conjunction: a word used to join clauses or words in the same clause or sentence, for example *and, but, or*

conjunctive adverb: an adverb that links independent clauses in a sentence, or links ideas between two sentences – for example, *finally, therefore, moreover,* to show cause and effect

conjunction: a word that joins two words, phrases or clauses in a sentence

connective: a word or phrase used to link sentences

connotations: the emotional or sensory associations of a word or thing – for example, a flag can immediately make someone think 'my country'

counter-argument: the opposite or contrasting viewpoint

determiner: a word that specifies a noun

dialogue: a conversation between two or more people in a piece of writing

homophone: words spelled differently but which sound the same

idiom: a typical phrase common to a language: for example, *dead funny* meaning 'really funny'; *a right laugh* meaning 'a lot of fun'

imagery: words or comparisons that create a mental picture

inferring: reading between the lines and drawing conclusions from subtle clues

interview: a conversation in which one person asks the other questions on a topic or aspect of their life

irregular verb: a verb that does not follow the standard patterns

jargon: technical terms that people unfamiliar with the subject would not know

main clause: the main part of a sentence that could stand as a sentence on its own

metaphor: a powerful image in which two different things or ideas are compared without using *as* or *like* (*my fingers were tiny splinters of ice*)

monologue: a speech, in role, by one character without interruption

noun: a word for a person, thing or idea

paraphrase: a rewording of something that has been said or written

pathetic fallacy: when a writer reflects human emotions in natural features or objects: for example, *the balloons swayed happily* or *the leaden clouds hung heavy above the figure crouching on the moorland path*

personification: when a thing or idea is described as if it has human qualities (*the storm bared its teeth and roared with anger*)

perspective: the particular angle or direction from which something is seen or experienced; it can also refer to someone's attitude towards something

preposition: a word that describes the relationship between people, things or places

pronoun: a word that takes the place of a noun

rebut: to 'knock down' a counter-argument

register: the level of formality in a piece of writing

regular verb: a verb that follows predictable patterns in forming tenses and agreeing with subjects

relative clause: part of a sentence that usually explains or adds detail to a preceding noun

rhetorical: designed to have a powerful effect on a reader; rhetorical questions are intended to create impact rather than elicit information (*Should we simply forget the awful suffering and hardship?*)

semantic field: vocabulary or set of terms closely linked by subject or usage

simile: a vivid comparison of two things or ideas using *as* or *like* (for example, *the hoarse voice sounded out like sandpaper on a broken brick*)

slang: very informal use of language (may include dialect words), often common to an area, city or group of people

standard English: the most widely used form of English that is not specific to a particular location or region (e.g. in standard English, you would say *we **were** going* not *we **was** going* and you would use the word *argument* rather than *tiff* or *barney*)

subject: the 'do-er' of the verb action in a sentence or clause

subordinate clause: a clause that does not make sense on its own; not a complete sentence

synonym: a word that is identical, or very close in meaning, to another word

synthesise: bring two ideas together to make a new one

tense: form a verb takes to show the time of an action

theme: a recurring idea within a piece of writing

tone: the way you vary your voice and language to suit your audience and get your meaning across (e.g. express a certain emotion or create a particular mood)

topic sentence: a sentence that introduces or sums up the overall idea or focus of a paragraph

verb: a word that expresses an action (*go*) or a state (*feel*, *like*)

Text acknowledgements

We are grateful to the following for permission to reproduce copyright material:

An extract on p.8 from *The No.1 Ladies Detective Agency* by Alexander McCall Smith, Abacus, copyright © 1998, 2005 by Alexander McCall Smith. Reproduced by permission of David Higham Associates Ltd and Anchor Books, an imprint of the Knopf Doubleday Publishing Group, a division of Penguin Random House LLC. All rights reserved. Any third party use of this material, outside of this publication, is prohibited. Interested parties must apply directly to Penguin Random House LLC for permission; An extract on p.11 from *Q & A* by Vikas Swarup published by Doubleday, copyright © 2005 by Vikas Swarup. Reproduced by permission of The Random House Group Ltd and Scribner, a division of Simon & Schuster, Inc. All rights reserved; An extract on p.14 about Jack Petchey from *P-Leisure Magazine*, p.14, Autumn Winter/No 10, p.14. Reprinted with permission; An extract on p.21 from *The Salt Road* by Jane Johnson, Viking 2010, Penguin Books 2011, pp.1-2, copyright © 2010 by Jane Johnson. Reproduced by permission of Penguin Books Ltd; Baror International, Inc.; and Anchor Canada/Doubleday Canada, a division of Penguin Random House Canada Limited; An extract on p.30 from *Set in Stone* by Linda Newbery, published by David Fickling Books, copyright © 2006 by Linda Newbery. Reproduced by permission of The Random House Group Limited and David Fickling Books, an imprint of Random House Children's Books, a division of Penguin Random House LLC. All rights reserved. Any third party use of this material, outside of this publication, is prohibited. Interested parties must apply directly to Penguin Random House LLC for permission; An extract on p.38 from Rough Guides Dubai, copyright © 2018 Rough Guides, https://www.roughguides.com/destinations/middle-east/dubai/. Reproduced with permission from APA Publications (UK) Ltd; An extract on p.39 about Dubai from https://www.visitdubai.com/en/articles/best-beaches, copyright © 2018; Extracts on pp.40-41 from "Social media is harming the mental health of teenagers. The state has to act" by June Eric Udorie, *The Guardian*, 16/09/2015, and "Social media gets a bad press, but it was a lifeline for me" by Grace Holliday, *The Guardian*, 24/04/2017, copyright © Guardian News & Media Ltd, 2018; Extracts on pp.43, 203-204 from *Losing my Virginity: The Autobiography* by Richard Branson, published by Virgin Books, copyright © 1998, 2002, 2005, 2007 by Richard Branson. Reproduced by permission of The Random House Group Limited and Crown Business, an imprint of the Crown Publishing Group, a division of Penguin Random House LLC. All rights reserved. Any third party use of this material, outside of this publication, is prohibited. Interested parties must apply directly to Penguin Random House LLC for permission; Extracts on pp.44, 45 from 'Confessions of a high rise window cleaner' by Carolyn Morris, *Metro Toronto*, 07/02/2011. Reprinted with kind permission of the author; An extract on pp.47, 48 from "J Hus - 'Common Sense' Review" by Joe Madden, *NME*, 15/05/2017, http://www.nme.com/reviews/album/j-hus-common-sense-review, copyright © Time Inc. (UK) Ltd. All rights reserved; An extract on p.49 from "Restoration of a king's art is long overdue" by Ben Macintyre, *The Times*, 27/05/2017, copyright © The Times / News Licensing; A speech on pp.82-83 by Angelina Jolie from World Refugee Day, 18th June 2009 Washington DC; An extract on p.89 from *Tales from Kulafumbi: Diary of a Nature Lover's blog* by Tanya Trevor Saunders, www.wildernessdiary.com. Reprinted with kind permission; An extract on pp.92-93 from "Mountain Goat kills Hiker" by Alex Robinson, *Outdoor Life*, 19/10/2010, copyright © 2018. Reproduced with permission of Outdoor Life. All rights reserved; An extract on p.94 from "First, catch your feral kitten. Then call in the experts" by Patrick Barkham, *The Guardian*, 07/11/2016, copyright © Guardian News & Media Ltd, 2018; An extract on p.112 from "Fracking: the pros and cons", *Country Life*, 23/05/2013, copyright © Country Life Picture Library. Reproduced with permission; Extracts on pp.130, 135, 138-139 from "Undiscovered south-east Asia: remote towns and secret beaches" by Nathan Thomson, Ling Low and Thomas Bird, *The Guardian*, 10/05/2017, copyright © Guardian News & Media Ltd, 2018; Extracts on pp.144, 145 from *A Game of Polo with a Headless Goat* by Emma Levine, p.71. Reproduced with permission of MBA Literary Agents on behalf of Emma Levine; Extracts on pp.146, 147 from *The Rough Guide to The Italian Lakes*, p.4, copyright © Rough Guides. Reproduced with permission from APA Publications (UK) Ltd; An extract on p.149 from *Welcome to Crete, 6th edition*, p.4, copyright © 2016, Lonely Planet. Reproduced with permission; An extract on pp.150, 153 from "Review: In Documentary 'Maidentrip,' Laura Dekker Looks for Paradise in a Sea that Never Ends" by Beth Hanna, www.indiewire.com/2014/01/review-in-documentary-maidentrip-laura-dekker-looks-for-paradise-in-a-sea-that-never-ends-194139/ An extract on pp.154-155 from "Lynx could return to Britain this year after absence of 1,300 years" by Damian Carrington, *The Guardian*, 07/07/2017, copyright © Guardian News & Media Ltd, 2018; Extracts on pp.164, 170-171 from *The Beach* by Alex Garland, Penguin, 1997, first published by Viking 1996, Penguin Books 1997, copyright © 1996 by Alex Garland. Reproduced by permission of Penguin Books Ltd and Andrew Nurnberg Associates Ltd; An extract on pp.179-180 from The *Old Patagonian Express* by Paul Theroux, copyright © 1979, Cape Cod Scriveners Co., used by permission of The Wylie Agency (UK) Limited; Extracts on pp.193-194, 209-210 from "Should pandas be left to face extinction? " by Chris Packham, *The Guardian*, 23/09/2009, and "Mass tourism is at a tipping point – but we're all part of the problem" by Martin Kettle, *The Guardian*, 11/08/2017, copyright © Guardian News & Media Ltd, 2018; An extract on pp.246-247 from "How printed books entered a new chapter of fortune" by Sam Dean, *The Telegraph*, 15/07/2017, copyright © Telegraph Media Group Limited 2017; An extract on p.253 from *From Stepney to St Tropez* by Peter Gould, 2007. Reproduced by permission of Mike Gould; An extract on p.260 from *Writing a Novel* by John Braine, Methuen. Reproduced by permission of David Higham Associates Ltd; An extract on p.307 from "Brady's Bad Bite: in his own words" by Brady Barr, National Geographic, http://channel.nationalgeographic.com/wild/dangerous-encounters/articles/bradys-epic-python-encounter/. Reproduced by permission of National Geographic Creative; and An extract on pp.310-311 from *My Family and Other Animals* by Gerald Durrell, copyright © 1956 by Gerald Durrell. Reproduced with permission from Curtis Brown Group Ltd, London on behalf of The Estate of Gerald Durrell and Viking Books, an imprint of Penguin Publishing Group, a division of Penguin Random House LLC. All rights reserved. Any third party use of this material, outside of this publication, is prohibited. Interested parties must apply directly to Penguin Random House LLC for permission.

Image acknowledgements

The publishers gratefully acknowledge the permission granted to reproduce the copyright material in this book. Every effort has been made to trace copyright holders and to obtain their permission for the use of copyright material. The publishers will gladly receive any information enabling them to rectify any error or omission at the first opportunity:

(t = top, c = centre, b = bottom, r = right, l = left)

p7: George Doyle/ Getty Images; p9t: Weinstein Company/ BBC/ Hbo/ Kobal/ REX/ Shutterstock; p9b: JI de Wet/ Shutterstock; p11t: Sergieiev/ Shutterstock; p11b: CHI-Photo/ Nick Cunard/ Rex Features; p12: CHI-Photo/ Nick Cunard/ Rex Features; p13: CHI-Photo/ Nick Cunard/ Rex Features; p14: Christopher Elwell/ Shutterstock; p15: Eric Isselee/ Shutterstock; p16: Sunlike/ Shutterstock; p17: Jason Politte/ Alamy Stock Photo Stock Photo; p18: EmiliaUngur/ Shutterstock; p20: Dmytro Kohut/ Shutterstock; p21: Pier Photography/ Alamy Stock Photo; p25t: Romiana Lee/ Shutterstock; p25b: Uber Images/ Shutterstock; p27: Granger, NYC/ TopFoto; p29t: irin-k/ Shutterstock; p29b: Folio Images/ Alamy Stock Photo Stock Photo; p30: llaszlo/ Shutterstock; p31: Bruce Rolff/ Shutterstock; p32: Songchai W/ Shutterstock; p33: Andrjuss/ Shutterstock; p34: Dieter Hawlan/ Shutterstock; p35: Maksimilian/ Shutterstock; p36: Nataliia Antonova/ Shutterstock; p38: INTERPIXELS/ Shutterstock; p39: Umar Shariff/ Shutterstock; p41: Antonio Guillem/ Shutterstock; p42: pinkomelet/ Shutterstock; p43: Sipa Press/ REX/ Shutterstock; p44: CharlineXia Ontario Canada Collection/ Alamy Stock Photo; p47: WENN Ltd/ Alamy Stock Photo; p49: Georgios Kollidas/ Shutterstock; p51: Pixsooz/ Shutterstock; p53: Eric Isselee/ Shutterstock; p55: Lukasz Janyst/ Shutterstock; p56: Odua Images/ Shutterstock; p57: Sergey Novikov/ Shutterstock; p59: Dinodia Photos/ Alamy Stock Photo ; p61t: Monkey Business Images/ Shutterstock; p61b: enciktat/ Shutterstock; p62: Marcel A. Mayer/ Shutterstock; p63: Anton Gvozdikov/ Shutterstock; p65: servickuz/ Shutterstock; p66: By NAN728/ Shutterstock; p69: monticello/ Shutterstock; p71: ANCH/ Shutterstock; p73: Cultura Creative (RF)/ Alamy Stock Photo; p74: Andrea Izzotti/ Shutterstock; p75: Panther Media GmbH/ Alamy Stock Photo; p77: RosalreneBetancourt 6/ Alamy Stock Photo; p78: itanistock/ Alamy Stock Photo Stock Photo; p81: David Grossman/ Alamy Stock Photo Stock Photo; p82: Bloomberg/ Getty; p84: Friedrich Stark/ Alamy Stock Photo; p85: Monkey Business Images/ Shutterstock; p86: kyslynskyyhal/ Shutterstock; p89: Mitchell Krog/ Shutterstock; p91: imageBROKER/ Alamy Stock Photo; p92: Alexander Demyanov/ Shutterstock; p93: carlosobriganti/ Shutterstock; p94: hecke61/ Shutterstock; p95: Vitalfoto/ Shutterstock; p96: Kate Aedon/Shutterstock ; p97: mangostock/ Shutterstock; p99: Roman Samborskyi/Shutterstock; p100: Cultura RM/ Shutterstock; p102: Katiekk/ Shutterstock; p105: keith morris/ Alamy Stock Photo; p107: Blend Images/ Alamy Stock Photo; p108: PicturesofLondon/ Alamy Stock Photo; p110: Alex Mit/ Shutterstock; p111: ssuaphotos/ Shutterstock; p112: Eye Ubiquitous/ Alamy Stock Photo; p115: Adrian Sherratt/ Alamy Stock Photo; p116: Thomas Andreas/ Shutterstock; p119t: Oramstock/ Alamy Stock Photo; p119b: Byelikova Oksana/ Shutterstock; p120: davemhuntphotography/ Shutterstock; p121: Paul Aniszewski/ Shutterstock; p123: SPUTNIK/ Alamy Stock Photo; p125: Phototalker/ Shutterstock; p126: goodluz/ Shutterstock; p129: gpointstudio/ Shutterstock; p131: Gabe Taviano/ Shutterstock; p132: Degtiarova Viktoriia/ Shutterstock; p134: J. Breedlove/ Shutterstock; p135: Gaertner/ Alamy Stock Photo; p137: Goran Bogicevic/ Shutterstock; p139: ian cruickshank/ Alamy Stock Photo; p143: wavebreakmedia/ Shutterstock; p145: Asianet-Pakistan/ Alamy Stock Photo; p146: Alice Tanya/ Shutterstock; p149: Aetherial Images/ Shutterstock; p151: AF Archive/ Alamy Stock Photo; p155: Rudmer Zwerver/ Shutterstock; p156: Soru Epotok/ Shutterstock; p159: Lolostock/ Shutterstock; p160: Anton_Ivanov/ Shutterstock; p163: Westend61 GmbH/ Alamy Stock Photo; p165: Patryk Kosmider/ Shutterstock; p166: Dr Morley Read/ Shutterstock; p168: B. Franklin/ Shutterstock; p170: Hamizan Yusof/ Shutterstock; p172: Artit Thongchuea/ Shutterstock; p175: Preto Perola/ Shutterstock; p177: panitanphoto/ Shutterstock; p179: Cal Sport Media/ Alamy Stock Photo; p180: Richard Wareham Fotografie/ Alamy Stock Photo; p183: Alex Peña/ Getty; p184: Hero Images Inc./ Alamy Stock Photo; p187: Hero Images Inc./ Alamy Stock Photo; p189: Image Source/ Alamy Stock Photo; p192: dbimages/ Alamy Stock Photo; p194: Foreverhappy/ Shutterstock; p197: dangdumrong/ Shutterstock; p198: MediaWorldImages/ Alamy Stock Photo; p200: Ammit Jack/ Shutterstock; p202: Featureflash Photo Agency/ Shutterstock; p204: Sipa Press/ REX/ Shutterstock; p207: Ira Wyman/ Getty; p209: allOver images/ Alamy Stock Photo; p213: Prisma by Dukas Presseagentur GmbH/ Alamy Stock Photo; p215: g-stockstudio/ Shutterstock; p216: Gajus/ Shutterstock; p219: allesalltag/ Alamy Stock Photo; p220: Sean Pavone/ Alamy Stock Photo; p223: Nature Picture Library/ Alamy Stock Photo; p224: SingjaiStock/ Shutterstock; p225: Galyna Andrushko/ Shutterstock; p227: gengirl/ Shutterstock; p229: Brandon Alms/ Alamy Stock Photo; p230: Asya Nurullina/Shutterstock ; p233: darikuss/ Shutterstock; p235: Prezoom.nl/ Shutterstock; p237: Robin Beckham/ BEEPstock/ Alamy Stock Photo; p239: Sergey Novikov/ Shutterstock; p241: Pressmaster/ Shutterstock; p242: Bildagentur Zoonar GmbH/Shutterstock; p247: Mike Hayward/ Alamy Stock Photo; p248: Bambax/ Shutterstock; p251: Prokrida/ Shutterstock; p252: Ronald Sumners/ Shutterstock; p253: Atomic/ Alamy Stock Photo; p254: Nikolay Vinokurov/ Alamy Stock Photo; p256: dpa picture alliance archive/ Alamy Stock Photo; p257: Sharath Rajashekhar/ Shutterstock; p261: Maria Dryfhout/ Shutterstock; p262: Vinicius Bacarin/ Shutterstock; p265: Robert Maynard/ Alamy Stock Photo; p267: Helen Sessions/ Alamy Stock Photo; p269: Hero Images Inc./ Alamy Stock Photo; p271: Stuart Monk/ Alamy Stock Photo; p274: imageBROKER/ Alamy Stock Photo; p277: Monkey Business Images/ Shutterstock; p279: Bob Daemmrich/ Alamy Stock Photo; p280t: Syda Productions/ Shutterstock; p280b: bibiphoto/ Shutterstock; p281: Neirfy/ Shutterstock; p283: Racheal Grazias/ Shutterstock; p284: dpa picture alliance/ Alamy Stock Photo; p285: Jacob Lund/ Shutterstock; p287: Fedor Selivanov/ Shutterstock; p288: Geraint Lewis/ REX/ Shutterstock; p291: Dennis Hallinan/ Alamy Stock Photo; p293: Robert Kneschke/Shutterstock; p294: Debby Wong/ Shutterstock; p296: James Boardman/ Alamy Stock Photo; p300: Kaspars Grinvalds/ Shutterstock; p301: WENN UK/ Alamy Stock Photo; p305: John James/ Alamy Stock Photo.